ON EDUCATION AND FREEDOM.

Harold Taylor

President, Sarah Lawrence College

ON EDUCATION
AND FREEDOM

Abelard-Schuman

New York

CONTENTS

ACKNOWLEDGMENTS

A part of "Moral Values and the Experience of Art" was published as a pamphlet by the Museum of Modern Art, New York, in March 1952; "Moral Leadership and Education" appeared in the *Yale Alumni Magazine* in February 1952; parts of other chapters appeared in the *Fiftieth Yearbook on General Education* of the National Society for the Study of Education, February 1952; in *Women, Society and Sex,* Sheridan House, 1952; in the *Nation,* October 3, 1953; in the *Tenth Yearbook of the John Dewey Society,* Harper and Brothers, 1950; in *Moments of Personal Discovery,* Harper and Brothers, 1952; and in the *Teachers College Record,* March 1949.

ON EDUCATION AND FREEDOM

INTRODUCTION

MOST of the topics discussed in this book have come up in the regular course of my work in education, and some of them have to do with subjects I had not thought about in any sustained way until impelled to do so by the circumstances of the work itself.

Before I became involved in administering a college, I had taught philosophy for five years at the University of Wisconsin, and although I had the pleasure of expressing myself to my students, my colleagues, and the president of the institution on the subject of what was wrong with the University, this was a pleasure indulged in without intellectual cost or personal disadvantage, and it was not necessary either to be consistent or to be responsible for doing anything about education itself. The most that could happen to a faculty member who criticized the curriculum as worthless or totally lacking in everything liberal education needs would be that he might be asked to provide a new one, which he could decline to do. Or he might be put on a curriculum committee where his ideas for reform would be washed away in the stream of alternatives provided by those with opposite views and a higher faculty rank. If he criticized the isolation of students from the faculty, he might find himself on a committee to study the counseling services, with his office full of students who agreed with him. But little more would be demanded.

For instance, no teacher of philosophy is compelled by the circumstances of his post to have firm, clear, and distinctive views on the education of women, universal military training, the possible college enrollment in 1965, the proper kind of asphalt tile for music studios, the best way to meet the communist threat in the Far East, whether communists should be allowed to teach, the role of the humanities curriculum in Western society, the wage scale for porters and cooks, how to put your hands on a million dollars, or even on what the aims of education are. The teacher of philosophy has only to describe the nature of reality, the extent of human knowledge, the destiny of man. He teaches his students to move safely through the world of ideas, himself secure from the threat of ever having to do anything specific about the ideas he advocates.

I discovered abruptly that this state of being is not possible for a college president. Such a man must make up his mind about many things which otherwise he would probably ignore or shirk, and he must have views on a number of things about which he has not had a chance to make up his mind. Fortunately, I had already acquired strong convictions about education, based on the defects I had discovered in my own, and had taught a large enough number of students to know that the field of education was full of interesting cases, and was open to improvement. But I was not prepared for the fact that a person who is held responsible for an educational institution must also take a kind of institutional responsibility for his own philosophy, and that to bring up an educational idea for discussion is to run the risk of having it tested in a real situation.

This has given me a feeling of distaste for all abstractions and for all ideas which are advocated loosely with no indication that the advocate has any clue as to how they can be carried out. Conversely, I have learned to cherish ideas which are helpful and interesting, and can be put into practice. I have never believed in the separation of thought and action, or the idea that educators and intellectuals should simply produce thoughts which it is the duty of the rest of the world to act upon. Those who do serious thinking must take responsibility for the effects of their own thoughts. I believe that the human being acts, thinks, and acts again, continually checked as to the accuracy and value of his thinking by the necessity of acting on it. If the intellectual—writer, teacher, scholar, educator, or artist—isolates himself from the real experience of the people living in his own age, he is cut off from the checks and tests which can correct his errors and from the source of ideas which can enrich his thinking. If the teacher is isolated from the experiences of his students and from responsibility for the consequences of his ideas in their hands, he is cut off from an understanding of education itself.

This isolation does exist in American higher education, and seems to me to be a major defect in the system. The university administrators arrange matters of educational policy, a curriculum of proper subjects is arranged by a committee, textbooks are written to cover the curriculum, and the teacher becomes a member of a staff of experts doing what the university asks of him in lecturing, marking examinations, and performing other technical functions. It is possible for most college teachers not to think about education or about what is actually happening to their students, and therefore to have no educational philosophy of their own and no feeling of responsibility for the educational policies of their university.

There are many reasons for this. The most important is the drastic increase in numbers of students and the consequent growth of mass educational needs which have had to be met in a hurry. In this situation, it has been much simpler to work with standard courses organized by the university for everyone and taught by the standard methods of lectures, examinations, grades, and points of credit. As a result, the educational policies, whether for the whole university, for separate divisions, or for separate departments, are seldom made by individual teachers. As the universities have become larger, there has been a tendency to concentrate more and more authority for policy in the hands of the administration. With the increase in student numbers has come an increase in the financial needs of the universities and a consequent emphasis on the business and financial side of university affairs. This has meant more and more authority, not only for the administrative part of the university but for the boards of trustees and boards of regents. In some of the state universities, with twenty thousand to thirty thousand students, and budgets of thirty to forty million dollars a year, the ascendancy of the authority of boards of regents has become marked, to the detriment of faculty responsibility for education, and an ultimate loss of quality in the education of the student. The major forces are all in the direction of submerging the individual teacher and the individual student in a mass of rules, formulae, administrative authority, and academic bric-a-brac.

One remedy for at least part of this difficulty is to give faculty members more responsibility for solving their own educational problems. There is a difference between a teacher and an educator. The true teacher is an educator: that is, he not only teaches, but he plans for the education of his students and makes his own decisions as to how he will teach and what he will teach. He has responsibility for what happens to his students through the effects of his teaching. But the teacher who has no responsibility for making educational decisions about his own students is not an educator. He has no opportunity to become one. Education and teaching then become separated.

Education is often used as a complete term for a special kind of mental activity which is said to take place in schools and colleges, and it is assumed that everyone knows what is meant. There are people who are educated and there are people who are not. Those who are educated—that is to say, those who have been to school and college—are believed to have higher intellectual ability, higher intelligence, and a great many more advantages than those who have not. This is not necessarily the case. The uneducated intelligence may be sharper and more creative, the free intellect appears in informal places, the educated do not necessarily share more widely in social and material advantage. Truck drivers and carpenters, to cite two examples, sometimes have more wit and more money than college professors. The possession of a college degree does not guarantee the owner a high salary, although it usually prevents him from being happy with a low one.

More strictly defined, but still too narrowly, education is a subject discussed by "educationists" or "educators"; it is a program administered by boards, principals, presidents, deans; it is a subject taught in schools of education; it is an abstraction which has aroused the interest of the most diverse groups in the country, from the American Legion to the Communist Party; and as long as it is considered to be an abstraction to dissect rather than a name for what happens when teachers teach and students learn, it will continue to be misunderstood. The teacher in the classroom and on the campus, talking with students and conferring with his colleagues, is in the middle of the whole educational enterprise. He is the one who should discuss teaching and education, write about it, and plan it, whether he is an anthropologist, a chemist, a philosopher, or a poet. Teachers should not merely be allowed to make educational policy. Making policy should be considered their duty as teachers. Otherwise there are few sources of ideas for education except those from the professional educators and administrators who are unavoidably one stage removed from the process of teaching. Nor is there likely to be an awareness of the need for educational thinking on the part of the faculty members themselves.

I say this because of my own experience, first as a teacher who wrote some philosophy, and then as a college president who found that everything about education tends to raise philosophical questions. There is very little occasion in most American colleges and universities for the teacher to talk and write about education, or even to talk and write about students, although most teachers have views on both subjects. There is also little occasion for students to talk and write about education, although they too have sharp and important things to say if they are encouraged to do so.

Anyone who has ever joined a school board, a Parent-Teacher Association, a parents' committee, a board of trustees, or who has a child in school or college, will discover within himself a great many ideas about education. On analysis, they will turn out to be ideas about philosophy and personal values. You may begin a discussion of where to find the money for new records for the school music library, but before the discussion has continued for ten minutes, questions will come up involving aesthetic standards (Who will choose the records, and which ones will they be, "Peter and the Wolf" or "Rudolph the Red-Nosed Reindeer"?), political standards (Was one of the children's record companies accused of having a director who belonged to organizations cited by the Attorney General as subversive?), public policy (Why doesn't the tax rate provide enough money for records without charging the parents, and where does all that money go anyway?), educational policy (Why do public schools teach music instead of concentrating on the fundamentals? or Why do children dance and do rhythms?), moral values (Aren't these teachers pampering the children by letting them do just as they please?).

Similar questions are raised whenever education is discussed. Every question that comes up in education ends in philosophy. Or, to put it another way, the questions end in a final question, By what standards shall we decide, and whose standards and principles shall we follow?

Some degree of knowledge about education is necessary before standards will have meaning. For example, one of the first things to know about education is the matter of what changes it can actually produce in human nature. This suggests the immediate question, What changes in human nature are most desirable? How do we decide whether or not a change is for the better or the worse? If it is possible to change human nature through education, is it not dangerous to allow the teacher to change the child in whatever way he chooses? If the teachers are not to decide, who should? Parents? Clergymen? School boards? College presidents? Congressmen? The Daughters or Sons of the American Revolution? If you believe that human nature can and should be changed, what do you say to those who believe that the whole matter is settled by the Deity or by Freud before the child goes to school? Or what do you say to those who believe that the inherent qualities in the child will flower into something beautiful and rare, if only the child is allowed to do anything he pleases?

Again, these are philosophical questions, although often in the heat of community debate they do not seem to be. The demands which parents make on education depend on their view of life and human nature. If the views are rigid, if they consider human nature basically sinful and life a process of purification of original sin, they want a formal, rigid education with a minimum of freedom. If the views are romantic and benign, and human nature is thought to be fundamentally good, parents want a free and easy educational program with the maximum of freedom for the child. If the views are materialistic and prestige-ridden, and life is considered to be a process of getting ahead in American society, the parents will demand conformity to a social pattern, and the development of a standard American commercial personality.

Variety of demand from the welter of philosophies which exists in each community then descends on the school and the college. The modern teacher in the modern world must cope with the attitudes of his society. These include not only the attitudes and wishes of parents, but those of principals and school superintendents, privately organized groups, the churches, the state legislature, the United States Congress, the newspapers, the general public and, in the case of colleges, the alumni. For the teacher in the school, the closest relation is with the family in a particular community setting where opposing ideals and values may be in conflict. There are families which accept the whole of television, radio, cowboy suits, movies, and space-ships as a complete answer to the community needs of the child. There are others who want the schools and colleges to give indoctrination in Americanism as a substitute for an understanding of American democracy. Many of those who make such demands have no children of their own.

In the midst of the tugs, pulls, and pushes, the teacher must keep his own center of gravity and his own belief in his mission. That mission is to keep alive in his society the use of the free reason, the ideal of enlightenment, the ideal of human betterment. He does so in a modern America where social, cultural, and political forces are producing tensions which distract many American citizens from a concern with these ideals. It is the duty of the teacher and the educator to make certain that the attention of the American community is centered on the development of a philosophy for education which keeps these ideals in full view. His failure to do so may lead to the imposition of a philosophy with radically different values to which all education will be forced to adhere.

The continual search for a philosophy has been the mark of serious education ever since schools and colleges were organized in place of home instruction. When children were educated entirely by their parents at home there was no problem of philosophical conflict between home and school, religion and secularism, school and society. The children were taught the entire philosophy of their parents, and when they learned to read and write, they read the books their parents had in the house, often the Bible and the complete works of Shakespeare. But as soon as institutions are formed to teach skills, ideas, facts, and opinions, differences emerge in the philosophies of teachers and parents, educators and society, and there are varieties of philosophy in every book and every subject confronting the modern student. It is no wonder that now, at a time of intense international conflict, and in a century in which all the values which make up civilization have been attacked and defended, doubted and debated, shattered and rebuilt, the questions of what philosophy education should have, what philosophy we should have, and what ways education can take to develop moral values in American youth, should be dominant.

Most of us who have been at work in college education have been asked to talk about the question of moral values, and a great deal has been written about it. Four chapters of this book have to do particularly with that subject, and the other three have to do with it indirectly. Much of the current discussion among educators is based on the assumption that moral values are fixed principles and codes of conduct known to philosophers, spiritual leaders, and educators, to be given to young people, who are presumed not to have them.

I disagree with this point of view. I believe, on evidence, that college students already have the beginning of a moral philosophy, and that in many ways it is more attractive than those recommended to them by their elders. Moral values are not fixed principles. They are ways of acting, modes of feeling and thinking, which are learned by children and adults through experiences with parents, friends, relatives, teachers, clergymen, business, their communities and life in general. The values change from person to person both in the way they are stated and the way they are lived. But the standard of judgment about their worth is based upon the way the values show themselves in positive acts of honesty, kindness, unselfishness, and respect toward the thoughts, feelings, and physical well-being of other people. A moral principle exists insofar as it is expressed in such acts. The morals, moral values, ways of thinking, and ways of behaving are different for this generation of college students than from those, for example, of the 1920's. But they are no less moral by the test of humanity and idealism by reason of that difference.

If college youth agreed to and acted upon all the moral exhortation currently being thrust upon them and actually became the kind of persons they are constantly being urged to become, I do not believe that anyone would enjoy them very much. They would be too much alike, too entirely predictable, too sanctimonious, too compliant, too uninteresting, too dependent, and too illiberal. I believe that in this matter American education is moving in the wrong direction, and I refuse to believe that the dominant tone of the older generation with its caution, its hesitancy, its insecurity, its conservatism, its fears, its public relations program for American virtue, and its nationalist dogma, has a compelling vision of life to present to American youth. What youth needs is breathing space, wider views, freedom to grow, encouragement, evidence of faith, leadership in humanitarianism and idealism, and the feeling that the future is to some degree open.

The young have been told often enough about the duties and the threats of contemporary life. They were born in a depression, grew up in a world war, and spent their adolescence in the cold war. They are ready for what comes next, they act responsibly, know their obligations, and need more than anything else the encouragement to become themselves and the means to achieve their own independence. The parent who has sufficient confidence in his sons and daughters of college age to encourage them to be themselves is usually the parent of children who have the qualities most parents would like them to have.

There are many things learned which are not taught, and some which cannot be unlearned. Children catch their values through the atmosphere, and are infected by courage and cynicism, love and hate, generosity and meanness, snobbery and kindness, selfishness and unselfishness. The formal part of most college programs has very little to do with such values, the life on the campus very much. Students are on the whole tolerant and liberal, and wish to do what the college expects of them in the matter of their attitudes. They will fit themselves to the social situation which the college arranges for them. Since liberal education is intentionally designed to liberalize and humanize each generation of the young, it is essential that the social situation be one congenial to liberal and democratic attitudes.

Yet there are college communities in America divided into exclusive groups which imitate the worst features of a stratified society: with wealthy, white, Gentile students living only with one another, while across the road or down the street live Jewish students in an equally segregated fraternity; in another part of town in boarding houses live the "independents" and the scholarship students, where sometimes Negro students are allowed to live as well. Tennis players are sometimes bought, at the age of fifteen, three years before entrance, to attend universities. Football players are offered cars, houses, salaries, for registration at particular institutions. Young women often select one another for admission to the sanctity of a sorority by estimating the value of the candidate's fur coat and other items of equipment, and by inquiring secretly into the financial position of the candidate's family. There are sorority rules forbidding any social contact with college men other than those from a selected list of eligible types.

This system of moral values is conducted under the auspices of college authorities, in the North, the Midwest, the West, the East, and the South, all in the name of liberal education. In many cases the students, who have found such moral attitudes revolting, have changed the situations to those more in keeping with their own principles, often against the efforts and attitudes of the older generation and the educators.

Or, to take another example, I believe most scholars and teachers would agree that the greatest value in the study of the liberal arts is gained when study is undertaken for the sake of its intrinsic importance to the student, and not because of external factors and pressures, whether the threat of low grades and academic disapproval, or the promise of competitive success, social recognition, or academic prestige. Most teachers also know that the credit system, the examination system, and the grade system are corrupting influences in American higher education, and that they furnish means by which students are put under the severe pressure of competition for prestige and for the external symbols of intellectual success. The result is that some spend more time in trying to beat or cheat the examination system itself than in learning what a college has to teach.

I find it hard to forget the student who came to me early in my teaching career to complain that she had not been given a grade of A for her essay examination in philosophy. She said that this was my responsibility and the fault of the course. If I had been of any consequence as a teacher, I would have taught her properly and the correct grade would have been forthcoming. Did I mark on a statistical curve, with a certain percentage of top grades, middle ones, and failures? If so, she claimed membership among those at the top. If not, my standards were personal, whimsical, and unjust. Had she not answered every question? Had she not read every assignment, made notes on every book, attended every lecture, said something in every discussion? She condemned my act as one which had marred her college career, had blotted an impeccable record with a B, would damage something called her grade point average, would keep her out of an honorary sorority, and would have to be explained to her friends, her mother, and her fiancé.

The difficulty in the situation was that she was right. She had been playing the game according to a set of rules laid down by the system, and I had suddenly changed the rules. Her university education had taught her a value system which included social and intellectual snobbery, and an artificial standard of intellectual achievement.

Among the central moral values around which so many others revolve is the value of critical intelligence. This it is the proper business of the university and the college to develop. Yet by its nature the conventional program of higher education directs the students' attention away from it. Everyone has noticed that fact, most people deplore it, but the educational reforms seldom touch it. Sometimes the reasons for not touching it are positive, and the idea is advanced that the agitations of competitive struggle for high grades are good for the students and furnish a motivation which would otherwise be lacking. Occasionally it is recommended as educational discipline and as preparation for the real world of competition in society. But most of the time it simply continues because the system is convenient and can be adapted to masses of students. I do not see how we can talk intelligently about developing moral values until we look at the specific ways in which the universities and colleges educate their students, and until the teachers themselves examine the quality and content of student learning to judge its worth and to find ways of improving it.

The reforms in the college curriculum during the postwar years have been made with too little concern for the individual student and the process of his learning. The attention of faculty planners has been concentrated on the materials of knowledge and on the question of what young Americans should know. This has led naturally to further concentration on the various departments of knowledge, and there has been a great deal of shifting around of departmental courses. In the absence of a coherent philosophy, other than the natural cohesion of similar subjects, it has been assumed that the welfare of each department in the college should be a central concern of the planning.

Accordingly, representatives of various groups within the faculty have been assembled into committees on curriculum. Often a philosopher and psychologist have been added for additional insight. Occasionally a creative writer has been attached, to write the statement of aims, and to make certain that the prose of the report itself is sufficiently abstract to include any point of view favored by the reader. These committee members have arranged matters so that due regard is paid to each subject and each department, and a rational order is established for the business of distributing students fairly throughout the departments. The fact that the new curriculum is now in operation from Los Angeles to Cambridge is a tribute to the seriousness of purpose, ingenuity, diligence, and sound tactics of the American academic community. It preserves intact the heritage of the past, the departmental system, and the conventional system of higher education.

But we should remember that the value of the system is to a high degree illusory. It is based on what could be called the three illusions of innocence of the American educator.

The first of these is the optical illusion. Merely because a hundred to fifteen hundred students are sitting in a lecture room all staring in one direction at a man talking, their eyes open, their hair combed, their notebooks in front of them, it is an illusion to believe that anything intellectually profitable is necessarily happening. What usually happens is that the internal life of each student goes along in its own way, alternately dreaming or listening; calculations are made about whether anything said will be on any examination; notes are taken such as "Get laundry tomorrow, see Joe re week end"; pictures are drawn, or elaborate diagrams of concentric circles: I have seen some very careful and delicate drawings of Plato in full color as a result of some of my own classes in philosophy at the University of Wisconsin.

The second illusion of innocence is the illusion of the examination. Merely because students are able to pick out the correct words from groups of five possible choices, because they can remember answers and facts for a sufficiently long time to locate them once a week, or once a month, or once a term, it is an illusion to think that the student has therefore shown himself to be educated. What has actually happened is that the student has borrowed someone's notes, looked up past examinations, looked in textbooks which he underlines interminably, consulted fraternity brothers, and has packed his head hastily with all the odds and ends of information which his preparation has turned up. Once he unpacks his head at the examination it is quite often empty again for some time.

The third illusion is that students are irresponsible, and that since they are still in the process of learning, they do not know how to conduct their own education or to assess the value of the one provided for them. This is the worst illusion of all. Students do know about their university. They can tell anyone who is interested which are the bad teachers, which are the entertainers, which are the good teachers, which are soft-hearted, which are left- or right-wing, which are dull, which ones care about students, and which ones they consider useless. The students do this best when they talk among themselves. They advise one another capably and well. In every student group there is a body of knowledge and wisdom about the whole educational system. There is also accurate information provided concerning the various ways to beat the system.

All these sources of educational thought should be tapped for the use of the university. The most important single reform we could undertake to aid the student is to give him responsibility, and greater freedom to carry it out. Because of the attitude of educators in the past, there has existed an exclusive concern for storing up knowledge, and for handing it over, intact, as a direct transaction from teacher to pupil, which has led to the many evil practices connected with lectures, textbooks, examining, and grading. Unless the effort of the teacher is in the direction of engaging the student in the process of knowledge, rather than in persuading him to accept the product already made by others, all the reforms of curricula are vain.

Nor do I think that college education can be planned intelligently until educators are aware of the general character, stage of development, and state of mind of the students they are called upon to educate. The present generation is much more mature about itself than previous ones. It was born in a difficult time as far as the external world of politics and social change is concerned, but a better time from the point of view of family attitudes. Earlier generations of parents and teachers held to a fairly stiff philosophy of child-rearing, and the first lesson to be learned by children was the lesson of obedience. The obedience was based not on an understanding by the child about why he was being asked to obey, but on the idea that the authority of parents and teachers was one of the facts of life. The family, the church, the school, the college, generated a set of rules which were based on obedience and were not to be questioned but to be accepted and acted upon. Young men and women in college were given social and intellectual rules to which they had to adapt or be dismissed from college.

Over the past fifty years, the area of freedom for young people in the family, school, and college has radically increased, and a new relation exists between parents and their children, pupils and their teachers. The relation is an easier one in some ways, but a harder one in others. It is easier in the sense that children and parents are much more frank and friendly with each other, there are open feelings of affection which would have been considered soft and spoiling in an earlier generation. The members of families have accepted one another with understanding of one another's weaknesses and the appreciation of virtues. The relations are sometimes harder because of the shift of authority away from the parents and teachers, and because very often the authority has no center; attempts by parents to help decide personal matters for college students are often rejected merely because they are made by the parents.

All family relations have loosened, and the young adult judges his parents as he judges others, not on the grounds of filial piety, but on the grounds of personal merit. He inclines to take his parents for granted, along with their financial support, their duties toward his welfare, without any apparent increase in his awareness of his own responsibilities and duties with regard to them. In advanced cases of adolescent sophistication, parents often receive advice from the children themselves as to how the parents can bring them up more successfully.

These characteristics of the young are often considered to be signs of irresponsibility, ingratitude, and rampant selfishness. The characteristics can be irritating, but are not indications of moral decay or lack of personal integrity. The attitudes have been learned, partly through the new family life. They come as a result of increased self-consciousness. The young people have assessed accurately the responsibilities of contemporary parents toward their children, without having learned the corollary lesson as to the duties and responsibilities of the children. These have also changed, and the lines of duty are no longer as clear as they were, in the minds of either parents or their children.

There are a great many gains for the young people in the changed attitude to children and the family. But there are some losses. The young often fail to take advantage of the wisdom and advice which their parents could give. Since they are no longer as dependent as before on the attitudes and wishes of their parents, they place a much greater reliance on the adolescent folkways they know than on personal standards held by the family. The young people have now gained independence of family dictation; they no longer find it necessary to rebel. The result is that without an authority to rebel against, some are living beyond their emotional means. They have cut themselves away from the family guidance and have not yet found a substitute, either in themselves, in their teachers, or in society in general. In situations like this the tendency is for young people to conform to the existing social and personal habits of the age group to which they belong. When they come to college they need an education which deals with their tendency to group conformity, and their desire for a center of intellectual security. They need to be educated into independence of group standards and to learn how to go it alone. This means that one of the first needs to be met is the need for intellectual and emotional self-confidence.

Whatever else the colleges do, they must take into account the independence and freedom the student has already won, and which he is not willing to give up. He is suspicious of anyone who asserts an authority over him, intellectual or otherwise, and is contemptuous of those who teach with a condescension toward students, or who demand assent to particular ideas.

The contemporary college student does not feel a sense of intellectual or social distance between himself and college professors. Like parents, college professors are considered as individuals with certain roles to play, to be judged by the things they say and do; and although the student usually recognizes his own duty to listen attentively and to fulfill the college demands for proper study, the respect he gives to the opinions and attitudes of college professors is based on his own judgment of their worth. He resents any effort to coerce him, either by administrative rules or by imposed ideas. To educate this generation of college students it is foolish to try to restrict intellectual and social freedom in the hope that this will produce firm commitments to doctrines taught in a didactic way. What is needed is an expansion of student freedom and a way of teaching the student to handle his own affairs, and to make himself responsible for the welfare of others.

During the past ten years, the American college student has demonstrated the fact that he is a responsible person, and an individual of some maturity. When put to the test, he has handled his own affairs. He has chosen a career and often worked at it in college. As a student, he has edited newspapers, run businesses, fought a war, chosen a wife, married her, supported a family, voted for a President. He has traveled abroad, organized conferences, studied college curricula, conducted student government, replaced dean's discipline by student discipline, written articles, educated foreign students, conducted seminars, and advised Congressmen. On their part, college women have shown equal responsibility and maturity. They have married during college, raised families while studying, traveled to Europe by themselves, paid their own way, worked as waitresses, published stories, served in student government, played in stock companies, taught school, organized nursery schools, worked in social agencies, served in hospitals, worked in politics.

These are the men and women we are called upon to educate. They demand serious treatment and they need the help of teachers who will take them seriously as young adults. If they are treated in an adult manner, they respond in an adult manner. If not, not.

The purpose of liberal education is to make people free and to keep them that way. I do not mean free to do anything they wish, but free from the handicaps of ignorance, intolerance, and illiberalism, and free to enjoy their own lives and to enrich the lives of others. The major issue in American education is whether or not the colleges and schools can remain free, from political, intellectual, or economic dictation. If they take as their task to teach students how to be free and how to think for themselves, in doing so they will build their own defenses against outside control and will teach the rest of society that freedom is the moral value on which the democratic system rests. If America does not learn to know this through the schools and colleges, there is no other place in American life where the values of democratic morality can be regenerated and recreated in each generation.

I hope that some of the questions raised in this book may persuade other teachers and other people interested in colleges to examine themselves for their own educational ideas, and to think about them, talk about them, and try them out in practice.

Some of the chapters were first written as addresses or articles, and then rewritten afterward in the light of comments in discussion and further thoughts of my own. I have not tried to join them together as consecutive chapters, and each has to be read as a separate discussion of topics related but not linked together. I am grateful to David Driscoll, Esther Raushenbush, and Alastair Reid for their kindness in reading various parts of the manuscript.

HAROLD TAYLOR

Holderness, New Hampshire
August, 1953

Chapter One

MORAL VALUES AND THE
EXPERIENCE OF ART

I BEGIN with a question set by Socrates, drawn from a familiar passage in *The Republic*.

Do you hold the popular belief that, here and there, certain young men are demoralized by the private instructions of some individual sophist? Does that sort of influence amount to much? Is not the public itself the greatest of all sophists, training up young and old, men and women alike, into the most accomplished specimens of the character it desires to produce?

When does that happen? Whenever the populace crowds together at any public gathering, in the Assembly, the law courts, the theatre, or the camp, and sits there clamoring its approval or disapproval, both alike excessive, of whatever is being said or done; booing and clapping till the rocks ring and the whole place redoubles the noise of their applause and outcries. In such a scene what do you suppose will be a young man's state of mind? What sort of private instruction will have given him the strength to hold out against the force of such a torrent, or will save him from being swept away down the stream, until he accepts all their notions of right and wrong, does as they do, and comes to be just such a man as they are? [1]

[1] Plato, *The Republic*, Book VI, translated by Cornford (Oxford University Press, New York, 1945), p. 199.

The clear answer is to teach the young to be free and to think for themselves. Until a man can do so he has no strength to hold out against the torrent and he will be swept down the stream. The question of how to teach him is more complicated, although we know how to begin. We do not begin by telling him what he should think and how he should act. We begin by making him know that we care about what he thinks, that we believe in his power to reach truth, that he is at liberty to make errors, that we are not afraid of where his thoughts might lead him. Until he feels completely confident that while he is learning he may say what he thinks without punishment or hindrance, he cannot begin to learn how to be free.

It is true that the public itself is the greatest of all sophists. A sophist is a man who makes the worse seem the better cause, a man who makes arguments not to establish the truth but to make a lie seem plausible. This is something which the public does, whether we like it or not. In contemporary American life, there are so many public pressures which bear down on the individual American citizen that it requires a serious and sustained effort of will to think, and even to feel, independently. It requires a deep sense of personal confidence to express independent conclusions once they have been reached.

Yet the pressures, once they have been seen as threats to individual independence, may produce their own reaction. There is no better way to arouse the American citizen than to order him around or to tell him what to think. Although there are many people in this country who would like to organize us more thoroughly and tidy up the freedom we have by a little more control, we still reserve the personal right to plunge our own way into our own mistakes and discoveries, in art, philosophy, education, or politics; and we suffer fools to tell us what to think and what to do, because in this country when a fool tells us what to do, we do not necessarily have to do it.

It is only in response to a challenge, a question, or a threat that we are forced to state our principles and to stand on them. Few are interested in gentle declarations in favor of virtue. Everyone is interested in vigorous statements of principle when principle is challenged by attack. The defeat of public sophistry begins when the citizen states his private truth and defends it by the laws of evidence.

It is often forgotten that all truth is private and all convictions are personal. Truths are known by individuals, one at a time, who believe one idea to be true and another one false. It is forgotten too that learning is a private affair taking place within the individual consciousness. The individual human being learns and becomes educated. Formal education is not something done to him. It merely surrounds him with the possibility of learning. The teacher and the educational institution are the means by which his inner life changes its character and content; the learner is the agent by which the changes occur. The teacher's first duty is to show his students how they can arrive at their own honest principles and then to teach them that the test of principle is in human action.

The teacher must therefore reach the individual consciousness of his students, penetrate beneath the surface of the slogans which cover the public mind, and set in motion those spontaneous and fresh insights which lead toward personal truth and personal value. This is the beginning of philosophy and of true education. We in America reject the idea of giving to our students a single pattern of truth which everyone must accept. When we succeed in moving the private consciousness into a condition of honest inquiry, we have begun the process toward a philosophy and an education which the student himself will complete.

There are moral values to be found in the student's experience which he cannot avoid accepting—the value of reason, of honorable conduct, of co-operation. If he refuses to accept them, he cannot remain a student. There are other moral values—courage, independence, charity, generosity, sensitivity—which he may not find in his experience as a student, but which he should find there if he is to be truly educated. The students themselves are ready to move toward the ideals which the liberal arts can teach them. They have values of their own which are sound. What they need is leadership toward new values through which they can enlarge and mature the outlook they already possess.

II

I am tired of hearing that moral values have disintegrated in the Western world. I am tired of hearing that the modern world has deprived life of its certainties, that the ideals of classical civilization have been shattered. I am weary of writers who claim that we are lost, bewildered, frustrated, neurotic, decadent, uncertain, threatened, insecure, immoral, corrupt, and generally doomed. Some people are. Some aren't.

We are, after all, living in our own world, in our own time, with our own values. It is, above all, an interesting time, if a little more dangerous than usual, and if its values are not indentical with those of the upper class, or philosophical set, in classical Greece, or are not identical with those of the emperors, soldiers, consuls, and working writers of the early Roman period, or with the ecclesiastical group of the medieval period who burned their heretics or shut them up in other ways for the ultimate benefit of humanity, or with the nineteenth-century groups who got along by keeping the workers in a state of economic and social insecurity, I find that I can face this fact cheerfully, and look for new values which can work more satisfactorily for everyone than the old ones used to do.

The disintegration of older values in favor of new has been

going on for the past three thousand years. In the twentieth century we are much more self-conscious about it, and with an acute awareness of our own history and the reasons we have come to be as we are, we have fallen into doom-ridden ways of talking about the certainties of the past and the horrors of the future. The reason the past is certain is that it is dead. For the modern citizen, this is too great a price to pay for certainty.

Beneath everything we say about our own age is an unconscious acceptance of the idea that the past was somehow normal and stable. The times have never been normal. They have been what they came to be by the efforts of the people who worked at it, who fought, spoke, thought, believed, planned, disagreed, agreed, and who were active within the limits of their own history to set the standards of the normal for themselves and for the future. The social forces, the necessities of history, are forceful or necessary only as individual human beings make them so, or allow them to be so by accepting the habits inherited by their generation. How else does history happen?

We have, among many other warnings, Mr. Toynbee's that history is working out its present phase at our expense, and we have Mr. Toynbee's assurance that when civilizations appear to be at their most healthy, prosperous, and blooming, they are actually rotting away at the core and are about to begin a radical decline. Those ignorant of this fact, or those who protest against it, are simply unaware of the inner dynamic of history. The rosiest apple contains the biggest worm.

On this point Mr. Toynbee is either wrong or right. In all questions of this kind referring to the present and where it is going, no philosopher or historian has better than a 50% chance of being right, although there are many who, with solemnity and without humility before history, predict decline as a professional occupation. Since the idea of decline cannot be verified except by going on living in order to see what will happen,

I suggest that, for the moment at least, we simply turn the theory around the other way, and by a happier logic, which has just as much chance of being true, accept the idea that when civilization seems to be at its worst stage, it is actually at the beginning of its best and most promising. In this way, we can face the future with grace and a modest hope, and with an amount of historical dignity equal to that of any historian.

At the same time, it is of first importance to recognize that our present time has special qualities, and that it is not just another period of the sort which followed wars in the past. The prime fact is that for the first time we have the means, and to some degree the will, to destroy the whole of contemporary civilization. The age is marked by its use of power, violence, terror, death, and intimidation as the standard means of settling social conflicts, with a sharp decline in the use of persuasion, appeal to moral values, and respect for personal rights. It is of course marked by an enormous increase in the development of new ways of bullying people into thinking required thoughts through the mass media and political coercion. Its favorite words are confusion, tension, and action. It is marked by the growth of politics to an overwhelming size in the scale of human concerns. But perhaps more significant than any of these things, and in large part as a result of them, it is marked by a continuous assault on the privacy and the moral confidence of the free-thinking individual. The nature of the assault is to drive everyone into line, to force agreement to policies, ideas, and acts which have been determined by state, public, or group authority.

There is an ultimate privacy of the moral conscience which is at the center of all personal values. If that privacy is invaded by force, coercion or threats of coercion, the effect is to dry up the flow of action and ideas from which new moral values come. With the loss of that privacy, moral and intellectual self-confidence is lost as well, and the individual hesitates, examines, analyzes, and is silent. It drives the individual within himself, and detaches his inner life from his outer action. He then says things which he does not mean, and, under compulsion, does things which he does not intend, and which produce an inner conflict and a secret embarrassment. The destruction of the human personality begins to be possible when that privacy is threatened, and the destructive element in social and political life begins to damage the individual citizen when a society allows the threat of coercion to go unchallenged.

Some of these threats are to be found in the assaults on the twentieth-century child through education. Sometimes the attacks are made under communist auspices, as in Eastern Europe and the Soviet Union; sometimes under fascist auspices, as in Spain and Argentina; at other times under organized bigotry, as in the United States. We should remind ourselves of the identical pattern to be found in each instance of assault. The first act of an authoritarian group, whether communist, fascist, or just plain patriotic, after it has seized power and control of the army and police force, is to capture the universities and the schools. Later come the capture of the artists and the writers. The pattern in all instances is simply this: tell the citizen what is valuable, what to think, what to do, and by psychological, political, or physical means coerce him into believing that what he has been told is true. Whether or not he knows it to be true is not important. He must be required by the authorities to make the correct public response to questions asked as to what is true, good, and beautiful.

We who believe in democratic education know what are the moral values which we want our children to accept and to fulfill in their lives. We want them to be honest, fair-minded, just. We want them to enjoy their lives, and to have a sense of purpose about the way they live and the experiences they choose.

We want them to be sympathetic and generous in their attitude to other people, to other cultures, and to other countries than their own. We wish them to be sensitive to the beautiful and the ugly, in actions and objects alike. We want them to believe in individual rights and human freedom, and to have a breadth of knowledge and a way of finding the knowledge they do not have. There are a great many ways in which these qualities are learned, and a great many different kinds of people who show them—composers, poets, scientists, farmers, workers, teachers.

This is not necessarily a matter of college education, since the qualities of the desired kind seem to develop well in other places. Values are learned, not always consciously, through the particular set of situations in which people spend most of their time, by the direct and indirect personal influence of parents, teachers, friends, and employers. The value of things and ideas is learned by the immersion of the individual in the stream of human relations which make up his daily life. The value of democracy is learned not merely by the study of its history or its character, but by learning what it feels like to be democratic. The value of a painting or a poem is not learned by hearing it described and praised, although that may help, but by responding to it personally. Unless the personal response is present, nothing has happened.

The beginning of moral values is in the child when he first explores his talents and desires. His mind and the rest of him all grow together as he plays with clay, rides his tricycle, learns to read, and wrestles his friends. When we think of children we think of them in terms of their possibilities, their needs, and their efforts at understanding. A genuine sense of wonder exists in each child, and each one, if he is given a chance, asks about the origin of the objects around him, and why things happen as they do. The child continually looks for values and for truth, and his search leads him to the important issues. These are the issues of what is good and what is bad, what is beautiful and what is ugly, and what is true and what is false. He asks for help, and wants to know from us what answers we can give him.

We cannot avoid giving answers. But we can avoid forcing the answers upon him as a form of revealed truth. We can also avoid cutting up the answers into different departments of knowledge, and classifying what he learns as subject matter—science, art, philosophy. We tell him as much as we can about what he asks. It is only when the child becomes involved in an educational system that he learns that there is a difference between science and art, poetry and fact, knowledge and values. When, as parents or as teachers, we are face to face with the very young child, we try to teach him to live in his world by making him understand the relations between one thing and another (philosophy) how to deal with himself and other people (psychology), what are the names and descriptions of various things (science), how to enjoy life (the arts), how to interpret the influences exerted by his parents and their friends (social science), how to count and do abstract thinking (mathematics), how to imagine people and situations (literature), and what are some of the more desirable ways to behave (the humanities).

In dealing with the young child, fortunately, it is almost impossible for us to separate the development of his mind from the development of the rest of him, since it is very clear that his mind is that part of his person which helps him to explore his world successfully and to satisfy his own hunger for knowledge and understanding. The way in which we measure the intelligence and moral qualities of children is by observing the way in which they respond to their own situations, the liveliness of their interest in the world around them, the readiness with which they grasp the meaning of what we say to them and what they say to one another. This of course involves the things they know; but the things they know are never subjects, or academic disciplines—they are things they have learned through living them. We immediately recognize the fact that in children there is a close relation between personality and intelligence, environment and emotions, mind and body.

As parents or teachers we wish to help the child change and grow in the ways signified by his talents. We must set the moral structure of his life widely enough to allow freedom of growth, and firmly enough to prevent diffusion of his impulses into a chaos of indecisive values. We need to bring to the education of older children and of young adults, in fact to our total program of education, the insight and knowledge we have gained about human nature from the study of the very young. This means, among other things, that we will have to stop acting as if human nature is everywhere the same; we will have to deal with students one at a time, and take as our aim the release of the talent which lies within each person.

I suggest therefore that we look at the whole of education as a series of different experiences, some of them more useful and interesting than others. Children and adults will continue to have experiences whether we wish them to or not. If the public is the greatest of all sophists and is capable of the highest degree of corruption, it is also the greatest of all educators, since it surrounds the child and the adult with continual experience from which the individual learns.

III

The difference between a school or college and all the other institutions of society is that the school or college selects a particular kind of experience for the individual according to an idea of what it wishes the child to become. The difference between the school and society is that the ultimate concern of the school is with moral values, or with the idea of what the child ought to become and what man ought to be. Society as it goes along is concerned with such matters only occasionally, and has made educational systems in order to transmit and recreate its own ideas from generation to generation.

What is the basic value in our American society which we want to transmit? What single item can be said to distinguish our value system from any other?

If we have to choose one single item, it must be freedom. The political structure of any society is modified or formed to support the demands which the citizens make for the attainment of certain values, and it is because of the ideal of freedom that we have organized our particular form of democracy. Having organized such a society, we have *needed* the idea of freedom to serve as a social goal and a social motive. Freedom in this system is not a luxury or a by-product of the society. It is the necessary and distinctive characteristic of this particular social order. It follows therefore that the educational system which serves our social order has as its primary duty to teach children to be free, and to believe in freedom as a personal and social ideal.

How can this be done?

Not simply by the study of patriotic American history or a study of the Constitution. The only way it can be learned is by living with it and in it. This involves a shift in the theory and practice of education.

As one aspect of the self-consciousness of the twentieth century, we have become interested in the ways in which personal characteristics are developed, and have formed new theories about human nature. The classical view of human nature holds that the individual human mind is identical throughout the whole of the species: the human being contains a mind composed of a mental substance in about the same way that an egg contains a yolk. Just as there is, in nature, a universal method for hatching eggs by placing on the nest the curriculum of the universal hen, so there is the classical curriculum, everywhere the same, which, if placed properly, can guarantee the hatching of rational certainty in the universal student. Although, in the classical view, the body may change and may vary from person to person, and may occasionally get the mind into trouble, it has only incidental relations with the mind, and thus has little to do with education or the development of character. For this reason, a major part of traditional education consists in wrestling with the body, keeping it out of the way, curbing the emotions, trying to make students learn in spite of themselves, and trying to keep the natural desires of the human being from interfering with the intellectual processes.

The flaw in this theory of human nature is that the values we actually hold have their roots deep in the body, and that desires, ideals, sex, sensibility, anger, joy and a number of other useful assets, play their own part in the incidents of the intellect. It is important to add immediately that the intellect, or mind, is a great aid to us in achieving the ends toward which our desires would have us move. The intellect also gives us considerable help in deciding in which direction we would like which desires to set about moving us.

A modern theory of human nature is therefore much more complicated. It accepts, for example, the influence of social environment on the personal character of the individual. It accepts the existence of an area of the unconscious as a significant part of the total personality. It assumes that there is a direct relationship between childhood experience and character in later life. It accepts the fact that motivations and talents are different from person to person, and different in each person at different times in his life. In other words, it accepts as observably true that each individual human being is a special case, and that if education is to be effective, it must deal with the emotional, the intellectual, and social needs of the individuals it is serving.

All this has a close relationship with the idea of freedom. A large part of the experimental work which has been carried on in modern education has had to do with the ways in which children can learn to become free, and, in becoming free, learn to discipline themselves to the needs of others, to the needs of their society, and to personal needs of their own. We know a great deal more than we used to know about the relation of the creative arts to the emotional development of children, and we know enough to say that creative work and experience in the arts has a generous contribution to make to the full maturing of the individual, or, as the matter is often put, to the development of a free personality. By this is meant a personality capable of reacting spontaneously, satisfactorily, and independently to new or to familiar situations.

Political, social, and economic freedom are of course the condition of personal freedom. The ideal condition allows the individual to choose courses of action among a rich variety of alternatives without the restrictions produced by hunger, class stratification, authoritarian rules, poverty, and economic insecurity. But once external freedom is assured to the extent that the individual citizen can share actively and without inhibition in the formation of public policy, the matter of personal freedom comes up again. How can the young learn to use their freedom? If there is no one to force the student to accept rules about what is good and bad politics, what is good and bad conduct, what is good and bad art, how does he make up his mind?

The answer is that he has to learn how to do it as part of his total education. To be free in the sense of being able to make independent choices means that the free person must know a great deal, must be sensitive to a wide variety of experiences, and must have enough confidence in his own judgment to assert it and to learn how to correct it through further experience. It also means that he must have learned to respond to other people and other ideas, different from his own, rather than reacting against them, and that he has learned to accept differences as natural rather than as a threat to himself and his whole style of life.

The psychological study of human nature has also turned up some important relations between rigidity and flexibility, dogmatism and liberalism, freedom and authority, as factors in the character structure of the individual. We have a clearer idea of the way in which personal rigidities are related to authoritarian ideas. The study of the authoritarian personality has gone far enough to show that those who are opposed to freedom for others and who want a controlled and ordered society have a standardized way of behaving toward many different kinds of situations, all the way from child-training to modern art. Such individuals show hostility to all groups and kinds of people who are different from themselves, consider the world a dangerous and threatening place, give exceptional emphasis to social power and social status, and are both socially and personally insensitive to the needs and wishes of others.

The extraordinary fact is that there is such a close relation between a hatred of liberalism in political and social terms, and a hatred of modern art, modern education, modern literature, and modern life in general. It is not hard to understand why people object to politicians whose ideas they do not like, or who might involve them in higher taxes, or why the people who detest state control of anything also object to price control. But why there should be such incredible outbursts against modern art, or modern education, why abstract painters should be considered more likely to be subversive than the realists, why representational sculpture should be considered more patriotic and more American than mobiles, why political criteria should be used to judge works of art of any kind, requires a great deal of understanding. It also requires a great deal of patience on the part of the artists, museum directors, and teachers who are attacked.

What has the modern artist done to deserve the epithets of Congressmen, columnists, war veterans, conservative sculptors, clergymen, and museum directors? Essentially what he has done is to say, Here is the way I see contemporary reality, this is the way I wish to work, these are the things I present for you to see, this is what I believe about art, this is what I have learned, I intend to go on working this way, consider it, look at it, enjoy it, with my compliments.

As far as I can see, the conduct of the artist is impeccable; he makes no claims except through his work, he threatens no one. Like the modern educator, he is experimental in his approach, and his work stands or falls with the results of his experiment.

The conduct of the observer, however, when he comes to the gallery or to the school, is a matter for the observer to determine for himself. If he screams with rage, if he feels himself threatened, insulted, or badgered, if he shouts that contemporary reality is not like that, if he cries for the *Sistine Madonna*, if he calls for the police or a Congressional investigation, this reveals something in him, not in the artists, the art, or the educator. The majority of those who comment unfavorably on modern art and education do not actually go to the galleries and the schools, and the act of looking at sculpture, architecture, or children themselves is not a necessary preliminary to denunciation. Modern art along with modern education is merely said to be corrupting, enervating, decadent, and communist, because, as one happy little band of critics put it, the work is dangerous "to the whole philosophy of national normalcy."

Certainly. It is dangerous to rigidity, smugness, conformity, and sterility. It starts from different assumptions, and moves to different conclusions. It refuses to take its orders from outside the areas of aesthetic judgment, or from any other source than the individual creative idea. It asserts the value of free expression, in whatever medium and in whatever form the artist and educator find valid and creative. When the work fails, it fails for its own reasons, not for the reasons assigned to it by those who reject its right to exist.

Yet for the past twenty-five years, bitter denunciations of modern art and the modern artist have been made on exactly the opposite grounds. The most recent one came from a Congressman who, in taking the present Soviet line on "formalist" art, bundled together a variety of museums and galleries, along with the artists themselves, as the conveyors of "distortion, frustration, and a spirit of rebellion," in addition to acting as vehicles of Soviet and communist propaganda. Included among those accused of modernism was one conservative museum whose director had himself denounced modern art shortly before on the grounds that (a) it had been rejected by the public, and (b) it was having a widespread pernicious influence.

But in the field of the general denunciation of pernicious influences, I believe that the National Sculpture Society's statement of January 1952 about politics, art, sculpture, and anarchy makes a particularly important contribution. The statement reads, in part:

In many of our schools and colleges, the students are being systematically indoctrinated in the philosophy of imaginative anarchy in the creative arts. . . . Unfortunately, by destroying an ideal of beauty, endeavor, and discipline in the artistic expression of a people, the very foundations upon which this national achievement rest are being undermined. The so-called "modern" artists claim that they represent the New age, and the tremendous changes it has brought. We most heartily repudiate this claim, in the name of the sound, normal American people.

In its form, its content, and its urgency this protest is a crude model of a frequent protest in America against modernism as a philosophy and an attitude, or, to put it more broadly, against the modern world and what it now contains. Hostility to modern art and modern artists is a symptom of a deeper and wider antipathy which includes hostility to advanced ideas in every quarter. The protest against progressive ideas in education, against the relativism of social science, against the dominance of science as a way of knowing, against the obscurity of poetry, the complexity of literature, and the disappearance of absolutes, is the rejection of a modern world in which ideas new in this century have emerged from the past.

In another sense, it is a rejection of modern man himself, the complexity of his self-awareness, his demand for individual freedom, and his explanations for his own behavior. The attack on modernism, which occurs in every century, is the present symbol of a period in which people have become tired of complexity and difficulty and look for simplicity, clarity, and stability. The intellectual movements of this century have been successful in the analysis of human nature, society, and truth itself, until, on the one hand, philosophy has been able to show that there can be no philosophy, psychology has been able to show that there is no simple human act, and, on the other, science has been able to show that the universe has no specific beginning and no end, and that it possesses a degree of unpredictability which was not formerly suspected. Twentieth-century movements have been less successful in putting back a synthesis to replace what has been torn down.

IV

This century does in fact represent a break with the past. The break came as the result of revolutions, in politics, society, industry, culture, and intellectual affairs. The study of society through anthropology, economics, and sociology loosened the tight pattern of natural laws for human behavior and exposed the fallacy of thinking that all societies and all human beings are alike. Such studies provided a new map of society and a new concept of culture, and have had a devastating effect on the absolutes of moral value.

Philosophy and psychology gave a new dimension to the idea of human nature and a new definition of truth. The experience of knowing was no longer a camera-eye technique by which a mind inside a body received pictures of an outside world and developed them in its own darkroom. The truth was not everywhere the same. The relentless and rapid movements of science over one problem after another, with the use of science to enlarge the whole social and physical world and to bring communication throughout its parts, were cultural phenomena which cut us away from the past. The mass media then brought a partial awareness of contemporary society to masses of men and women who knew no society or century other than their own. This has sealed them off in a separate point of time and history in the twentieth century.

The dislocation of images, the refusal to accept classical rules of art, and the appeal to private experience, all became part of the break artists and writers made with the past. They changed the look and feel of the older reality to which Western civilization had become accustomed. At the same time, we found ourselves with larger and larger collective societies which seemed to develop social laws of their own, while we became less certain of our own power to control them. Add to all this two world wars and an international economic depression followed by renewed revolution, and the break is definite. One can understand the dominant wish to return to the past and to reject a modernism which tries to encompass the total confusion.

Yet a rejection of the real world is not a solution of any consequence. Modernism can be understood only as an attempt to represent the modern world in new and truthful ways. Its basis lies in the acceptance of the reality of the present world. In architecture it does not refuse science, it joins science and art in a new synthesis; it does not reject mass man, it invents new forms of living to accommodate him; it does not reject the industrial revolution, and sigh for cottages, it accepts with delight the new materials and new ideas which technology makes possible. In poetry, sculpture, painting, and dance, modernism does not deny the reason, form, or classical aesthetic values; it simply drops some of the old, having become aware of it and weary of it, and invents new ways of synthesis of modern ideas in new forms of expression. It has new things to say which cannot be said in the old ways.

Modern education does not reject the classical tradition by a concern for the child in his present existence. It is rejecting the past in terms of its failures, and looks ahead to the use of everything it can find about human behavior in order to improve the quality of teaching and learning and to increase the reach of education. Modernism in education accepts the child as he is, and goes on from there, to what he can become, accepting also the fact that truth cannot be certain, that the good can never be absolute, that what comes next is more important than what failed yesterday, that the modern world has in it not merely the seeds of its own destruction but the seminal ideas for its own growth. In keeps itself open and friendly toward the world and toward human nature.

But in doing so it does not deny the traditional virtues, nor the value of the disciplined intellect. On the contrary, the modern teacher and the modern artist both know that the creative act demands, as a condition of its successful accomplishment, the most severe intellectual discipline, and that to live as a moral independent it is necessary not merely to believe in moral principle but to know enough about the conditions of each moral situation to be intelligent about it. The teacher and the artist have a common aim, to open up the way to free development and growth—the one in the life of the child, the other in the form and content of the arts.

V

Modernism as a philosophy is romantic and restless. It denies the authority of the state, of politics, of moral absolutes, or of brute power to decide the goals of human life and the rules of conduct for individuals, whether in their personal lives, in their society, in their art, or in their education. It finds the pessimism of the classical attitude boring and destructive, the rules of classical absolutes inhibiting and deadening, and the classical interpretation of life a distorted image of what exists in reality. The classical message, that all this has happened before and that there is nothing much we can do to change it, that human nature goes along its own way, darting here and there but always returning to the same thing, falls on unwilling ears. Modernism accepts the philosophy of process and puts itself on the side of nature and the upward thrust of individual energy against the downward weight of history, and believes that if there is room to grow, and room to correct mistakes, the good will be accomplished.

To the conservative, the classicist, or to those who want to trim down hope to a minimum of aspiration, this is naive and woolly romanticism. They say that you cannot trust the young, or the uneducated, or those who will not recognize traditional rules to make their own formulae for personal, social, political, or aesthetic behavior. Nor can you trust a philosophy which leaves all the ultimate questions unanswered, and the particular rules of human conduct uncodified. In practice, it is said, the philosophy means merely that those who are liberated then control those who liberated them, science controls civilization, popular standards control culture, the masses control the former élite, the modern artists control the museums, labor controls management, children control their parents.

It would be a very foolish philosophy which left itself with no control for the unbridled release of human energy, and which had no form or direction. The fact is that modernism achieves its standards and its direction through the work of its own critical intelligence, not through external convention or tradition. Eric Newton states the recurring problem of such philosophy when he says:

To liberate is not always desirable. Freedom is a dangerous gift, and for the creative artist freedom from obligation to represent may be fatal. Indeed, unless he exchanges that freedom for another kind of obligation, it is certain to be fatal. What makes a sculptor great is not his act of rebellion against the old formula . . . but his subsequent act of submission to a new formula of his own invention. Without a formula of some sort there can be no order, no discipline, no harmony; and without these, there can be no art. That is true of all power, human or inhuman. Water, for example, unless it is canalized, will spread itself into a useless, unattractive marsh. Harness it, imprison it, and it will turn dynamos or light cities.[2]

The teacher whose outlook is modern no longer feels the necessity of rebellion. The rebellion was successful and he won new ground. He has found new ways, new formulae of his own invention, and his efforts are now used to enlarge and defend his discoveries against those who want him to go back to the old and others who want him to give up his independence and method of critical thinking. The teacher is an artist who can

[2] Eric Newton, *The New York Tims Sunday Magazine*, August 11, 1952, p. 17.

teach the art of learning and who can guide his students to experience of the arts themselves. The experience of art is one which quickens the human consciousness to a greater sensitivity of feeling and a higher level of discrimination among ideas and emotions. There is not simply one kind of art or subject which lends itself to this experience, whether modern or traditional, a painting or a theory, sculpture or science. The art objects and subjects themselves are the occasions on which individuals, either the artists and thinkers who made them or the observers and readers who re-create them, can move more freely into areas of experience which were formerly unknown.

We cannot destroy the ideal of beauty or of truth except by crushing the artists, thinkers, and teachers themselves, or by forcing their expression into insincerity by the demands we make for " normality" and conformity. The experience of liberal arts, for the child in school and for everyone else, is an experience through which one can gain insight into what it means to be free in emotional response and free in the choice of ideas. The experience of the arts is a way of enriching the total quality of human experience, and of reaching a precision in the choice of values. It is a particular kind of experience which requires for its fulfillment a discipline freely undertaken, a knowledge firmly grasped, a heightened consciousness, and an intensity of interest in the creative and imaginative aspects of human life. It is not an experience which takes the artist or the thinker out of the material world or out of the context of his society, but one which moves through contemporary reality into newer levels of awareness of what human society is.

The moral value of art, and of education as an art, lies in this process of discovery and in this contribution to the richness of human experience. Its value lies in drawing attention to aspects of the world other than those connected with material, social, or political power. Experience of the arts leads into discussion of ultimates, into questions of truth, into serious philosophy, since the response evoked in each of us becomes part of our way of looking at the world and part of our stated and unstated vocabulary of response.

The ideals of the spirit of humanism are carried not in manifestoes, catalogues, or proclamations, but in the minds and hands of the creative thinkers, the scientists, the artists, and the teachers. Through them and through their work we find a continual reassertion of the invincibility of the human intelligence in its continual struggle with ignorance and bigotry. This provides its own proclamation of freedom—freedom for the imagination, for the reason, and for the human personality. Those who catch the meaning of this freedom through their experience with art and free thought possess an antidote against despair and a weapon against oppression.

We teach the meaning of freedom when we teach the young to explore the world of the imagination. We thus give the private instruction which can enable young men and women to hold out against the torrent. We need no explanation or defense of the arts; all we need do is to practice them and to enjoy their benefits. The process of creating a poem, a play, a painting, a book, or a mature and independent student is a discipline imposed, not from without but from within, and it need answer to no one for its final form. The art of teaching draws upon the finest human qualities—sympathy, imagination, affection, understanding—and it raises the level of human consciousness by its presence in our culture. It is an art which enhances all other arts, and restores the intellectual vitality, the self-confidence, and the moral dignity of the contemporary individual. By the imaginative reconstruction of human experience it can show that human life is greater, more noble, more wide-ranging in its possibilities than the particular embodiment it now takes in the politics and disorders of the present moment.

Chapter Two

THE COLLEGE PRESIDENT

THERE are few men and women who receive as much advice as the president of an American college. The advice comes from politicians, journalists, radio commentators, Congressional committees, businessmen, alumni, trustees, students, parents, deans, faculty members, and people he meets on buses. Much of it does not reach the president directly but is blown on the winds of private talk. There are people, some of them strangers, who will quickly advise him about raising money, how to get rid of subversives, how to aid free enterprise, what to say and what not to say, what subjects to teach, how to discipline the younger generation, what to do about communism, and how to encourage free thought without worrying anyone about its consequences. The inner content of a great deal of this advice, no matter what its outward form, is, Don't do anything. It will be either expensive or dangerous.

Other items of public advice are contained in speeches, magazine articles, and newspaper reports, although here the college president is not usually mentioned by name or office, but is addressed by the generalization "Higher education in this country must . . ." followed by a wide variety of interesting predicates. It is encouraging, although wearing for presidents, that so much serious interest is taken in the work of colleges. The colleges and universities now provide the center for intellectual and moral controversy formerly occupied by religious institutions when the Protestant movement was struggling to gain and hold its independence, and the freethinkers were struggling to gain independence from the Protestants.

There is hardly a single problem or controversial issue, economic, religious, philosophical, political, social, scientific, or aesthetic, which in one way or another fails to receive serious and troubled attention in the contemporary American college. In a very real sense, the college has become a testing ground for ideas and values, and a community in which the major issues of American life are analyzed, investigated, and exposed to public view.

Because of the volume and intensity of the advice and interest, and in view of the seriousness with which higher education is now treated, the college president must be his own man. That is to say, he must make up his own mind about what he thinks his college should be and where it should be going. Otherwise other people will run the college for him by the volume and intensity of their advice. Or the college will not be run at all, but will simply wallow in its own tradition.

There is a difference, of course, between acting on conviction after learning all one can from other people, and indulging in a private dogma. The one is principled action, the other merely arrogance. Mr. Robert Hutchins once pointed out, wittily, although I believe mistakenly, that the university president must either be strong and disliked or weak and tolerated —either an office boy or an administrator. Mr. Hutchins went on to point out that the proper president is a philosopher in action, by which he implied that the president should keep his time and mind free to think up decisive things for the faculty and other educators to do.

I am reluctant to disagree with this view, although I find it necessary to do so. The college president will find that no matter how much abstract thinking he does, the educational ideas resulting from the process will only be as good or as helpful in improving education as other people believe them to be, and as other people feel impelled to carry them out. The president will also find that a great many ideas which seemed to be of very deep significance when first written down become much less so when placed in the middle of a faculty discussion.

The fact is that a college or university is made up of a variety of individuals with diverse points of view about ultimate and immediate truth, but all of whom agree in a general way that the search for ultimate and immediate truth is the final aim of the institution. In this situation, the president, selected by a board of trustees which forms a "jury whose favorable verdict must be secured," may have his own particular sets of truths firmly in hand, but he will refuse to act as if the search for ultimates had ended successfully with his own conclusions about them. He will act so that the quality of thought, the quality of personal relations, and the quality of student learning in his institution are constantly working toward a higher level. It is his sense of what constitutes a higher level which must be clear and unequivocal, and his attitude toward his colleagues in the faculty and in the board of trustees must be one of alliance with men and women of good will, each of whom, it must be assumed, is equally interested in raising the level of quality in the daily life of the university.

There have been universities in which the weakness, incompetence, amiability, insensitivity, or willfulness of a president has created situations in which the faculty or board of trustees has organized itself so strongly that the president is put in chains. There have been other colleges in which one arbitrary act or one weak and foolish act by a president has caused the whole institution to decline. Of the two, the weak action is the more disastrous, since the opposition aroused to strong action and the arbitrary use of authority often livens up the community and generates new ideas. Continuous amiability in a president, the negative passion for having no trouble, leads to a mediocrity in the intellectual and social environment of any college. At best, individual trustees or faculty members with strong views or a talent for faculty intrigue may rise to the occasion and seize power, either directly or indirectly. But the controversy and general disturbance which result will deflect a great deal of useful emotional energy into useless activity.

The first necessity for the university and its president is therefore a clearly seen and strongly held conviction about its aims. If the college or the university is to teach students to think, add to the store of knowledge, search out the truth, and put old and new ideas to the test of critical intelligence, the president must be a person with the will and the capacity to achieve these ends. If he demonstrates some capability and a serious commitment to the aims of his institution, the faculty will forgive him many errors and will support his general effort. The way in which his acts are judged should be, What effect does this have on the education of the students? On the faculty? On the quality of life in the college community? The strength of the president is measured by the degree and kind of help he receives unasked from his colleagues in carrying out the aims of education. His contribution to education is measured by the opportunity he provides for every student, faculty member, trustee, alumnus, and employee of the college to move the institution toward its goal.

II

When the university movement first began some eight hundred years ago, universities were composed of scholars who elected one of themselves to act as leader. Occasionally the students administered their own education, to the point of employing their own faculty and moving their premises from one place to another.

In the United States in the middle of this century, we have now reached an opposite position. The administration of colleges and universities has become so complex a problem in finance and personnel that governing boards have often sought, in their appointments to the presidency, the services of men with business and administrative records, and, in many instances, have not considered scholarship or educational experience as essential to the post. The governing boards, composed of businessmen, industrial executives, lawyers, or political appointees of the state, incorporated by charter to control education, now frequently act in the manner of corporation executives employing an executive officer. The president is employed to administer funds set aside to hire a staff of experts to instruct young Americans in the proper professional skills, intellectual and social habits, and academic folklore of American society. Qualities of scholarship, learning, and humanity are not considered relevant to this task, and in some cases are considered hindrances. What is said to be required is sound business sense, good public presence, a talent for never annoying anyone, and a reputation for political and social respectability. In special cases it is considered necessary for the president to have been very well known by the general public for work in a field which has no connection at all with education.

So much has come to depend on the financial success of the university that it is impossible for a college or university to advance in its proper work without a continuous and efficient program of money-raising and a continuous series of projects designed to increase the annual income. This has now come to be accepted as a major responsibility for the president. Many of our American universities have become institutions in which the academic, student, and employee affairs are conducted by autonomous vice presidents and deans, who, since they deal with day-to-day policy-making, are more directly in touch with the university than the president.

This would perhaps be less serious if administration by vice presidents were confined to business matters. But often the educational policies are administered entirely by the president's assistants, and the new kind of president, a man who has not grown up in the hard world of faculty controversy, and the hopeful world of faculty planning, is shut away from the knowledge he must have if he is to decide most of the important issues which finally come to him. With the internal life of the university in the hands of assistants, deans, and departmental chairmen, and the external life directed by the pressures of trustee, legislative, alumni, and public bodies, the president then actually does occupy the position of a very expensive office boy, for his university and for his society.

It is often said, in justification of the manager-president, that his skill in public relations, fund-raising, business management and general administration is needed so that the university can gain the financial backing it must have for the improvement of educational quality. This argument contains a dangerous fallacy in its separation of financial policy-making from educational leadership. The former can control or destroy the latter. The administrator of a business organization can move from a post in making rubber tires to one involving plastic cups without endangering the new business he is entering, since there are experts who can be employed to advise him on production, and the public relations and promotion of a product follow a familiar pattern.

In the case of education, so much depends upon the philosophy and knowledge of those responsible for decisions that the college administrator who is ignorant of the processes and subtleties of the educational system itself has no clue to the kind of advice he should be seeking, to the kind of expert he should be employing, or to the fact that he is dealing not with a product but with a process.

We had a sensational display of work by a managerial president not long ago in an American college, in which a young man who had done very well in electrical appliances, and indeed wished to introduce some of them into his college as an aid to education, applied simple business practice to the incredibly complicated area of college faculty affairs. With the aid of a board of trustees, also equipped with experience in business efficiency, the president discovered a sizable deficit in his next year's budget, and solved it by announcing that there would be fifteen to twenty fewer teachers on the pay roll during the coming year. By the time this solution to a recurring college problem had worked its way to a conclusion, the college had a new president (after having had two serving concurrently for a short period), a new board of trustees, had become involved in a lawsuit, and retained only remnants of its deficit and most of its faculty. When last heard from, the new president was sending around grains and bottles of campus sand, gathered from the campus grounds, with a view to obtaining gifts from graduates still sensitive to their former environment, and the former president was employed by a foundation to help give money away —a less complicated and dangerous occupation than that of administering it for educational purposes.

In college or university life, the quality of the institution depends upon the character and values of the persons who are appointed to the administration and faculty. This in turn determines the qualities of the intellectual and social environment into which the student comes, and, accordingly, determines the direction and quality of the educational growth of the students. Lowell at Harvard, Harper at Chicago, Gilman at Johns Hopkins, Wilbur at Stanford, Van Hise at Wisconsin, Hadley at Yale, had in their bones the ideals to be achieved through their universities, and knew how to set about bringing to the universities the kind of men and women who were devoted to achieving those ideals. Without experience of the professional standards and ideas of the scholar and teacher, the administrator is badly equipped to choose the educational policy-makers themselves.

Nor can he command the respect of those who look to colleges and universities for educational leadership, unless he can show by his public statements and educational policy that he is in fact exerting that leadership. The policy of assigning business or fund-raising executives to university posts in place of scholars and teachers is shortsighted even in terms of the business and fund-raising work itself. When that group of people known to fund-raising agencies as potential donors (a group which seems to consist of everyone with an income above forty dollars a week) are presented to a university or to its president or to his representatives, no one in it wishes to feel that he is meeting a fund-raiser or a business executive, or even a general. Most of all, he does not wish himself to be considered a potential donor, or victim, of a campaign, or an assault. He is a citizen, conscious (or unconscious) of his responsibilities toward education. The function of a university is to educate, and the head of a university must be an educator.

The graduates of American colleges and the members of the general public give their support to universities because of the university's educational program, not in order to recognize the efficiency of the administrative organization. As a matter of fact, when the administration becomes too efficient, organized, and smooth, with squads of orderly administrative people settling all the problems, it usually does so at the expense of individual responsibility on the part of the faculty, and is quite likely to remove the color and flavor from the institution itself. What appears to be a sound and efficient administrative practice may be the exact device calculated to take the vitality out of the college community. We need only think for a moment of the ease with which it is possible to administer and correct objective examinations, that series of correct and incorrect grunts, to realize that ease and efficiency can work against the interests of education.

Most American colleges and universities are overorganized. Too much is arranged by administrators, too little by the teachers and students themselves. The overorganization runs straight through the curriculum, the student body, the departmental system, the personnel services, and the whole institutional mechanism. Nothing is left to chance, everything must be arranged. Whenever a new idea shows its head, whenever a small body of knowledge shows symptoms of independence, whenever a new problem emerges, it is immediately seized upon and organized into a special category with its own administrator and its own specialists. As soon as this is done, people begin to worry about specialism, and immediately a new department is organized with a new administration in order to bring together all the disintegrated pieces, until there are now specialists in non-specialism, experts in integration.

Many American educators are in the grip of a passion for efficiency. They cannot bear the sight of an idea lying around loose without its own place on a chart of the institution. Business efficiency, when it sets to work on the intellectual life of students and teachers, prevents them from dealing with one another in natural and informal ways and takes away from the teachers the responsibility of solving their own educational problems. This in turn makes it impossible to have the kind of community life which will give to students the sense that learning is an informal and personal affair, that scholarship depends on the easy exchange of ideas and opinions, and that education is not something administered in lumps but something which grows in the warmth of a friendly community. There is too little opportunity left for students to educate one another, and the idea of administration is an idea about manipulation of students in and out of courses, record keeping, mechanical speed, streamlining, and policy-making.

The administration in the ideal university would be one which kept out of the way and made it as simple as possible for students and teachers to spend time together profitably, and to conduct their intellectual transactions in their own ways. This would give us a student community of the kind described by Cardinal Newman, where "the conversation of all is a series of lectures to each, and they gain for themselves new ideas and views." [1]

The president of a college has in the long run to build a community which carries the students along by its own momentum without the necessity of being steered, pushed, or organized by any particular set of administrators who are said to be in charge. The true college community "will give birth to a living teaching, which in the course of time will take the shape of a self-perpetuating tradition, or a *genius loci*, as it is sometimes called; which haunts the home where it has been born, and which imbues and forms, more or less, and one by one, every individual who is successively brought under its shadow." [2]

We all know that the strength of a college depends upon the way in which everyone connected with it—students, faculty, alumni, and administration—identify themselves with the institution and feel that they belong to it. It is only when there is a strong feeling of belonging that the ideas and values of the institution are accepted by its students. The most common mode,

[1] John Henry Cardinal Newman, *The Idea of a University* (Longmans, Green and Company, London, 1929), p. 146.

[2] Newman, *op. cit.*, p. 147.

and also the most trivial, of developing attitudes of loyalty and commitment is the easy mob appeal of football teams, basketball teams, and the attendant rituals of pep rallies, bonfires, whiskey drinking, and organized shouting.

This is quite openly a manipulative device, of the same order of significance as outdoor advertising, flashing electric signs, military parades, and soap advertisements. The program of enthusiasm is conducted by a staff of professional experts, publicity writers, coaches, scouts, pep leaders, alumni directors, and, in some cases, college presidents. The latter have been known on occasion to put on football helmets and address student rallies the evening before a game is to be played, to attend football practice regularly, give newspaper interviews about the chances for the team this year, and to take with them, in visits to alumni in cities around the country, films of the big team in action, and to supply comment for the benefit of the alumni.

There is a direct relationship between the donations of alumni and the success of the football team in institutions which adopt this method of engendering commitment to themselves, and sometimes a direct relationship between such success and the appropriations passed by state legislatures for university purposes. The financial danger in this kind of system is that only one team at a time can be the champion, and there are always losing teams.

The philosophy of those who sponsor such methods was stated with clarity and conviction in a statement issued by an American college not long ago.

. . . Tearing apart the common, stock defenses of college football—"physical education," character training, money making, President —— declared that "football in America has not been so much over-emphasized as underrated and misunderstood." He explained that football and other intercollegiate sports are not physical education, for those who need it are the ones incapable of performing on varsity teams.

Intercollegiate football, President —— continued, is "an emotionally integrating force" around which the loyalties of students, faculty, alumni, and friends of a college rally. As an allegorical comparison he used the national stars and stripes which is the symbol of national unity.

Speaking in terms of the church-related small college, President —— expressed his feeling that neither philosophy nor Christianity is capable of becoming the integrating element on the modern campus. Football is the one universal experience which all elements of a college enjoy, whether in playing or cheering.

I do not believe that I have become personally embittered by the fact that in England no one other than the immediate family and intimate friends of the players ever came to watch our rugger games, or that it was possible to gain a place on the tennis team by telephoning to the secretary of the tennis club and notifying him that you were available for matches. But I find the president's statement hilarious and at the same time frightening. It is frightening because he has stated a commonly accepted truth which most college presidents would shrink from mentioning.

But it is equally true that where values of a different kind have been developed by the faculty and its president, the students and the alumni respond to them with genuine enthusiasm, without damaging their own enjoyment of athletic contests when they are well performed, or endangering whatever feelings of excitement they may have when teams from their own institution do well. My own view is that the only way in which students become seriously identified with their colleges and universities is by the personal relationship which they have with the faculty and with other students. There is only a certain amount of emotional energy available for institutional devotion, and when it is drained away by the obvious external devices of football-style loyalty, the students naturally assume that this is the intention of the educational institution, and this is the aspect of the institution to which they attach the free-floating loyalty which they wish to give.

Within a few years we may find that the students themselves will cure the evils of this system. Some of the football players are now refusing to allow themselves to be exploited as commercial attractions by the universities and are reserving their football talent for professional games only, on the grounds that the salaries are higher and they have more time for their studies. One famous athlete in an American university dropped out of intercollegiate football recently for this and other reasons, and remarked: "When the whole purpose of a game becomes so confused that players try to inflict injuries on each other, then I say football has lost its appeal as a sport." Another university player told me recently that he prefers playing with the professionals because their standards of sportsmanship and professional ethics are so much higher and would not allow them to injure other players deliberately.

III

The major flaw in the organization of most of the large educational institutions is the impersonality of the academic program and the almost complete lack of opportunity for the students to learn through personal relationships to identify themselves with the values and attitudes of their teachers, which, on the whole, are the values of the thoughtful scholar and the liberal thinker. Here again, I believe that the college president has considerable responsibility, and that by making it possible for both students and faculty to share in the formation of educational policy a great deal of the impersonality can be cured, and a different attitude to college education can be fostered in the student body itself. In this kind of system, the college president behaves as chairman of a committee of the whole, not as an administrator who makes policy with the board of trustees, or administers policy made for him by that body. He is a faculty member with additional responsibilities.

In making decisions, he is not deciding for himself on the basis of his administrative authority what everyone else must do: he is choosing particular courses of action from the many alternatives which, in the view of his student, faculty, and trustee associates, show most promise of contributing to the total aim of the community. His ability to get things done, in any democratic institution, depends upon the trust which his associates place in him, a trust which either develops or declines on the basis of the daily decisions he makes throughout each year. When he presents a point of view of his own, it must be one which he is prepared to argue on its merits, not as a presidential point of view from which there is no retreat. His best means of achieving the leadership which his college needs is to spend time with his colleagues in the faculty and to give encouragement and practical support to ideas which they develop together.

This means that for a president, the actual administration of a college makes serious and heavy demands on his physical and emotional energy. The luxuries of impatience, annoyance, spontaneous comment, sudden enthusiasms, hates, prejudices, personal tastes, discouragement, and weariness are the privilege of the faculty and students, not to be enjoyed by the president. Letters which one might write as a faculty member to a colleague become suddenly charged with hidden meanings when written on the letterhead of the president's office. Casual remarks made in the middle of a noisy dinner party abruptly become the View of the Administration. All of this has a chastening effect on the president, and will improve his character unless, of course, he becomes cautious, circumspect, and domesticated.

It also means that each part of the college community must be self-governing. The student body must be given responsibility for governing its own affairs, not simply in the trivialities of social decorum, sports, and college dances, but in matters of basic policy connected with their campus lives—the legislation and administration of student discipline, the educational policies, the planning for courses, the problems of social relations. The administrative staff and employees should also have representation in the policy-making of the institution, either through union delegates, or through committees within the college system. The faculty, through its own elected committees, and through its representation on the board of trustees, must be self-governing in forming educational and administrative policy.

The whole community can then be interlocked by joint committees of faculty and students, trustees and faculty, administration-students-faculty, with the president as liaison officer. The usual chart of organization has to be scrapped to remove the chain-of-command, with its board of trustees in a large square at the top, joined by a thin line to a president, who is tenuously linked to anonymous persons lower in the hierarchy and contained in squares marked students, faculty, employees, deans, alumni, vice presidents. What we need is a movable set of symbols to represent the individuals who make up the institution. The process by which they work is organic, not linear. If we must have a chart, it would be drawn as a circle with the student at the center.

A number of aims can be achieved simultaneously if the college is organized to spread the authority around the community rather than keeping it at various levels of the conventional academic hierarchy. In the first place, a different attitude of faculty to students is created, simply by the new organization. When responsibility is actually given to the students for educational planning, for legislation affecting student behavior, for decisions about campus policy, they rise to it, and their own relation to the members of the faculty becomes one in which they are not the recipients of an education handed to them by their teachers, but one half of a relationship of student and teacher in which both halves have equal though different rights, and equal though different duties. The duty of becoming educated is placed in the students' hands, the duty of providing the guidance and the materials of education is placed in the hands of the faculty. The division into separate groups—faculty with their intellectual authority and educational demands, and students with their own private world and their own set of interests—is no longer possible.

Santayana has described what is too often the situation on American campuses in his description of Harvard at the beginning of the century. "The young had their own ways, which on principle were fostered and respected; and one of their instincts was to associate only with those of their age and caliber. The young were simply young, and the old simply old, as among peasants. Teachers and pupils seemed animals of different species, useful and well-disposed toward each other, like a cow and a milkmaid; periodic contributions could pass between them, but not conversation." Then Santayana goes to the center of the educational problem with the statement, "Their tasks and their pleasures divide people of different ages; what can unite them is ideas, impersonal interest, liberal arts." [3]

The unity between students and faculty provided by a joint interest in ideas and the liberal arts is essential to any serious educational program, and cannot be achieved without an organization of the intellectual community on a basis of shared

[3] Santayana, *Character and Opinion in the United States* (Charles Scribner's Sons, New York, 1920), pp. 52-53.

responsibility. It is from the discussion by students and by faculty of the means and ends of their joint educational program that the best kind of curriculum planning can be developed. This is not a matter of adding and subtracting subjects, either at the request of students or of faculty, but a matter of raising questions as to whether or not certain means and ends in the work of teachers with students are those which, on close examination, show promise of educational advance and more productive learning.

Curriculum committees themselves should not be isolated from the flow of information and suggestion which can come from students, or from any section of the faculty. That flow of idea and suggestion is likely to be stopped if, in the academic hierarchy, graduate assistants, young instructors, or assistant professors are rated in intellectual as well as financial categories, each of them farther away from the central power of the departmental chairman, the dean, and the president. Good ideas are likely to be buried, simply because they are thought to come from the wrong category of human being.

The departmental chairman, who is usually conceived as the third unit in a triumvirate of educational powers composed of himself, the dean, and the president, should be a chairman in the more informal sense—the person who conducts meetings, who deals with the correspondence, and who leads the discussion of educational policy in conjunction with his colleagues. The purpose of departmental meetings should not be to discuss business items and administrative detail but to discuss education and the advancement of learning in the student. The chairman should be responsible for insuring such discussion, and the departments themselves must take the responsibility for the general education of those students who work in the area of their subject matter.

The evil in the organization of universities by departments is the separation which they give to the subjects in the curriculum and the isolation of the work of one department from another. Rather than planning jointly for the sake of the students whom they all teach, departments plan the presentation of their subjects, often without realizing that in doing so they are cutting up the students' experience without reference to the ways in which it needs to be put together.

Each department is a small college. There may be as many as one thousand to four thousand students in attendance, and a roster of five or sixty faculty members. If the department behaved in the manner of a college, and dealt with the total education of the student rather than with that small part of it represented by one subject, it could break down the isolation which now exists between departmental units in the university system.

Within each department it is possible to try many experiments in teaching. For example, each department needs a satisfactory solution for the problem of dealing with freshmen courses. The introduction which a freshman receives to the subject offered is usually the only knowledge he gains of it through the rest of his university or college education, yet it is usually planned as if it were the first unit in a chain of courses leading to a doctorate degree.

Individual faculty members, or groups of two and three within the department, can be asked to work out new courses of their own, rather than relying on a departmental curriculum with a complete syllabus which new faculty members are asked to teach. Otherwise, the department begins to assume the attitude of a group of men and women who have invested their intellectual capital in a given subject, and who act competitively and defensively on its own behalf, both in scholarship and in teaching.

I believe that it is the chairman who must provide leadership in the improvement of teaching and in the discussion of education within his department, and that it is the responsibility of the dean and the president to meet with the chairmen and with the department members for policy discussion in order to keep the relationship between the teaching and the administration direct and educationally useful. If, in addition, the individual faculty members have the direct responsibility and the freedom to try their own ways of improving the education of the students whom they teach, the vitality of educational discussion is bound to increase, with a consequent improvement in quality of student learning. The administration of the institution will then shift away from a central authority of administrative officers and toward the authority of individual teachers.

As institutions grow in size, and as the administrative details grow in number, the distance between one department and another, one division and another, one professional school and another, between the administration on the one hand and the faculty and students on the other, is likely to assume the proportions of a chasm. It is only by serious efforts to create a democratic structure, with direct responsibility in each section of the university for its part in solving the day-to-day problems of student learning, that the chasm can be bridged. Otherwise, the teacher in the university is a person who is thought to have discharged fully his responsibility for students by making scheduled appearances before classes. The rest of the educational process is then left to the accidents of the extracurriculum.

The larger the university becomes the greater is the isolation of the president from his students and faculty. The isolation can be remedied only by the president's own initiative. He must retain close connection with the students and faculty by whatever means can be devised. In the case of President Conant, this took the form of teaching courses in science and working closely with members of the college faculty and graduate schools in educational planning. In the case of other presidents, it has been achieved by conferences with students and faculty on matters of university policy, or the continuation of scholarly work by the president in the field of his special competence, and by close association with his colleagues who are scholars in that field. The problem is one of deciding on the disposition of a limited amount of time, and the best means of spending it in the interests of the institution. If too much of it is spent in official duties which have no connection with the actual educational program, the loss is a genuine one for the university and a serious one for the personal development of the president.

It is clear that under any system of organization the president is in the midst of a complicated network of personal relationships, and has to interpret each part of that network to each other part. Not only is he responsible for the relations between himself and his faculty, between himself and the board of trustees and alumni, between himself and the students, but also for the relation between the faculty and the trustees, the students and the faculty, the faculty and the alumni, and the relation between all of them together and the image of the college they project to the general public. Do the graduates want to know what the students are thinking? Do the faculty want to know what the trustees have to say? Do the parents and trustees want to know what the faculty are doing? The president must have them all in mind. Not only that, but he must anticipate their questions, and accordingly must inform himself accurately and fully about the work which each section of the college is carrying on.

There is no way for the president to become fully informed about his institution other than by spending the bulk of his time in it, and by remaining intimately connected with the daily work of teaching and learning. The absentee president, continually speaking in public on all subjects, the president who has his eye on some other public office than the one he holds, the president who travels continually to conferences on education, or who travels continually to raise money for his college, quickly loses the most important part of his experience, his experience with his own students and faculty.

It is very easy for a college president to begin living beyond his intellectual and emotional means. All he need do is to succumb to requests to make speeches while the daily round of university duties makes it impossible for him to read or to think about what he might be able to say. In the rate of consumption of all national products, the consumption of speakers occupies a high place. The principal quality the president needs—provided he has already met the test of sheer physical energy, the ability to stay awake after dinner, and the ability to look at a chicken patty surrounded by peas without wincing—is the quality of humility and the ability to detect the subjects on which he is not informed.

To put the matter bluntly, he should talk about what he knows or not talk at all. If he knows a great deal about education, he may also be informed about other matters as well, since education is connected in one way or another to most of the important issues which now concern American society. But when the president speaks in public about education, or about his college, his remarks should come as a result of close acquaintance with the ideas, beliefs, and actions of the students and faculty with whom he associates. He must go to school to his own colleagues, who, because they are teaching and because they have the opportunity to spend more time with students and with educational ideas in practice, know more about the realities of education than he does.

When the president makes statements about American education, or the American student, as he can scarcely avoid doing, he should ask himself: Which particular parts of American education are you talking about? Which teachers? Which students?

Would the teachers and the students agree with what you are saying about them? Do they act and think in the way you say they do? The college is a continual course of instruction for the president, as well as a testing ground for any ideas he may have of his own. If he considers his college in this light, his own education is much improved, and his public statements will at least be free from the rhetoric and cliché of educational discourse, and will have at most the ring of truth about them.

IV

In all forms of administration, I have a prejudice in favor of the haphazard and a taste for organic disorder. Although I am for answering mail promptly, dealing with things as they come up, and being generally helpful, the image of administrative virtue which I cherish is of Sir Richard Livingstone, as President of Corpus Christi College and Vice Chancellor of Oxford University, seated at a twelve-foot desk, partly hidden from view by piles of books, manuscripts, flowerpots, and papers, answering his mail by hand and calling upon a member of his faculty with a head for figures to add, subtract, multiply, and otherwise deal with the items of the annual budget. In order to arrange this happy situation it is necessary to be attached to a college at least five hundred years old, heavily endowed with regular income, with a student body of no more than one hundred. It does, however, furnish an ideal toward which one can hope to move.

The fact is that there is a serious danger not only to individual institutions, but to the country's intellectual and cultural life, in substituting administrative executives for learned men in positions of educational leadership. Monroe Deutsch, Vice President and Provost-Emeritus of the University of California, has stated it clearly. "The college presidency," says

Deutsch, "is in danger of becoming the normal refuge of persons of prominence who are 'out of a job.' Senator Robert A. Taft proposed that substantial pensions be set up for retiring Presidents of the United States so that they could afford to 'accept dignified but often low-paying jobs such as college presidencies.' " [4] How can we hope to find leadership through American education if the college presidency is considered by trustees to be a resting place for public figures temporarily unemployed?

We are already presented with continual displays of intellectual poverty by the public figures who address us. The Senators, Congressmen, and political leaders, with only a handful of exceptions, are committed to party projects and opportunities. Their public statements are often deliberate evasions of intellectual and moral responsibility. Leaders of business enterprises who make public statements—and there are more of them who do so than ever before—are largely committed to the financial interests of a specific corporation, to a particular economic and political point of view, and lack the training and experience of disciplined intellectual effort from which original statements regarding the public welfare can come. In any case, their statements are often written by members of a public relations staff trained in journalism and advertising. The military leaders are by training and occupation prevented from giving sustained thought to social issues and cannot be expected to reach sensitive and informed conclusions about cultural change. Although the institutions of organized religion are not designed to develop secular social criticism, good social comment comes from their leaders.

By default, the editorial writers of weekly magazines, the radio commentators, the newspaper columnists, a few university

[4] Monroe Deutsch, *The College from Within* (University of California Press, 1952), pp. 11-12.

professors, an occasional Supreme Court Justice, and a handful of university presidents are those who have been left with
the task of moral leadership on matters of public policy. One of
the reasons why Adlai Stevenson's remarks on public policy
during the 1952 presidential campaign received the praise of
such a variety of social critics was that they had serious intellectual content at a time when this was a comparatively rare
phenomenon.

In this situation it is of first importance that the educational
leadership of the country be in the hands of those whose continual concern is with the place of knowledge, scholarship,
science, and liberal values in contemporary civilization, and
whose natural sympathies and attitudes are tolerant and helpful toward the inquiring mind and the freedom of educational
institutions. From where else can this intellectual leadership
come if not from our universities? It is an intellectual and moral
stance we look for, one which is on guard against the attack by
society on the liberal values which make civilization itself worth
having, a stance for the protection of society from its own vices
and weaknesses.

This protection is necessarily the task of educational leaders,
not of managers, administrators or fund-raisers, no matter how
distinguished they may be in their extracurricular activities. The
person who can establish, protect, and encourage the creative
work of the free intellectual is one whose own experience has
taught him to understand and cherish the ideals of scholarship.
The intellectual himself has been alienated from the wider areas
of American social policy. His social criticism and political
action are not organically related to contemporary political and
social change. Nor is he consulted, except in a technical sense,
by the country's business, political, military, or government
leaders.

By an intellectual, I mean the person whose main occupation

lies in the field of scholarship, science, study, research and the learned professions. Such a person does not share any longer in political action groups of the kind organized during the 1930's and early 1940's, since, in the post-McCarthy era, by doing so he exposes himself to defamation and attack by political pressure groups who impugn the essential integrity of his motives and talents as a scholar. He has withdrawn himself from direct participation in the formation of public policy, and in some quarters is actually suspected of a kind of occupational subversion because of his interest in the intellect.

But the intellectual, considered as a teacher and college administrator, does have a direct relationship to the formation of beliefs and ideas within the educational system itself. The college president exists in order to make it possible for the teacher to transmit and transform the knowledge he possesses. This is the prime fact of his occupation. The managerial president, having absorbed the clichés of an unexamined world, is capable only of repeating them with an air of solemnity whenever the occasion is provided. Ghost writers, whether from the faculty or the public relations office, are of help only in preventing the grosser forms of error, but cannot disguise the evidence of an intellectually sterile past. The danger is that paucity of ideas when publicly revealed by educators has a direct effect on the attitude of the general public, of the scholar, and of the student.

How can the young men and women in our universities catch the spirit of learning, respond to educational ideals, and grow to respect the values of liberal thought if they receive only secondhand and borrowed concepts for their moral guidance? How can the teacher gain a sense of identity with the university of which he is a part, or feel the pride he must have in his own calling, if the spokesman for his institution fails to win the respect of the intellectual community? The danger lies in a beginning of cynicism toward education itself.

The aim of higher education is to develop certain attitudes and values in students, to make certain that each generation carries along with it a thoroughgoing respect for democratic institutions and for the worth of human knowledge. This is true equally of technical, professional, or liberal education, since once the attitude to knowledge itself is established, the educational task is comparatively easy. Students who are clear about what it is they want to know, and who are seriously interested in knowing it, present the least amount of difficulty to the teacher, unless, of course, all the things they wish to know are trivial. Most students, however, are not clear about what they want to know. They are ready to accept any form of knowledge which the institution considers appropriate. They are ready to accept it, that is, if it can be seen to justify itself by the use to which it can be put, the personal enjoyment it affords, or the interest it evokes.

In his beginning stages, as I have tried to point out in other chapters of this book, the student is usually not experienced in making distinctions among values. It is in learning to make such distinctions that he needs a "higher" education. It is fairly easy to convey information to students, and if this were all that higher education had to do, it could operate most effectively through television, correspondence courses, simple textbooks, and mass lectures. In the matter of values, however, it is the day-to-day life of a university community, where students and teachers talk and work together, and where their personal relationships involve them in a common educational purpose, that students learn to make discriminations between truth and falsehood, good argument and bad, good style and bad rhetoric, and where they learn to develop their own intellectual character. The ideal university is one in which there is general recognition among students and faculty alike that the work they are doing together is a significant part of the development of their own civilization.

Judge Learned Hand has given an eloquent and compelling expression to this ideal in his remarks to the members of the Harvard Club at its 1952 annual dinner. He said in part:

Many years ago, like you, I sat in the halls of Harvard and brought out of them whatever I did bring out. One man carries away one thing; another, another; some, perhaps, nothing. For myself I learned and took away . . . a creed which has endured and whose conviction has grown upon me as the years have passed. You were not taught it in words; you gathered it unwittingly from uncorrupted and incorruptible masters. It was in the air; you did not affirm or proclaim it; you would have felt ashamed to demonstrate the obvious. You came to know that you could hold no certain title to beliefs that you had not won; and indeed you did not win many. But that did not so much matter, for you had come into possession of a touchstone; you had learned how to judge a good title; and, although tomorrow might turn up a flaw in it, you believed that you could detect the flaw. And chiefly and best of all, you were in the company of those who thought that the noblest of man's works was the pursuit of truth; who valued the goal so highly that they were never quite convinced that the goal they had reached was the goal they were after; who believed that man's highest courage was to bet his all on what was no more than the best guess he could make; who asked no warranties and distrusted all such; who faced the puzzle of life without any kit of ready-made answers, yet trusting that, if they persevered long enough, they would find—in the words of John Dewey—that they might safely "lean back on things." [5]

The values implicit in these words are connected in intimate ways to the whole tradition of scholarship and learning, from the time in history when scholars first came together to make their own communities, to the present American university. It is in the transmission and re-creation of these values that the university has its true function.

On the other hand, if the university merely provides instruc-

[5] Learned Hand, *The Spirit of Liberty* (Alfred A. Knopf, New York, 1952), pp. 258-259.

tion in subjects at a certain price, the emphasis is automatically placed on business and administrative arrangements, and people with administrative talent, whether teachers who administer courses, or deans who administer teachers, are those best qualified for employment by the institution. The students pay for slabs of subject matter, and take them off as quickly as they can in order to find their own employment in a position which requires the certification of a college degree. The faculty member signs a contract to dispense the subject matter for as high a price as the competitive bidding for services in the current faculty market allows, and carries on his own research in order to become a more attractive piece of academic merchandise in the eyes of the purchasing agents, or college presidents and deans.

In this institution, the role of the president is to buy as much instructional talent for as little as possible, to manage the hotel and auxiliary enterprises of sport and the physical plant, and to report to the board of trustees, to the state, or to the general public, on the number of customers served, and the amount of money in the bank. There is no basic difference between this kind of university and any other commercial enterprise. A group of owners want something done, they hire people to do it, dispense a standard product through textbooks, lectures, and the credit system. There are many whose idea of a university corresponds to this model. It is only through the leadership of our universities by those whose basic commitment is to the life of learning and scholarship that their number will be lessened.

V

There is a deceptive likeness between the structure of an American business corporation and an American university—they are both chartered by the state, and are both in the hands of a board of trustees. Although the likeness stops there, it confuses many people, among them trustees. Several of the Regents at the University of California during the past few years have acted as if they were members of the board of a corporation which hired salesmen and technicians to market America. Regents at the University of Texas acted in exactly the same way several years ago. There is nothing which can anger a member of a university faculty more than to be told what to do by a trustee. If a faculty member is to act strictly in accordance with rules and authority, it must be the authority of a democratic community whose rules the teacher accepts as the condition of his work. Even an autocratic college president has quite limited power, since he too must work according to rules set by the academic community.

But in the case of managerial presidents working with authoritarian trustees, the teacher is quickly placed in the position of an employee hired to carry out educational goals set by non-educators. In actual fact, the university is the instrument by which a society plans its future, keeps in touch with its past, and criticizes its own present. The society which wishes to advance in a creative way, solving its problems by the use of intelligence rather than by submission to political and social pressures, will make certain that its universities are supported and are free to carry out their function of criticism, creative thinking, and the transmission of the society's own past. To do otherwise would be to commission an architect to build a city and then forbid him to draw his plans.

In a communist state, all education is under political administrators who set policy and impose it. Teachers are employees and servants of the state. A similar situation exists in fascist states. In American society, the theory of control is that it should be neither by the government, by the church, nor by any particular power group. The public board of trustees, and the colleges and universities entrusted to their direction, together represent an independent third element between the state and the general public. In the case of the state universities, the state, through its elected executive officer, the governor, appoints a board of officers to set educational policy. Such boards have the right to pass on all appointments to the faculty or administration, and all details connected with educational administration. In the case of colleges sponsored by religious organizations, the state charters a board of officers presented to it by the religious organizations themselves. In the case of private institutions, the state charters a group of private citizens to act as officers of the university, and to conduct its affairs within the framework of the state constitution.

Both theoretically and practically, it is within the latter institutions that the greatest possibility for freedom from outside control exists. But whether or not an institution is formally organized as public or private, it serves as a public institution and is supported morally and financially by the citizens, through the fact of tax exemption in the case of private and parochial colleges, by direct taxation in the case of the public ones. The college is carrying out a commission given to it by the constituted authorities of its society.

The college therefore has the responsibility of remaining closely aware of the needs of its society and of the individuals within it. The crucial question is, Who shall decide on the needs, and who shall decide how they should be fulfilled? On the one hand, we do not wish to hand over all responsibility to an élite corps of professional educators who then decide what is good for the country and its young people. On the other, we do not wish to give to political-minded or dogmatic individuals and groups within our society the power to dictate what should be taught and what should be learned. It is on this point that most of the controversies turn in the matter of academic freedom. It was the issue of who is responsible for directing education which was at the center of the recent bitter controversy at the University of California. A loyalty oath was the occasion on which the issue was raised. Do Regents have the right to dictate to teachers and to interfere with the democratic community of self-governing scholars? The California controversy was not primarily a matter of loyalty oaths, but was a defense of freedom for education from political interference, carried on by educators against a political authority duly constituted but arbitrarily used.

The college president who is in fact an educator is not employed by a board of directors to carry out their wishes and demands. Nor is he the servant of the alumni, who, in the mind of a recent alumnus of Yale University, should have the responsibility and power of a group of stockholders who should control policy and who should vote as stockholders to grant or withhold funds. The graduates of a college are those who have received its benefits and privileges for a sum of money vastly below the cost to the university, and who owe it their support and understanding, as well as their informed criticism. Neither they, nor the general public, nor any organized group in it, may dictate what should be taught and who should teach.

Nor is the college president the servant of the government, responsible for fitting an educational policy, whether about politics, economics, foreign policy, or religion, to the demands of politicians and government authority. His responsibility is to the Constitution of the United States, to the laws of the country, to the charter of his institution, and to the freedom of students, faculty, and citizens to speak, write, and think the truth they find in their own experience. He is a member of a community of scholars whose task it is to keep alive the ideals and practices of a free society by the exercise of authority granted to him by a board of trustees.

I have said that in the midst of the welter of advice, opinion, and pressure from every quarter, the college president must be his own man. His educational duty is to decide issues without regard to pressures, in the interests of the education of his students and the integrity of his faculty. In the current situation in higher education, the external pressures on him come from four quarters—from boards of trustees, from alumni, from privately organized groups in the general public, and from the government. It would be wrong to assume that all such pressures would drive the president and his university in the wrong direction, or that the members of all boards of trustees are wrongheaded reactionaries who are out to take autocratic control of presidents and education alike. Most are responsible conservatives who take their duties seriously and who resent the interference of others in the proper exercise of their authority and that of the president. The weakness in the constituency of most boards is that they draw their membership from too narrow a segment of American society, and do not contain representation from a diversity of cultural, educational, and economic groups.

It is when appointments to educational bodies are made for political and financial reasons and when the appointments disregard the qualifications of the members for service to education that the trouble begins. The president has the responsibility of acting as an educator for the board itself, and of presenting issues for discussion and decision in such a way that the educational principles are clear and the lines of authority marked. He must act on educational matters as a representative of education, scholarship, the teaching faculty, and the students. When his authority as an educator is challenged in an issue where his educational principles and those of his faculty are at stake, he must hold to his principles at whatever cost to his position as president. Otherwise there remains no principle on which educational policy can be made.

The example most immediately to hand is that of the University of Illinois, where a Board of Regents, fortunate in the quality of educational leadership their University had been receiving from its President, formally expressed a lack of confidence in President George Stoddard, who subsequently resigned. The points at issue were fourteen in number, varying from charges that there were "Reds" at the University to the fact that Dr. Stoddard was connected with UNESCO and spent too much of his time away from the University on its business. The classical situation of American education, celebrated in James Thurber's *The Male Animal* and elsewhere, developed at the University, with the combination of a former football-playing alumnus and a politically ambitious chairman of the Board lined up against the educator. The real issue was stated inadvertently by the Governor of Illinois, William G. Stratton, who said (in reply to a newspaper reporter's request for comment), "The Board sets the policy for the University. The trustees have felt that Dr. Stoddard was attempting to originate policy instead of its coming from them."

The faculty, as represented by the chairmen of departments of the College of Letters and Science, condemned the Regents' act, and praised President Stoddard for his "stand for honesty and integrity in education" and for his character "as a man of progressive programs and ideas." Other members of the faculty analyzed publicly the qualifications of the Board members and noted that several of them were lacking in the essentials of educational leadership.

In other words, in a conflict of educational policy between an educator with his faculty on the one side and a Board of Regents on the other, the Board of Regents won by insisting on its own policies, devised by men without educational qualifications for making them, over those of the persons appointed as scholars and educators. This in spite of the fact that there was every indication that the President's ideas were sound and, over a period of years, had raised the quality of the work at the University.

The attitude of the members of the Illinois Board of Regents represents the ultimate point in mismanagement of education by an accredited body. The function of a Board of Regents is not to make educational policy or to prevent the President from making any, but to do everything in its power to encourage the President and his faculty to make policy which is in consonance with the needs of the students and of the state which the University serves. What this means in practice is that, according to the Illinois Board's action, the administration and faculty of the University are to be clerks in the service of a group of men whose talents lie in fields other than those of education. It is comparable to the board of directors of a hospital dictating to the staff surgeons the proper methods of the operating room.

As a major part of their duties, the president and the board of trustees are also responsible for informing the alumni and the general public about the educational policies of the institution, and for listening responsively to criticism made of it. But they must never forget that it is the institution and not the alumni which makes the policy. Every college president receives strong letters from alumni demanding the dismissal of certain teachers, or threats of withholding financial support unless certain courses are taught or certain other courses are not taught. The example of Harvard University in recent years when confronted with such threat is one to hearten all educators and to serve as an example of educational integrity. The threat was published with the reply of the Harvard Corporation—that Harvard policies were made on grounds other than those of possible loss of university revenue.

With regard to political pressures from the state or federal government, it is clear that the only course of action for a university and its president is to distinguish sharply between educational policy as formed by teachers and educators, and government policy as formed by politicians. Education is not an instrument of national policy, nor are teachers to adopt curricula and doctrines set down by political mandate. During a national emergency, in the event of total mobilization for war, at a time when every institution in the country must devote itself to the defense of the country against an attacker, the colleges and universities have a reason for devoting themselves to national policy. But if education is to take its orders from either the legislative or the executive branch of the United States government, it has lost its function in our society.

Educational policy can be made satisfactorily only when there is a genuine understanding on the part of boards of trustees or regents as to the true function of a university in a democratic society, and of the way in which that function is fulfilled. In order to carry out its mission, a university *must* operate with rules set by the academic community, and not by doctrines imposed from a board of governors. Otherwise, the university is rendered impotent in the area of its own creative growth. The function of the university trustee is to act as the mediating instrument between the university and its society. The trustee exists, as does the university president, to make available to society the contributions of the scholar and teacher.

In a brilliant presentation of his views on the role of the trustee in American universities, Mr. Wilmarth Lewis of the Yale Corporation made the following remarks about the general rules of the university community:

Rule One is that the scholar is a citizen of the Republic with the same rights as other citizens.

Rule Two is that the trustee must not think of the scholar as an employee.

Rule Three is that once a scholar is wrapped about in the magic mantle of "tenure" he is invulnerable to attack unless it is proved that he is immoral, incompetent, or a traitor.

Rule Four is that the scholars choose their own colleagues and teach what they please in their own way.

Rule Five is that scholars do not use their classrooms to indoctrinate students with pet isms, their own or the trustee's.

There are many other rules, but these five are perhaps the most important ones for the trustee to learn because they are the rules that he will have to defend most frequently when performing his function of liaison between the scholars and the graduates. If he is to be a successful liaison officer it is essential that he rid his mind of lingering doubts about the honesty and decency of the American scholar. To be a convincing liaison officer he must get himself to the point where he believes in the right of scholars to hold views that he may hate. To be an enthusiastic liaison officer he must have the co-operation of the faculty. They can reassure him by being as mindful of their obligations to the university as they are of the university's obligations to them. They know that a scholar wears the label of his institution, and that he should be careful not to allow his personal prejudices and activities to embarrass it. There will always be a few who flout this principle, and it is part of the trustee's education to recognize that he must not attempt to punish them for their inconsiderateness, but leave them to their long-suffering colleagues who have their time-honored methods of dealing with them.[6]

If these judicious and sensitive remarks were understood and acted upon by the governing bodies of all American universities, there would be little occasion for the deplorable waste of human talent which occurs whenever the rights of scholars are challenged by attempts at suppression. The suppression of such rights can lead only to a weakening in the moral and intellectual strength of the university system. Indeed, it would be fatal to the growth of American society if those who wish to inhibit and

[6] Wilmarth Lewis, Phi Beta Kappa Oration, delivered at Harvard University, Cambridge, Massachusetts, Monday, June 16, 1952.

suppress the scholar were allowed to prevail, or if those who are frightened by the expression of dissidence and the free discussion of radical ideas were allowed to dominate education.

Education is a polite form of mental exercise unless the student feels for himself the tang of original thinking, the bite of new ideas, and the heat of political and social controversy. The trustees and presidents of American universities are now the central group of individuals on whom we must rely to protect and encourage the independence and freedom of scholars and students. The trustees have, in fact, power to do so, and have, by their relation to university presidents, the opportunity to choose and to support educational leadership against the heavy and constant pressures now working against it. They have in their own hands the power to decide whether colleges will perform their true mission of sustaining and developing the values of liberalism and humanism, or whether they will become information agencies managed by technicians in the service of cultural orthodoxy.

Chapter Three

MORAL LEADERSHIP AND EDUCATION[1]

LEADERSHIP of the world, if it is to be accomplished at all by the United States, can be accomplished only in moral terms. Nations are not impressed favorably by the threat of military power and economic strength to be used against them, and the existence of such power does not induce respect, loyalty, and co-operation on the part of its potential victims. The rest of the world—that is, all those on whom the power is used—either scorns it or fears it, and makes alliances against it. The human race, considered as a very large number of individual human beings, judges world leadership by the quality of its ideals and acts, not by the numbers of its armies or the size of its production; by the reality of its effort to help, not by the extent of its capacity to harm. Leadership is in fact impossible unless it is directed toward fulfilling the needs of those who are affected by it and who respond to it. Anything else is forced co-operation or coercion.

---

[1] "Moral Leadership and Education" was delivered as an address to the Yale Political Union Intercollegiate Forum on World Affairs, *The United States as a New World Leader—In What Direction?*, Yale University, Saturday, December 1, 1951. It appeared in the *Yale Alumni Magazine*, February 1952.

I believe that this is the definition the United States must give to leadership and that it is a true definition, whether for the United States or any other power. Those who give world leadership an opposite definition, whether in this country or elsewhere, are bound to the logical conclusion that war and the destructive use of power are the only means of achieving the aims of contemporary society.

The question of world leadership is therefore primarily moral. By this I mean that the United States must ask itself the question, What do we really want? To expand markets? To dominate the world? To fulfill American self-interest? To help the world to fulfill its own needs? Every answer is enmeshed in every other.

But there comes a point in all policy making, whether in one's personal life or in national and international affairs, when a basic moral choice must be exercised. The choice is between working in the service of others or working in the service of self. In personal terms, to make a moral choice in favor only of oneself leads to a defensive, narrow life, the character of which becomes gradually more and more restricted and self-defeating, the rewards of which become more and more sterile. Exactly this happens in national and international policy. It is simply not possible to rest policy on national self-interest unless we are prepared to alienate the men and women of every other nationality except our own.

Nor is it possible to rest policy merely on opposition to the Soviet Union, since in that kind of game the Soviet Union holds most of the cards and has learned over the past twenty-five years the technique of playing them. Similarly it is not possible to make domestic policy on the basis of anti-communism, or to judge the worth of social legislation by whether or not it leads to an abstraction called a welfare state, collectivism, or some other sinister mental image. The world is not interested in such dialectic. It asks its hard question, What does the policy do for human need?

It is in this sense that I wish to use the words morality and leadership. They are used in personal terms, which when expanded into an approach to public policy become the same principle we know and recognize in personal experience, but transposed into the broader terms of international leadership. As we think of the inner tensions of the life of an individual today, we find that within each one of us the drama of uncertainties, confusions, and unrest is working itself out in a way similar to the drama of the outer world of society. The same anxieties, insecurities, and fears which bother each of us, and each of our leaders, are the things which plague the world, and we find the world reflected in ourselves and ourselves projected into the world. Then we realize suddenly that the whole mechanism of modern society is only a projection of ourselves—of our wish for freedom and security and our fear that we will not reach it. It is then clear that society is the enlargement of the individual and is the total result of the acts of millions of individuals, each one different, each one insistent on being himself, no matter how timidly, and each one helping to make the world take the shape it has now taken.

The personal morality of these millions of human beings is infinitely varied. But there is one ethical standard which appears constantly in every society and in every relation between two or more people. The standard makes the distinction between selfish and unselfish acts, and identifies the unselfish act as the one possessing moral content. International developments have put the United States in a situation in which the country is being tested by the rest of the world on just this point. The communists have succeeded in persuading a good many people that we always act selfishly from capitalistic greed; Senator McCarthy has persuaded most of Europe that we intend to act selfishly and blindly in everything we do. Under the double influence of hostility from abroad and the bitter attacks of native isolationists and anti-communists at home, Americans have become less certain of where they stand in the matter of co-operation with other countries and faith in the liberal tradition of their own.

At Sarah Lawrence College Miss Uta Hagen once spoke to the students of her work in Bernard Shaw's *Saint Joan.* In answer to a student question, Miss Hagen remarked on the deep effect of the play and of the life of Joan on herself and on the contemporary audience. "People find the play deeply disturbing," Miss Hagen said, "because it is the story of a human being who had such a deep faith in the ideals of her life that she died, and with her death European society was forced to examine itself for its absence of faith and of ideals. It is this lack of faith in principle which disturbs people. They want it, they recognize it in Joan, and want it for themselves."

I agree with Miss Hagen that Americans want to believe in principles. They also want to believe in their own country and in the quality of its moral leadership. But confusion exists as to whether we should serve the ideals best by conducting international affairs through the United Nations, or by dealing directly in power terms with each of the other countries of the world. Further confusion exists on the question of whether or not we should take responsibility for the rest of the world, either as a hard-headed policy of self-preservation or as an act of will on our part to live by American ideals.

I I

In this situation I would like to suggest for the use of students and citizens something called the philosophy of the unavoidable. Its doctrine runs as follows: Try to discover, as far as possible and as clearly as possible, what in our present international situation is unavoidable, beyond our control, and what are the necessities with which we have to deal. These would include the fact that 464,000,000 people live in China, another 450,000,000 live in India, Pakistan, and Burma, that none of them speaks the English language as the native tongue, that most of them know nothing about the United States. These facts and a number of others like them have a great deal to do with setting the limits of successful achievement of American aims.

Put these facts aside for the moment. Then decide what are the things which are avoidable, things about which students and citizens have live options, where they can make personal decisions which will effect changes. Work at the task of clarifying what are the things which *should* be avoided, then set about working to avoid them.

After a certain length of time, it is altogether likely that some of the things which formerly seemed absolutely unavoidable have been avoided—war, for example—and in the meantime the individual has been kept busy and occupied at tasks which give him the satisfaction of seeing results accomplished. This philosophy has the advantage that the person who holds it can be just as pessimistic and dramatic as anyone else about the horrors of contemporary life, the decay of the human race, and impending disasters of all kinds, yet at the same time he can be working at the cause and cure of particular evils which contribute toward the bigger ones, and can earn the right to be honestly optimistic.

In practice, this philosophy would have to take certain things for granted. The fact is that the world has always been in one or another difficulty. But before the middle of the last century, the difficulties were of comparatively manageable proportions, or at least seem so in retrospect. Since the revolutions of 1848, since the spread of mass education, and the increase in awareness by workers and underprivileged groups of their latent power for social reform, more and more material improvement is demanded by more and more people. Social changes which in former centuries would have required a half-century to produce now happen overnight, and only the countries where there are governments flexible and imaginative enough to keep abreast, if not in advance, of these changes can stay in power by peaceful means. The rest find it necessary either to accept a revolution, or to govern by means of a police force or an army.

The new factor in social history is the emergence of a mass revolutionary movement, coupled with the growth of intense nationalism on the part of Eastern nations who have gradually awakened to the possibilities open to them by the use of power in their own hands. The industrial revolution in Europe, the subsequent exploitation of the East for cheap labor and raw materials, the economic control of the world by Western powers, the superiority consequently claimed by the white races over the colored—all these have historical roots and are real aspects of the present situation.

An additional real aspect is the fact of social revolution. The Eastern countries are having one, a revolution based on the rejection of older moral values and an older social system which is no longer flexible enough to meet the needs of a new society. The lives of a billion Eastern people are not something we can direct from America. Their lives are taking a direction of their own over which we, as citizens, or as a government, cannot have direct control. The only control we can have is by the attraction we can exert in stating our ideals for social justice and acting them out in practice. There are many places in which we can act them out, in decisions taken at the United Nations, in the practical use of our Point Four program, in the attitude we take to the non-communist world. Among these places for action is one which is often forgotten in the excitement of international events—acts committed within the United States, in the daily lives of its citizens, and in the daily conduct of government affairs. These acts have an immediate bearing on world leadership. An attitude of social superiority of the whites over the colored people is built into the American social system. It is part of the problem of world leadership, as has been so often said, and it is an important aspect of the social revolution. Students have a part to play within our own country, in stating our ideals of social justice and acting them out in practice, through their attitudes to racial equality, their education, their campus life, their student organizations.

The student and the citizen needs a moral framework for his action and for his thinking about the world society in which he happens to exist. To exert moral leadership at any time and in any way it is necessary to know the conditions under which an act can attain its moral content. There are many possible frameworks in which the citizen's thinking can be conducted, some narrow, some generously large. One framework could be the economic, social, and psychological welfare of the people within the boundaries of the United States; another might be the material welfare of the Western community of nations; another might be welfare of all nations and everyone living. I recommend to your attention one such structure of unavoidables in which thinking and acting may profitably take place, that suggested by Pierre Emmanuel in a talk given at Harvard University some time ago.

What then is happening? We have entered into a period of mutation in history, which, tomorrow perhaps, will express itself by vast specific migration and the trampling under foot of the old values by new barbarian times. Our thought is unprepared for events of this order and magnitude; it is anguished and disconnected . . . at one moment conservative, at the next revolutionary, but always at odds with itself.

On one side we see souls who are highly and perhaps excessively individualized, but incapable of vital force and concerted action; on the other side are the almost indivisible masses moved by a confused aspiration, where each individual thinks and feels itself alive only when immersed in the mass force. These individualized beings and these masses use the same words, but not the same language. Supposing even the language of the first group has attained perfection in one kind of meaning. This meaning is the result of a long tradition of intellectual privileges patiently consolidated by an élite, reinforced by the existence of a corresponding social order. Yet this social order succumbs to its own contradictions, this élite is devoured by its own skepticism. A poet who sings for himself and for the three hundred or so readers who will each one of them honor his work with a mis-interpretation, cannot but doubt not only the necessity but the reality of what he writes; more precisely, he does not know for whom he writes, or, if he does, he no longer has confidence in this "élite" which has ceased to believe in itself.

We see happening today that which inevitably happens each time the number of privileged people diminishes while the mass of have-nots increases: this mass upsets the social balance, and with it, its intellectual guarantees, the weakened guardians of a language in-comprehensible to the masses because it tells them nothing which corresponds to their lived-through experiences. Of course it is always possible for anyone to acquire the old type of culture: but even if the great mass of people had the time to follow the path traced by this culture, they would not take it because their impulsion leads them elsewhere, down some other unpredictable path.[2]

What we in this country can do is to help to lead the impulse M. Emmanuel describes down a path which is to some degree predictable. To do so the basis of our leadership must be multilateral: not the basis of a single power, but that of a leader acting in collaboration with other nations to achieve common ends.

As one other aspect of the presently unavoidable, I would like to point out that the internal affairs of the Soviet Union are

[2] Pierre Emmanuel, speaking at the Harvard Poetry Conference, Harvard University, Cambridge, Massachusetts, August 29, 1950.

beyond the control of individual American citizens, and beyond our power to direct or to influence. This is partly due to the complete rejection by the Soviet Union of any exchange of ideas, objective information, or people between their country and ours. It is also due to the limitations placed on any country in influencing or directing the internal affairs of any other.

Communism in the Soviet Union, or Stalinism, is operating according to a pattern of internal power and organization which we can know only indirectly, and which we as citizens cannot touch. We can learn of the barbarism of Soviet politics and the manipulation and destruction of men and women for political and material ends. We can also learn to understand the meaning of communism as a political philosophy and a political program which is commanding the support of Eastern people, and not simply discourage students from dealing with it, or having them learn about it as a subject which can be studied only by denunciation. Communism is something we avoid in the United States, as it has been avoided in Great Britain, by understanding it, presenting valid alternatives, curing social evils by democratic planning.

But apart from learning to know the facts about communism and communist states presently in operation, we, as students and individual American citizens, have to accept the internal political situations in those states as beyond our personal control, and must turn our attention to our own political life to do what we can to insure that the system we advocate is always operating at higher and higher levels of human values and social morality. It is unwise for us to be negative and to do nothing more than to prove communism to be an evil, if in so doing we direct our energies away from committing acts which can show democracy to be a good.

The intellectual appeal of the philosophy of communism to those who are its converts rests in its dogmatism, its completeness, its simplicity. Those who turn, for whatever reason, to a dogmatic philosophy have found in communism a doctrine which provides the comfort of complete answers to every question. Once the idea is accepted that world society is split into two camps—the oppressors and the oppressed, the owners and the workers, the capitalists and the communists, the tyrants and their victims—the communist can then go on to accept the black and white moral system in which the United States and the West are always wrong, the Soviet Union always right. Such a system of ideas must remain morally repugnant to those of us whose values center in personal freedom and who cherish social justice for workers and for everyone else. But it does no good to say to those who are faced with tyrants to deny that they exist, or to say to those who have no political freedom that they may have to go without it.

I found a statement of the Communist Party of East Germany, adopted at the Congress of their Central Committee in March 1951, which seemed to me to represent a point of view and a policy which we should do everything in our power to avoid. The policy statement reads as follows:

In regard to cultural policy, the fight for peace, for the democratic union of Germany, and for the guarantee of our anti-fascist democratic order, is the centre of our entire work. Through our cultural policy men are educated to become true democrats, independent and responsible citizens and highly qualified professionals, who place their entire knowledge and ability in the service of peace, progress and democracy.

So far, there is nothing here with which we could disagree. We too speak of our cultural policy as one for educating true democrats who will work for peace, progress, and democracy. But then, the statement goes on:

This education can be carried on only through the relentless fight against the cannibalistic teachings of the imperialistic warmongers.

Every attempt to describe these enemy ideologies objectively is equivalent to the propagation of these ideologies. Therefore it is the decisive task of our cultural policy to effect a radical reversal in all phases of cultural life and to put a relentless stop to lukewarmness and compromise.

The significant point in this policy is that it expressly forbids objectivity, it demands that every time Western ideas are mentioned, they must be condemned in the tired clichés of communist rhetoric. There are individuals in this country who advocate similar treatment of all matters connected with communism, and who act as if any objective statement regarding the Soviet Union or Communist China implies disloyalty to America in the person who makes it. We must remember that one of our basic democratic values is the value of seeking truth objectively, without the interference of prejudice, whether from national or personal pride, and that our educational policy must be one which does not accept the communist perversion of objectivity as the democratic way of meeting the threats of communist ideology.

In other words, the honest search for truth, whether about communism, democracy, or American foreign policy, is a more important value to protect than the artificial value of propaganda technique. If we are to teach American youth to believe in their country and its moral idealism, we must do so by the development within their daily lives of a respect for honesty of expression and objectivity of analysis. This cannot be achieved by sheer anger in the face of ideas and policies which are opposed to our own. On the other hand, one can only suspect those who defend the historical necessity of all present situations, and who absolve the contemporary individual from any responsibility for political and social developments. As a country, we have wisdom enough to make our own political history, without relying on waves of the future to do it for us. My argu-

ment is that the individual citizens of the United States must
turn their attention to the basic moral choices for which this
country is responsible, and that we must act in terms of these
moral choices, in positive ways, with full conviction that the
honesty of the moral act will show to others the integrity of
our social system.

I I I

At this point we enter the area of the avoidable. It is of very
great importance to note the relation between what we do as
individual Americans in developing the moral values on which
our system rests, and what our leaders can do in projecting
these moral values into action on a world scale. Contemporary
American society, particularly its youth, is waiting for moral
leadership. The ideals of social justice, freedom and equality,
and personal integrity, form a cluster of values which lie at the
root of democratic philosophy. Unless these ideals are taught to
the young by vigorous and compelling example, they will wither
away from sheer neglect. Unless they are reasserted and re-
affirmed as basic values on which we stand, the world will
continue to find us confused, disintegrated, uncertain, and
reactionary.

A unique element in democracy, as compared with any other
political system, lies in the fact that its internal affairs are directly related to its external affairs, and the one works directly upon
the other. The leadership of this country cannot make policies
in relation to international affairs which deviate in any large arc
from the basic line of the country's thinking. Nor can it take
steps, unless it wishes to reject the democratic process completely, to assault the country's thinking by propaganda in order
to make us accept policies decided upon without reference to
the ideas and attitudes of the American people themselves. It

is the tendency of government and military leaders to work in this way which disturbs many of us who are now interested in the formation of public policy.

On the other hand, the impact of external affairs upon the internal life of this country has been direct and powerful. Over the past ten years changes have occurred in the intellectual and social atmosphere of this country as a result of challenges to us from outside. The challenges and the resulting changes have diverted our attention away from the ideals of social justice, freedom, and personal integrity toward the materialism of a power philosophy. Because of the challenge of the military power of the Soviet Union, our own military power has been re-established and increased. Sixty per cent of our national budget now goes for military defense. The increase has been necessary. However, with the increase in military power and the mobilization of the economy and manpower for defense has come an increase in the significance and attention given to the social and political thinking of military men, and to the respect accorded to the military point of view.

We have military men making policy in domestic and international affairs who know little about politics or the strategy of political democracy. We have civilian officials making policy in military affairs who know little about military strategy or about its use to achieve political ends. As a result, policy is made largely by military decision. One striking instance of this fact was seen in the hearings conducted on American foreign policy in the Far East after General MacArthur's dismissal by President Truman. It was not the evidence of the Secretary of State and his colleagues, or even the President's views as to the wise conduct of foreign policy, which convinced the country that General MacArthur's recall was necessary and that our policy of a limited war was sound. It was the testimony of the Chiefs of Staff, who argued simply from military premises and military expediency, not from the premises of moral leadership, social justice, or an American desire for co-operation with the United Nations for international peace.

The most significant piece of evidence of the shift toward a military point of view and a power philosophy is the size of our military budget for arming and rearming foreign countries as compared to the pitiful size of the budget allocated to aid for rehabilitation and social reconstruction. There are many of us who believe that if even one-third of the amount we now allocate to foreign military programs were redirected to economic and social reform, the leadership of the United States in world affairs would begin to assert itself with a strength and vigor sufficient to shift the direction of international events. A military program without a positive social ideal is a monster set loose which may attack its creators. In the end, it is the intelligent use of our power to achieve humanitarian ideals which will decide whether or not we can exert leadership in the maintenance of peace.

Similar evidence is to be found in other parts of the national life, evidence which shows a shift in the country's attention away from the arts and values of peace toward the skills and techniques of war. When public figures, too often the generals themselves, talk to us about world affairs and our duties and responsibilities, they speak of military posture, situations of strength, industrial production, and manpower, and one would assume that the whole of America has become a huge instrument for making war and that American youth is useful only as material to fill up the armed services. We have learned to refer to the adult population as well as to the youth as Manpower, or Human Resources, the counterpart of natural resources like coal, oil, or copper, to be used in mobilization of a military and economic instrument. The question is again a moral and social one—whether we should think of our military and economic power as an instrument of international service, whether decisions about foreign policy should be made for military reasons by military advisers or for reasons connected with the politics of democracy by those who have conducted sustained efforts to understand world needs.

This is particularly important to the state of mind of the country's young men in relation to their present military obligations. With the dominance of military thinking and the impact of defense mobilization, the young people respond with a kind of fatalism and passively accept a military world. They react to the idea of military service by saying simply, Let's get it over with, I don't care if it is necessary, wise, or stupid, but let's get it over with. At the same time, we find educators beginning to agree with the military that the best kind of education an eighteen-year-old boy can have is a period of two years in the armed services. It is natural for educators, in their desire to help in an emergency, to think of education as part of the national defense program. But what is so often missing is the realization that there is a crucial difference between national defense and national security, and that if the universities are considered only as training grounds for military personnel—in science, engineering, technical skills and research of all kinds—we have given up the only means this country has of developing a critical intelligence about political and social policies.

The total contribution of the universities is to keep a flow of educated men and women moving into the social system, and to keep American ideals and the quality of American thinking at an increasingly higher level. It is true that we must take account of the needs of the country for young men and women who will serve us abroad. But service abroad does not stop with military service. Is it not the true function of the university to educate those who will serve the United States, not only by carrying arms in its defense, but by carrying the liberal tradition and a deep understanding of human affairs, political and international, into American life, and into foreign countries where true representatives of our culture are so badly needed?

Whatever else the general public may say, it is the duty of the educator to keep the values of our civilization alive, and to develop in each new generation of young men and women a vitality of interest in social affairs and a concern for the welfare of our own and other countries. I have seen announcements of military-produced films which are designed to be shown in the high schools as part of a program to change the idea in the minds of the young that there is anything wrong with war, or that international peace is the ultimate goal of American policy. I have seen literature to be distributed in the high schools condemning the work of the United Nations and UNESCO as communist-dominated and dangerous to American values. I have heard the commercialism of intercollegiate football defended by college presidents on the grounds that the competitive pressures and rigorous physical discipline of the big league programs train young men to be better soldiers. Such moral confusion can be explained only by a lack of vision as to the aims of American education and the future of American culture.

IV

In response to further challenges from outside the country, another trend has developed along with the trend toward acceptance of military thinking as a guide to social action. Contemporary youth finds itself in an American society which is increasingly concerned with material and commercial values. This is partly due to the continuing and wearing pressure of economic anxiety, the constant worry over inflation, the taxes, the increased costs, the need for economic aid abroad, the repeated crises in the European economy, and the sheer size and weight of the economic and industrial mobilization for defense. These economic pressures have not had the effect, as the Marxists would prefer, of producing social contradictions and tensions which have split American society. On the contrary, they have produced an almost complete uniformity of political, social, and economic attitude. But they have had the effect of concentrating public attention on money values and economic status, until both capital and labor have united to organize a capital-labor economy which increases the economic status of each group at the expense of the general population. The pathology of an economically competitive society lies in the fact that if left to go unchecked it does concentrate attention on economic and material values at the expense of social ideals.

Whatever else may be true of our present economic situation, it has had the effect of applying its pressures to the thinking of contemporary youth. In the commercial world of college basketball and football, it is the offer of money, as well as the offer of other forms of recognition, which encourages young men to throw basketball games and to sidetrack their education in order to live the comfortable life of the advertised athlete. It is the acceptance of money values as a higher goal which corrupts the lives of public officials and sets so low a moral standard for the younger generation.

But deeper than this is the general effect of this value system upon the social and personal attitudes of young men and women. It is frequently noted among journalists and educators that young men are cautious, without the personal initiative to reorganize society, to experiment in new fields. They are seeking jobs with large corporations, large businesses, stable institutions, where a steady and secure income is already guaranteed and in which the personal and social security of the individual is certified by the board of directors. As a result, the areas of society

which need the services of our best young men and women are
neglected and ignored. The idea of public service, of the use
of one's education and talents as a contribution to the welfare
of others, is not presented convincingly by our national leaders.

We need teachers, social workers, civil servants, community
leaders, nurses, scientists, and educators to take care of the social
problems and the educational need of the whole of America. We
also need professional men and women—doctors, lawyers, engineers, public officials—who have the social conscience and the
personal idealism to work for other people and not merely for
power and money. In the present economic and social climate,
it is not the absence of moral idealism in youth which accounts
for their concentration on money and security, but the absence
of moral leadership among their elders, the absence of any but
military and baseball heroes, and the continuing presence of
economic pressures and economic lures. It is also true that the
effect of sustained bombardment of the sensibilities of the young
by magazines, movies, radio, and television is to deaden the
moral faculties and to lead the youth to conclude that American
life is money, crime, fun, and games. Higher education itself, in
attempting to solve its own economic problems, has often
yielded to the temptation to become a form of business institution and to forget its aims in the struggle for its means.

Closely related to this trend in economic and commercial
emphasis is the trend toward political and social conservatism.
Again, it is in response to challenges from outside the country,
and the pressures of national and international anxieties, that
the character of thought and attitude has moved in the direction
of rigidity, uniformity, and absolutism. In periods of great social
tension it is natural for many people to be worried about the
security of the country and the need for stability and control of
social conduct. But it is an ironic fact that exactly at the point
in the world's history when leadership from the United States

in the realm of social idealism is urgently needed, the pressures upon this country have become so great as to turn us back to doctrines of self-interest and of counter-revolution.

It is foolish and dangerous to allow a longing for security to blind us to the fact that we cannot gain security, either physical or spiritual, by demanding uniformity of thought from our citizens, and loyalty from our friends and allies. Loyalty will not appear upon command, and respect from other nations will not come from demands for gratitude and political allegiance. It can come only from a display of democratic attitude, and the display of honest effort to share our freedom and our ideas for social welfare with other people in other countries.

In America today, everyone agrees that contemporary society is in a bad situation. But few agree on what the situation is or why it is bad. In the absence of anything resembling specific information on this point, the easiest thing to do is to blame something or somebody—communism, imperialism, the United States, the Soviet Union, capitalism, labor, Stalin, Roosevelt, Yalta, Churchill, Alger Hiss, progressive education. In the United States when everything else fails, the custom is to blame education, and its product, modern youth. On the whole, this is an important and innocent aspect of the national habits and customs. Since the person who blames education can never be proved wrong, and since we can always count on a succession of young men and women, each of them doing something to outrage the moral sense of the preceding generation, this gives us an endless supply of moral indignation to be generated and distributed throughout the social system. "The denunciation of the young," says Mr. Logan Pearsall Smith, "is a necessary part of the hygiene of older people; it greatly assists in the circulation of the blood."

But during the recent past, a more sinister element has entered the practice of condemnation. Seizing upon one of the abstractions, such as communism, socialism, subversion, un-American-ism, or radicalism, as the reason for a decline in American values, people have begun to attack education as the carrier of these abstract diseases. From many quarters have come violent pro-posals to comb the textbooks, ban the speakers, investigate the teachers, standardize the curriculum, and tidy up the students, all in an effort to produce a patriotic American type of boy and girl, no one of whom could be distinguished from another, and each of whom would salute the flag, read the comics, watch television, play football, follow the *Chicago Tribune,* and never bother his little head about politics or any other matter which involves his own destiny.

The sinister element which has now entered is a widespread display of intolerance for intellectual and political dissent. It is also a scorn for intellectual activity in general. Those of us who are devoted to education and are working as hard as we can to improve it are pleased to have a flow of criticism from every quarter, since this is an important way in which we can remain in touch with the stated needs of modern society. But the present attacks, all the way from a bigot who disguises himself as a Yale man to organized groups who wish to protect the freedom of America by preventing teachers and students from having it, are attacks on basic moral values to which American education has always devoted itself.

I am describing this new political attitude, not with a view to deploring it, although it may be moderately clear that I do, but with a view to describing the present situation of our youth. It seems to me that the total effect of the militarism, materialism, and conservatism is to change the attitude of Americans to their own world. The change is away from the vigor and vitality of idea and action which we are accustomed to finding in American youth, and toward the compliance of the young with the ideas and attitudes of the older generation.

This change has been looked upon with favor by a number of intellectuals, among them Mr. Peter Viereck, who has given us the phrase "the revolt against revolt" to define the basic attitude of the present generation. I do not agree with this definition, nor do I believe that it is possible to describe the present state of mind of college students with the term "new conservatism." It seems to me, rather, that the older generation has presented youth with a cautious and conservative philosophy and is hoping vainly that the youth will respond to it. In a cultural atmosphere characterized by negativism, there are few leading ideas to which the youth can respond.

It would be more accurate to say that contemporary youth suffers from repressed idealism, having no opportunity to exercise political or social power in the present social system. For it is true, as has so often been reported, that independent thinking and positive social action are discouraged in the young, especially those who are in college, by the accusations and threats of accusation accorded to any person whose views are radical and whose interests are political. It is observably true that on the college campuses the intellectual tone of student and faculty life is subdued and muted by the repressive measures which have either been adopted or suggested for adoption by those who attack the educational system. Even in those institutions which are noted for the free and clear defense of faculty rights and student independence, individuals have been watchful and guarded in the expression of personal views, both in private and in public.

We are now working in the area of the avoidable, where decisions made in education, in our communities, and in our national life are genuine decisions about live options. Although we must work within the conditions imposed by our own situations, we are at least working with possibilities and not with foregone conclusions. When a community rises to the defense of its teachers and its school system and defends the rights of its citizens to enjoy the freedom to teach and to learn, it is making a positive decision about democratic values. When a school or a college refuses to give up its own right to choose books, speakers, and teachers by intellectual and not political standards, it is making a moral choice. Such decisions, multiplied and enriched by the company of other decisions about similar questions in political life and public affairs, reassert the moral values from which our youth can learn the truth of their own heritage.

This process of reaffirmation of American ideals can properly be called moral education. By education I do not mean only that part of it which is carried on formally in the schools and colleges. I mean the education for everyone which comes from community action, from the statements of democratic principle made by religious leaders, from the work of private agencies for social welfare, from newspaper editors who take a stand on issues of freedom, from publishers, radio producers, playwrights, educators, poets, businessmen—whoever makes the moral choice of defending personal integrity against its attackers, and of defending democratic ideals against authoritarian practices.

V

The cause of social justice and equality of opportunity is one to which Americans have always rallied. Throughout our system of higher education, college men and women have responded quickly to calls upon their energies. They have taken action themselves, often in the absence of leadership from their elders, in breaking segregation barriers against minority groups, in making democratic reforms in their college community.

The difficulty is that in the present national climate there is a latent hostility on the part of many university and public leaders to progressive ideas for educational and social reform, a hostility which occasionally breaks out in violent attacks on the philosophy of John Dewey. In a singularly uninformed piece of philosophical effrontery, *Time* magazine some time ago placed the blame for what it referred to as the moral confusion in our youth upon the educational ideas of John Dewey, and placed its hope for our future salvation on the shoulders of Mr. Robert Hutchins. Mr. Hutchins had won favor by advocating that we turn our attention away from contemporary society and toward the study of a list of books which he and his friends had been good enough to prepare for us.

There is obviously merit in any educational proposal which suggests that we all read serious books and think about what they say. But in the matter of moral values, so much depends on the relation between thought and action that the simple advocacy of reading is not an answer to the educational problem. Students who find that they can discharge their debt to the cause of social justice by reading about it are not likely to be worried by a segregated housing situation or an anti-Semitic fraternity when it occurs on their own campus. There is also a disadvantage in the fact that so many of the more respectable and weighty writers recommended in the book list as guides to humanity bring a European class and race consciousness to bear on cultural questions, and urge the superior virtues of a stratified society and a quiescent mass of citizenry. Even if we were to rely so completely on the power of the classical word to revive the moral enthusiasm of youth, we would need to extend the reading list in an anthropological and social direction, and perhaps admit, in addition, some American writers to the company of the classical moralists.

But what John Dewey suggested throughout the whole of his life was not that we give up reading any serious book of any period in history, but that we read such books in order to help with the matter of testing our ideas in action, that we bring moral and social issues to the center of the educational system, that we teach our students to recognize and solve moral problems in their daily lives. If this is moral confusion, it is the kind we should actively cultivate. The philosophy of education we need if we are to deal with moral values is one which relates the school and college directly to the society in which they exist, and attacks directly the social problems raised, whether in economic and racial discrimination, in the maintenance of civil rights, in the construction of a democratic foreign policy, or in any matter where moral values are at stake.

To do so we need all the wisdom we can muster from the great humanist writers of the past. But such wisdom will remain discursive, abstract, and conversational unless it is used and tested in the reality of contemporary moral issues themselves. The ideal of social justice can be taught, and when it so saturates the thinking of our youth that it becomes a natural and instinctive attitude to social issues, it then affects the direction and boldness with which this ideal can be carried to other countries and other problems. It gives the Voice of America something to talk about, it gives concrete expression to the claims of our political philosophy, and gives our national leaders something with which to back up the statements they are making to the people outside this country.

The ideal of freedom can also be taught. Freedom defined in the moral sense is closely related to economic, political, and social conditions. The young Negro cannot be free without the opportunity for education, for an occupation, for social equality. Nor can anyone in any country achieve freedom in its full moral sense unless he has the opportunity to become all that he is capable of becoming.

Freedom defined in a personal sense consists in an attitude, to oneself and to authority. It rests on the conviction that each person has the right to make up his own mind about the truth of an idea on the basis of the best evidence he can find, and that he must retain the right to choose his own ideas and his own course of action within the limits of an accepted social framework. In America today we need to strengthen our own conviction about the value of freedom before we can hope to encourage our leaders to act courageously in bringing independent ideas to the administration of foreign policy. Democratic leadership can only be as strong as the support it receives from the people it leads; and no maker of foreign policy, no State Department executive, can function in his true capacity unless the citizens he serves are secure in their conviction that freedom of thought is a necessary condition for achieving wisdom in political action.

There is great danger, both to domestic and foreign policy, in restricting the scope of political discussion in colleges by screening speakers, investigating teachers, and imputing disloyalty to dissidents. These are challenges to the very method by which truth is reached, and educators who fail to meet the challenges do so at their own peril and at the peril of our national security. The danger exists not simply because of the effect of repression on those who are trying to formulate public policy, but because of its effect on the attitudes toward freedom thus taught to our youth. Freedom will die if it disappears from the consciousness of one generation of our youth, if it is not taught as a living concept and an ideal for our youth to follow.

How can the contemporary student learn to value the ideal of freedom if university authorities prevent or condemn a campus effort to achieve it? How can the rest of the country learn to appreciate the inviolability of free speech if educators join the side of those who would prevent it? How can students at the University of California learn about loyalty to ideals of freedom when the Regents of their University give them constant examples of disloyalty to the principles of democracy? To quicken the imagination of the country to the cause of democracy, educators, citizens, and government leaders alike must act boldly and firmly whenever the practice of free thought and free speech is threatened. Only by their doing so can we be sure that American policies will be kept from the control of the ignorant and bigoted.

V I

The center of these moral ideals of social justice, freedom, and equality is the ideal of personal integrity. By this I mean consistency of action, consistency between what we say and what we do, a belief in the ideal of honesty and a commitment to carrying it out.

How is it learned?

By the example of integrity. By learning to understand and to feel the passion of the scholar for the rectitude of his intellectual conduct. By observing in action the selflessness of men who are willing to give up personal advantage in order to confer a public benefit. By living in a community of teachers and students where standards of honesty and humanity are revealed in the daily work of learning the liberal arts. The liberal art which is most worth teaching and most worth learning is the art of finding the truth and standing by it under pressure.

I can find no better way of expressing the hope and faith in this ideal than the expression given to it by André Gide, just before his death:

At a time when I feel in such peril, so besieged on all sides . . . the fact of knowing that among the young, even if they are few and in no matter what country, there are those who take no rest, who keep intact their moral and intellectual integrity, who protest against all totalitarian commands and undertakings which would subordinate, lower and subject thought or reduce the soul—for it is finally the soul itself which is at stake—it is the fact of knowing that these young people are there, that they exist, it is that which inspires confidence in us, the older folk; it is that fact which keeps me, so old now and so close to leaving this life, from dying without hope.

Leadership by the United States in the world today must be a leadership which relies on this hope, which stretches out to those people everywhere who want to have faith in us and our cause of social justice. Every one of us in the colleges can help to achieve this world leadership. We cannot run the world. But we can create the conditions within this country which will make it possible for our leaders to know that if they will only use our power for democratic ideals, they have a strong and vigorous nation of democratic citizens to sustain them and to strengthen their purposes.

Chapter Four

PHILOSOPHY AND THE TEACHER

Philosophy is a name for the process by which people come to make sense from the disorder of common experience. There are therefore philosophies of an infinite variety, no one of which is entirely true, since each philosophy takes the liberty of defining truth in its own terms, and the truth itself keeps a little ahead of each philosophy. There is, in addition, a variety of philosophies *of*, as distinct from pure philosophies—a philosophy of art, of life, of religion, of science, of society, of history, of literature, of education, and a philosophy of philosophy. The latter is an attitude taken by professors of philosophy at their annual meetings and in their communications to one another in the journals. It consists either of a genial skepticism or a cautious neutrality about all philosophies, and a tendency to believe that an idea which makes any claim to truth should be cut to pieces before your eyes. The philosophy of education suffers from some of the same disadvantages along with others of its own. It is often about itself, and is taught to people who go on teaching it. Occasionally, a philosophy of education breaks out in a classroom or a college, where it is subject to attack by people who say that it is either backward and dangerous to progress, or forward and dangerous to classical values.

But a philosophy of whatever kind, when it is out of the academy, is only as good and as important as it is thought to be by those who accept it, and is only as significant as the use people can make of it in organizing their own thoughts and actions, or in stimulating speculation which they enjoy. Knowledge and ideas are an outcome of living. Simply by existing, every person is forced to have ideas and knowledge of some kind, and to make up his mind about what he will or will not do—that is, to have values. Through his existence, the individual becomes aware of some of the conditions of his own life, and he agrees unconsciously with Ortega's "I am myself in my context." He feels himself to be part of some kind of process, and if he becomes more conscious of the different elements in that process, he distinguishes certain ideas and judgments as the focal points around which his explanations and preferences form themselves. By an increased precision about what it is he values, he gradually puts a world in order, and learns which of his ideas may be trusted. These ideas are constantly tested in experience for their trustworthiness, and can last only as long as they are proved to be worthy of trust, unless they are covered over by so many layers of sentiment, custom, or prejudice that they have become a dogma and are completely protected from practical testing.

But the principles and ideas which each person believes have no universal life of their own. They are individually created by each knower, and merely point to the places where other people may have similar experiences and where private truths may be confirmed or denied. The truth for each person is found in the process of knowing, not in any final forms which someone else has arranged for him.

Accordingly, philosophy is not simply a subject to be studied. It is a process of sorting out principles and experiences, and transforming them into new meanings. The philosopher is one who has developed an oversensitivity to the ordering process, keeps worrying about his own experience, and is not satisfied to let reality simply exert its own reality. His pathology is that he cannot leave things alone, that he sees relations among things normally thought to be widely different, and sees differences between things normally thought to be the same.

Each person begins to be a philosopher as soon as he pushes his ordinary questions past the point to which they usually go. Children are fond of asking questions about ultimates, although before they are grown they have usually learned to stop asking questions and to occupy themselves with other things. But the questions, whatever they are, must be the honest expression of a desire to know an answer. Otherwise they are a form of intellectual snobbery.

The purpose in the study of the philosophers is to find answers to questions which trouble or interest the person who reads. The philosopher will raise questions which have not occurred to the reader. But it is important to remember that the philosopher has his roots in the world in which people live, and is to be judged by the way in which he succeeds in explaining that world. There must be no barrier between the philosopher and the rest of the human race. The great thinkers are to be admired and respected, not as those who have left us to slip away into places where there are truths hidden from the rest of mankind, but as those who have carried on the process of thinking at a very high level with a great deal of imagination to a set of credible conclusions. From these thinkers, the individual can learn to value standards of reasoning and of insight, whether or not it is always possible to agree with the conclusions reached.

On the other hand, it must be noted that philosophers do shake the foundations of society, and the greatest philosophers are those who have given the foundations the hardest shaking, sometimes bringing them down. It is the mark of a civilized and humane community that it allows and encourages this kind of testing. It is also the mark of social wisdom that the most severe criticism of a society should be encouraged and not thwarted. As in the case of individuals, life goes forward in a society along unexamined and accepted lines and stabilizes at what appears to be a satisfactory level of achievement for all concerned. The level and the means of achieving it may or may not be satisfactory when new standards are applied. The true philosopher exposes in imagination and in prediction the consequences of thinking and acting in certain ways, and questions the customary forms of living. Taking certain particulars which he has found to be true in his own experience, he rises to generalizations which go beyond the smaller details of life and thought, and gives new suggestions, new explanations, new aims, to the human race. In a liberal community, philosophy is the self-correcting mechanism by which society and the individual can examine their own weaknesses, can take steps to overcome them and move in a new direction. In illiberal and authoritarian societies, a ready-made philosophy is applied with force by the rulers, and the philosopher becomes a sycophant who rationalizes whatever views are held by the state.

A mistake is often made in thinking that philosophers, because of their preoccupation with abstract thought, are harmless dreamers who live in the eternal while the rest of mankind copes with the temporal. But even a philosopher like Santayana, who made a philosophy out of this mistake, was not harmless. In advocating a detached and disenchanted life, and in deploring the moral dogmas of those who were too attached and enchanted, he damaged religious dogmatism along with all forms of Puritanism and disturbed, among other things, the piety of Boston, New England, and Harvard University. If philosophers were harmless, fewer of them would have been killed, burned, imprisoned, deported, harried, suspected, scorned, and feared in the exercise of their duties.

The fact is that the institutions of society have evolved to meet human need, and the forms they have taken in each society have depended on the interpretation given to those needs by social critics of all kinds and by philosophers. The great social philosophers have been informed and practical men—practical in the ultimate sense that they have sensed what is possible and attainable for man if he wishes to attain it. Their special contribution has been to draw together facts from many different quarters and to provide explanations of human motive and ideas for human betterment, or, in some cases, to provide ideas for the betterment of certain groups at the expense of others. Often, the philosopher's social contribution has been made indirectly by the establishment of new systems of abstract thought which have had no immediate relevance to social issues, but which have made fundamental changes in the total way of thinking characteristic of the age in which they lived.

The philosophy of an age, a culture, a period, or a civilization consists of a set of general ideas about the ends of human life and the principles of nature to which most people agree whether or not they have thought about them. A large part of the time, these ideas are not analyzed or understood, but are merely acted upon in an automatic way as a form of social custom. Yet the philosophy of each age or period of history does change, not because it is ever successfully refuted by the arguments of philosophers, but because a new set of ideas, more appropriate to the new social and personal needs which are always developing in every society, is advocated by those who think, speak, write, and act about these matters.

If they are advocated in an open society, and they turn out to be useful in meeting human needs, they are slowly accepted, and the recommended changes occur from generation to generation. If they show promise of improving the ways of thinking and living and yet are put down by force or by repression, they may serve as the intellectual and moral center for revolution. But in either event, the characteristic ways of thinking change from period to period under the joint influence of human need and creative thinking. The closed society tries to avoid such changes at all costs, and is willing to use all its agencies of control—police, army, political party, and educational system—to insure the continuation of one system of thought, one system of government, and one image of what human life should be.

In considering the variety of philosophers whose works have come down to us, however, there is no reason why we must give them all an equal respect. There are great thinkers of the past about whom it may be decided that they were simply wrong in what they said. There are others who have devoted themselves to many technical questions which need not concern us unless we too wish to become technicians in dealing with them. Other questions have been raised by philosophers simply because they have grown out of paradoxes between what was popularly accepted to be true and what was seen by philosophers to be false, or have grown out of problems which have since been solved by the accumulation of more exact information.

Those philosophers from the past who are important to any of us today are those whose questions, qualities of mind, and depth of insight have something to give to the solution of problems which continue to be raised in each generation, and which do not belong to any one of them. What is my responsibility? What should be my aim? How should I live? How should I act? How can I know the truth? What is most worth while? These are the personal questions of every generation. There are public and social questions which grow out of them, there are logical, metaphysical, scientific, and aesthetic problems involved, but the center of philosophy lies in personal questions of personal importance. Philosophy can bring content and criticism to thought and to experience. This is its use. As an instrument for giving direction to societies at large, it is the most practical of all studies, the most vocational of all subjects. One of the practical uses is to be found stated in a familiar passage by Walter Pater:

A counted number of pulses only is given to us of a variegated dramatic life. How may we see in them all that is to be seen in them by the finest senses? How shall we pass most swiftly from point to point and be present always at the focus where the greatest number of vital forces unite in their purest energy? [1]

The function of philosophy is to reveal what there is to be seen by the finest senses, to give shape and form and a sense of style to a life, to sustain the importance of certain values within human experience.

I I

Teachers of philosophy, when they are academically trained and at work in a college or university, seldom think of this function in their relation with college students. They do not practice the art of the philosopher himself; they mediate and administer philosophical ideas. In their hands, the study of philosophy has become not a means to the enrichment of life but a means to the possession of information. One of the reasons for this is pointed out by Mr. Squeers, who, in the course of some random remarks in *Nicholas Nickleby*, explains a neglected educational principle to a friend.

"Measles, rheumatics, whooping cough, fevers, agers, and lumbagers," said Mr. Squeers, "is all philosophy together; that's what it is. The heavenly bodies is philosophy, and the earthly bodies is philosophy. If there's a screw loose in a heavenly body, that's philosophy; and if there's a screw loose in an earthly body, that's philosophy too; or it may be there's a little metaphysics about it, but that's not often.

[1] Walter Pater, *The Renaissance* (Macmillan Company, New York, 1904), pp. 249-250.

Philosophy's the chap for me. If a parent asks a question in the classical, commercial, or mathematical line, says I gravely, 'Why, Sir, in the first place, are you a philosopher?' 'No, Mr. Squeers,' he says, 'I a'n't.' 'Then, Sir,' says I, 'I am sorry for you, for I shan't be able to explain it.' Naturally, the parent goes away and wishes he was a philosopher, and equally naturally, thinks I'm one." [2]

There are those in American academic society who play Mr. Squeers' game. The philosophers too often play the role of those plowing the arid ground of a special subject matter, or, in particular circumstances usually described as cutting across fields, share their subject matter with others who are not philosophers. The fact has been ignored that philosophy exists only because there are men and women who have thought deeply and hard about the conditions of their existence and the direction of their lives. Instead of inciting students to speculate, challenging them into independent thinking, stirring their imagination, teachers of philosophy have placed before them deliberate surveys, careful histories, and a set of philosophical problems, usually about the relation of body to mind, which were inherited from traditional sources, and are now used as a device for testing the memory. In the minds of most students, philosophy therefore remains a set of opaque signs and symbols, behind which are seated truth, beauty, goodness, and the famous philosophers.

This was not always the case in American colleges. The total college program was at one time devoted to the development of a philosophy, in which individual courses were parts of a coherent whole. The unity of the curriculum was obtained by the study of Greek and Latin classics, logic, rhetoric, and Christian ethics. Very few colleges have found a modern unity of curriculum which rests on a philosophy, either a philosophy of education or a philosophy of nature.

[2] Charles Dickens, *Nicholas Nickleby* (Chapman and Hall, Ltd., London), Vol. II, pp. 346-347. Cited by C. E. M. Joad, *About Education*.

With the influence of scientific thinking, the rapid increase in organized knowledge of all kinds, and the division of studies into small units of intensive disciplines, the professional philosopher, taken out of the world and into the academies, is a man more interested in logic than in ethics, more absorbed in private research than in the minds of young people, more involved with the academy than with the world around it. The moral and intellectual influence of the philosopher has thus declined, and his effect upon the education of the young is slight. He is simply one more exponent of the ethical neutrality to be found in the rest of the curriculum and most of college life.

Yet the need for a philosophy and a unity of knowledge continues in an almost desperate form. If the education of students is to mean anything at all, it must lead to a philosophy, and each part of the curriculum and the college life must have some relation to an educational aim. It is this unity of knowledge and principle which has been sought so urgently through the efforts at reform which have marked the past ten years of higher education. Certainly the classical unity of knowledge has been in ruins through the whole of this century, having been undermined by the intellectual and social history of the preceding one. In society the unity disappeared with the break-up of the class system, the spread of mass education, the radical shift in the material conditions of modern life, the revolutionary movements, the wars, the intellectual nihilism of fascism and the intellectual coercion of communism. Education was of course affected by these social changes as it was by the development of scientific thinking which ran a course parallel with the changes themselves. Philosophy and education felt the double impact of science and society. The grand style of the classical philosophers and poets disappeared, to be replaced by the empirical, subjective, analytical, and psychological methods of modern thinkers and writers. There came to be no single unity which could hold all systems, all facts, and all values together.

A large section of contemporary educational writing is devoted to deploring this fact, and to suggesting a return to the older unities, through religion, through the revival of classical learning, through medieval universalism, through the classic philosophical disciplines. I do not believe that the failure of the classical unity to hold contemporary knowledge together is to be deplored. It simply cannot do it, and that is that. The fact should of course be noted and a search for other unities begun. But if we have learned to be wise enough to accept the relativism of modern cultures, we must now learn to live with this knowledge and find a unity for education in a new way. In this situation, the teachers of philosophy have not provided the intellectual or the moral leadership to help in making a new philosophy of education, or to help youth find a modern philosophy strong enough to stand up against the antagonism of contemporary life to all philosophical principle. They have been busy with other matters, with commenting on the creative work of the past, catching each other out in mistakes of logic, analyzing the meaning of propositions, and, by making text-books for beginners, consolidating the ideas of the past into units of subject matter.

Accordingly, the creative gift has been lost. We look back to the golden era at Harvard when Royce, Munsterberg, James, and Santayana set the whole place moving with the vitality of their ideas. They advocated the ideas they believed in, they taught what they thought. We still look back to John Dewey, to Alfred North Whitehead, to William James, to Santayana, we continue to read Bertrand Russell while he restates himself, we shrug at the existentialists, shudder at the Marxists, tolerate the logical analysts, and wait for someone to say something interesting. As Arthur Miller has said of the American play-wrights:

. . . but we also had a group of rebels insisting on thrusting their private view of the world on others. Where are they? Or is everybody really happy now? Do Americans really believe they have solved the problems of living for all time? If not, where are the plays that reflect the soul-wracking, deeply unseating questions that are being inwardly asked on the street, in the living room, on the subways? [3]

The teachers of philosophy, of literature, of the humanities, seem not to be interested in such questions. Yet young men and women while they are in college are more interested in ideas and more sensitive to the biggest and most serious ideas they can find than at any other time in their lives. This is their chance, perhaps never to be repeated, for challenging every accustomed way of thinking, and for trying to find solutions to every big question. They expect to be interested in ideas, especially in philosophy, and they look for the excitement of it when they come to college. Too often their teachers, and in particular their teachers in philosophy, exclude the excitement of philosophical discovery and the fascination of real controversy about issues whose importance the students can recognize. In the colleges, the problems of philosophy have been detached from the problems of men and women. There is no way for the students to feel the human passion and the pulsing intellectual energy of the great thinkers, and no way for them to catch the spirit of the men who were willing to suffer and to die for the truth they had found. The students do not know and do not learn that ideas are won only through intellectual struggle, that ideas do not simply occur but have to be created, by peo-

[3] Arthur Miller, "Many Writers, Few Plays," *The New York Times*, August 10, 1952, Section II, p. 1.

ple who care so much about knowing truth that they are willing
to give up everything else to the search.

In the absence of such acquaintance with the way ideas are
made, the best students assume a negative attitude to all philosophers and direct their efforts toward demonstrating fallacies
in the philosophical systems. The rest of the students ignore the
whole enterprise. The same tentative, negative, and critical
spirit is found in the new generation of students with literary
interests. Under the influence of the new criticism, they prefer
to analyze the work of others rather than to produce creative
work of their own. Ambivalence and the refusal of commitment are characteristic of contemporary American literature
and American philosophy in the colleges.

As a result we have no philosophical radicals among the teachers or the students. We have none of the intellectual ferment
which comes when the advocates of new ideas state them with
enthusiasm and conviction. What students look for is a point
of view in their teachers, not in order to take directions for
thinking, but in order to have a point of reference around which
their own thinking can turn and about which they can argue.
Students also look for a philosophy which has some relation
to the real world in which they live and to which they can relate
their own experiences.

Aside from the outline of systems of philosophy in the history
of Western thought, what range of modern ideas is now available to students in philosophy? What modern philosophy now
taught might stimulate the kind of creative interest students
need? The difficulty is that modern philosophy as it is taught
to undergraduates usually appears as a unit of study in a survey
of philosophy in which the ideas of Plato and Aristotle dominate.
Along with a number of other modern philosophies, Marxism is
taught sporadically, in those colleges where educational policy
allows it, by economists and political scientists, not by philoso-

phers. But Marxism is seldom intellectually stimulating to American students of philosophy, partly because so much of its content is unconvincing to a non-class society, and partly because no one is likely to speak a good word for it. There is little intellectual challenge to students in a philosophy which is never advocated but only condemned. But its lack of vitality in challenging student thinking is due more than anything else to the fact that Marxism is taught as if it did not exist as a philosophy in a real world where whole countries and systems of government are in the process of civil war and revolution and are using its doctrine as a guide to action. The lack of connection made by teachers of philosophy between Marxism as a system of ideas and communism as a program of revolution gives the students no chance to find their own specific answers to the challenge Marxism makes to their ways of thinking.

Existentialism seemed radical and interesting for a little while, but not much was said about it in college classes of philosophy. When taught to students as an important intellectual phenomenon, it served to arouse more interest on their part in political thought, in questions of moral commitment, in the social responsibility of the artist and in a number of issues in metaphysics and ethics, than most other modern movements. As a philosophy, however, it has quickly become technical, pretentious, and obscure, and when it is taught at all, is taught historically, by the method of tracing its roots to other philosophers in the nineteenth and twentieth century. This has rendered it useless as a stimulant to philosophical, literary, or political discussion among students, and by itself it has lacked the staying power of a positive philosophy which can breed its own intellectual and social consequences and its own intellectual opposition.

In a similar way, logical positivism, although widely taught and widely practiced among the graduate students, has had no creative or energizing effect on philosophical thinking, since by its nature it very soon reaches Professor Wittgenstein's end of the road, "The philosophical treatment of a question is like the treatment of an illness," and sets out to trap creative thinking in a network of logical puzzles. The excitement of demolishing all arguments by logical analysis soon wears very thin and is likely to make philosophical prigs of the young. In any case, it ceased to be exhilarating to undergraduates some time ago and has only contributed to the negative mood of students toward philosophy.

Pragmatism, the American radicalism of the past fifty years, is now in bad repute, largely because of the consistent and often wilful misinterpretations given to it by its European and American critics. At one time the rebellion of Charles Pierce, William James, and John Dewey against traditional philosophy, and the radical way in which they confronted all philosophy with tests for truth which had not been suggested before with such vigor, created its own center of controversy and a series of opposing arguments. But now, the most fashionable criticism to make of pragmatism, or of naturalism, or of American philosophy in general, is not to say that it has reached a lull, or is gently drifting, but that it shows a lack of the tragic sense, is full of relativism, materialism, glorification of science, optimism, and is therefore a little vulgar. The trend is toward those philosophies from the past which assert moral absolutes, pessimism, a fatalism about human nature, a dislike of science, and a demand for order and control in society. The influence of this point of view on student interest in philosophy is once again negative, since it does not ask for new ideas from students or anyone else—it reminds them that the truth has already been discovered and that any comments they might make on it would probably be in error.

In this period of educational history for the colleges, it is ironic that William James, who was responsible for so much of the vitality and growth in American psychology and philosoophy during the early twentieth century, should be brushed aside as the proponent of a philosophy alleged to be one of expediency and compromise, at a time when the influence and reputation of his brother, Henry James, has reached a new peak. For William James, those qualities of mind and social attitude so perfectly represented by Henry James' life and thought were the precise qualities guaranteed to inhibit the vigor and thrust of creative philosophy. The mood of Henry James has captured the colleges. The philosophy of William James has eluded them. Whatever else his philosophy contains, James' message to educators and to philosophers states that each of them ignores the real world of empirical fact at his own peril, and that an education or a philosophy which separates the realm of thought from the realm of feeling, or the sphere of theory from that of action, will be incapable of achieving depth or breadth. If the philosophers and educators do not talk to men and women who want to hear them in ways which they can relate to their own experience, they will not be heard, and those in search of education and of philosophical insight will receive it elsewhere under less desirable auspices. William James expressed this view in the following passage:

The world to which your philosophy-professor introduces you is simple, clean and noble. The contradictions of real life are absent from it. Its architecture is classic. Principles of reason trace its outlines, logical necessities cement its parts. Purity and dignity are what it most expresses. It is a kind of marble temple shining on a hill.

In point of fact it is far less an account of this actual world than a clear addition built upon it, a classic sanctuary in which the rationalist fancy may take refuge from the intolerably confused and gothic character which mere facts present. It is no *explanation* of our concrete universe, it is another thing altogether, a substitute for it, a remedy, a way of escape. . . . [It] will never satisfy the empiricist temper of mind. It will seem rather a monument of artificiality. So we find men of science preferring to turn their backs on metaphysics as on something altogether cloistered and spectral, and practical men shaking philosophy's dust off their feet and following the call of the wild.[4]

The shortest comment to be made about philosophy in contemporary American education is that when the college regulations allow it, the students are shaking philosophy's dust off their feet and following the call of the wild.

III

When I first read philosophy in college, I read it as the history of certain ideas. I assumed, in the absence of any evidence to the contrary, that all ideas began with Plato, who gave currency to the basic philosophical questions, which were then carried through the minds of others, century after century, in regular order, like annual reports or monthly issues of a magazine. The ideas themselves were sometimes interesting, often not. They were collected into various systems, some starting at one point, some at another, and were ordered logically according to certain rules upon which everyone seemed to agree. A variety of systems had appeared, all of them justifiable, all of them, in a sense, equal, and the role of the student-philosopher was to recognize the systems by the names of the philosophers who had made them.

These ideas were not to be dealt with in terms of their ultimate value, their validity, their truth, or their contribution to human understanding. They were not to be criticized from any particular point of view, but to be understood, remembered, and known. Those systems which had appeared fairly recently

[4] William James, *Pragmatism* (Longmans, Green and Company, New York, 1947), pp. 21-23.

were to be studied last, if at all, and then only with a view to locating them in the tradition from which they had come. The master of all philosophers was Höffding, the textbook historian of philosophy, who had the whip-hand because of his formidable erudition and his talent for putting every philosopher in his proper place in the history of philosophy. Höffding's erudition thus enabled the student to answer questions. The fact that these were questions which only people like Höffding would ask seemed perfectly natural to me at the time.

Simultaneously with this philosophical reading, I was involved in reading literature from the same general point of view. Since the bulk of this reading was listed by educational authorities who seemed to me to have a passion for covering ground, I discovered quickly that it was better not to read the original authors but to go straight to the heart of the matter by reading Legouis' and Cazamian's *History of English Literature,* or some equally competent text in the field. In this way, I saved many hours of drudgery which might otherwise have come from dealing with the actual materials of literature and philosophy. This left me free for other pursuits which seemed important at the time, including athletics, music, poetry, novels, youth, life, and the general pursuit of happiness.

My difficulty was that none of the books or ideas in which I was interested were ever brought up in college, nor did they have anything very much to do with the philosophers and writers I was officially called upon to study. Although I kept this as a guilty secret for some years, it was not until I had been certified by various institutions, and had been called upon to teach what I had learned, that I realized that it was possible to hold a philosophical position of one's own by which other positions could be judged, or that the illicit interest which I had in what can only be called a philosophy of the present was in fact legitimate and in theory respectable. I had an inkling that this might

be true when I had discovered in London that almost everything said by my tutor, John MacMurray, could be easily dis-
proved by Susan Stebbing, to whom I went for instruction, and
that both could be shown to be giving predictable expression to
a social, economic, and political *Weltanschauung*, by Karl
Mannheim, whose lectures I attended.

It was a re-reading of David Hume after I had been teaching
students about him for two years which convinced me of what
I should have known all along—that it is necessary for a serious
student of philosophy to work toward his own point of view. I
came across Hume's sentence in the section of the *Treatise on
Human Nature* in which he traces the argument leading to his
own philosophy—"After the most accurate and exact of my
reasonings I can give no reason why I should assent to it."
Although I had read the section and the sentence several times
before, and, I have reason to believe, had commented successfully on it when asked to do so, it now took on a completely new
meaning. I realized for the first time that I had been philo-
sophically cheated by my education, that I had been playing an
elaborate game which I did not understand, and that I had
never seriously asked myself why I agreed to any conclusion
or how any claim to truth could be justified. I found that the
empirical way of thinking was most agreeable to my own, that
the most radical empirical thinkers were those who seemed to
speak the most truth, and that among the modern philosophers
William James had the most to say of consequence for my further education.

But more important than any particular conclusion was the
fact that I had found a sense of philosophical identity. I had
discovered that it was not necessary to accept systems of ideas
at their own valuation, that humility before all philosophies did
honor to none of them, and that each person capable of any
degree of sustained thought could, within the limits of his in-

telligence, develop a philosophical position of his own by which to judge himself, his world, and other philosophies. I cannot help feeling that it was the responsibility of my teachers at least to have pointed that out at some time during seven years of philosophical discipline.

On the other hand, I cannot help feeling that I should have noticed it, along with a number of other things, a little earlier. I came to realize later on that the attitude of guarded scholarship and strict moral neutrality is the mark of a particular kind of educational philosophy which tries to reach its goal of independent thought and liberal attitude in students by reliance upon tradition, and by presenting the sweep of human thought without a twinge of moral indignation or a twist of intellectual preference. It is the educational philosophy of detachment, a deliberate isolation of the student from society. The college is thought to be a calm place at the center of the storm, where, for a while, students can speculate, expand their knowledge, learn, and grow, with enough freedom from the pressures of social action and personal responsibility to be able to see things in a long perspective and with considered judgment. After the perspective is set and the mind freed from parochialism, the student will then be ready to tackle his society and his life in it.

This is a point of view which has dominated European universities, and, through their example, has had a heavy influence on American attitudes to higher education. It has had more to recommend it to European student bodies where political, social, and cultural awareness is acquired in the act of growing up in the special group of families from which the students are drawn. But even in Europe, as can be seen from new developments in the British provincial universities, the change in a student body now drawn from more families of lower income groups and fewer cultural and social advantages has meant a change in the attitude of the university toward its traditional curriculum. In the United States, the university cannot assume that its students are already able to make the connection between academic knowledge and cultural issues in contemporary society. In an earlier and less democratic period of higher education, it could be assumed that all students had similar experiences before coming to college and would be going after college to other experiences which they would also share in common. This has not been true for a hundred years, yet college education is still organized as if it were.

The student who comes to college full of trust, hope, and intellectual good-will deserves more from his teachers than the invitation to look with a cool eye at two thousand years of collected thoughts. The neglect by the teacher of philosophy to do more than this is one aspect of his larger failure to come to grips with moral and philosophical issues in the urgency of their setting in contemporary society. To ask students to live in the eternal before they have become located in the temporal, is not only to put the cart before the horse but to load it up with a pile of unlabeled baggage.

In effect, concentration in the classical philosophical studies meant in my case an isolation from the contemporary world and a failure to grasp the significance of the political and social events around me during the 1930's. I recall the sudden shock of discovering for the first time that the world was adrift when in 1937 I saw the march of the Welsh miners on London to protest the treatment of unemployed miners by the British government. I listened to the passionate speeches they made and suddenly realized that these men and their families were at the center of a contemporary crisis in which their moral dignity, their sense of justice, and their rights as human beings had been violated by a force beyond their own control. From that point on, I knew that men of this quality when aroused by social injustice are not to be put off with political answers which fail to reform the evils they face.

I believe that at the time I had read every social philosopher in the classical tradition. I had written essays, papers, theses, on the subject of political philosophy, on theories of the state and on ethics. I was prepared to write at some length on the nature of evil. But I knew nothing about the real situation of the world in which people lived. In my early years, nothing much had ever been said in my presence about the struggle between the haves and the have-nots, and although I knew of the existence of poverty, social distress, unemployment, and economic troubles because of our family situation and that of families in our neighborhood, I had never considered any of this as more than a natural situation in which most people found themselves. After the experience with the miners and similar ones which followed it, it seemed to me that there had been no meaning in a philosophical discipline so devoid of personal and social content. I had been taught to believe that the work of the scholar was to trace out the relation between one idea and another, and that ideas were interrelated in ways which had nothing to do with the lives of the human beings who produced them or the society from which they came. What I had conceived as a philosopher's world—the world of abstractions and concepts, of generalized experience expressed in categories—could now be seen as teeming with life, as if a microscope had turned up an invisible population which had never been seen before. I can only say in defense of my ignorance that I was young and that I had been misled by my education.

"There are some things which cannot be learned quickly," Ernest Hemingway said in *Death in the Afternoon*, "and time, which is all we have, must be paid heavily for their acquiring. They are the very simplest things and because it takes a man's life to know them the little new that each man gets from life is very costly and the only heritage he has to leave. Every novel which is truly written contributes to the total of knowledge which is there at the disposal of the next writer who comes, but the next writer must pay, always, a certain nominal percentage in experience to be able to understand and assimilate what is available in his birthright and what he must, in turn, take his departure from."[5]

To be able to understand and assimilate what is available in his birthright, the student must also pay his percentage in experience. What Hemingway says about writing is true of learning. Every novel which is truly written, every philosophy truly conceived, contributes to the total of knowledge available not only to the next writer and the next philosopher, but to the next citizen. In the case of the young citizen, especially the American who has seen little of the real political and social world, he cannot pay his nominal percentage in experience, he has not had time to earn his way. Although he must take his departure from the ideas and values which are available in his birthright, he has had neither the time nor the experience to live himself into them. He is unable to understand and assimilate the ideas and values of things he has never known, unless in some way they can relate to his experience. The student then has a double need, a need for literature and philosophy so selected as to reveal to him the world of ideas and values of which he has had no experience, and a need for guidance toward those forms of experience with society which can help him earn the currency by which he can pay for his birthright.

It is for reasons of this kind that many of us advocate the reform of liberal education away from the traditional curric-

[5] Ernest Hemingway, *Death in the Afternoon* (New York, Charles Scribner's Sons, 1932), p. 192.

ulum. Perhaps mine was an extreme example, or perhaps I was more than usually innocent, but it has led me to believe that the philosophy and the philosophy of education which treats ideas and students with this degree of aloofness is ineffectual. To divorce ideas from their natural ground in human experience and human society, to shut away the study of philosophy from contact with contemporary life, is to deprive education and the student of the most important means at their disposal for the development of philosophic insight and social responsibility. Unless there is an awareness within the college community that the work in that community is part of a larger work in forming the culture of contemporary civilization and in dealing with the problems of contemporary society, the student may train his mind to a razor edge of intellectual fitness, but it will cut nothing but air when it is sent from college.

My view of my own education was a delayed reaction. I found the arrangement excellent at the time I was involved in it, and only later did I discover that I had missed the central point of the whole enterprise. But how can young people know that true education goes beyond formal training, or that ideas are related to real events, or that the purpose of the liberal arts college is to enable students to run their own minds and their own lives, unless they hear about it from their teachers, and unless it is implicit in the structure and practices of life in the college community?

I believe that most ideas for the reform of education come as mine did, from the experience of people who react against what seem to them to be defects in their own education, and who advocate the virtues they have found there as the beginning of a new system. The ideas are usually recollected and transformed into theory or criticism after the education has been completed and then they are presented as a program of reform. Either that or they are the result of criticisms made by teachers and educators who do not like what they find in the system in which they are working. One new element which has been added by modern theories of education is to shorten the lag between criticism and reform by bringing a critical awareness of the educational process into the process itself. Another element is a concern for the attitudes of students to one another and to their world, in addition to their attitudes to intellectual accomplishments.

In practice, this means that educators in college must have some idea of the effect education actually has on their students, and that a degree of responsibility on the part of students for the curriculum and for educational policy is a natural part of college planning. The curriculum is in the process of development toward whatever form gives the most promise of achieving the best educational results. The curriculum does not take a finally established shape in content or in method, since its form will change according to the best judgment the faculty can bring to the correction of error and to the accomplishment of the aims of liberal education. This represents the opposite view from the conception of the ideal curriculum as a thing in itself to be given to teachers who are then to use it for their students.

The practical virtue of this theory of education is that it continually thrusts the educational problems into the hands of the teachers and the students, where they belong. It also thrusts the attitudes and views of the students into the full view of the faculty, where the extent of student knowledge or ignorance, maturity or lack of it, can be assessed and the curriculum can be planned accordingly. This means an atmosphere of experiment, or trial and error, of free expression of intellectual vitality, and of progress toward aims which students can understand. Philosophy can then be taught as a way of helping students to deal with questions, and can serve to develop points of view, and to teach students to think for themselves.

I V

The conservatism and negative tone characteristic of philosophy in the colleges is also to be found in contemporary trends in the philosophy of education. Educational theory in the colleges has turned against experiment, against progressive ideas and most forms of flexible curriculum, moving instead toward a set of required courses for all students. Everything has become much more formal. Progressive theory and practice in the schools has been so abused in certain quarters as to give the impression that it favors bad spelling, illiteracy, ignorance, kicking the teacher, and a scorn for the American flag. Progressive theory for higher education has been ridiculed as a system of doorbell ringing, newspaper reading, indulging in whim and bad manners, becoming psychologically disintegrated, and adjusting meekly to modern society. Occasionally, violent bigots will refer to it as encouraging communism, internationalism, and immorality.

An editorial typical of popular misunderstanding and written from the general point of view of Yale University at the turn of the century appeared in *Life* magazine two years ago, announcing that a counterrevolution had swept the country in educational theory, particularly in the colleges, and had swept the schools and colleges clean of modern philosophies. The result was said to be that the followers of John Dewey have been removed from positions of educational influence, with the implication that they are now to be banished to their own special hell, where they may spend their days being harassed by basket weaving, ceramics, bad sentences, and progressive parents. Meanwhile all students in college will study the works of the great Western thinkers in their chronological order, and the

well-disciplined, morally firm, good-spelling, and neatly-dressed
Great Books children will grow up to be the men and women
of the American future, ready to state a principle of Western
thought, or to quote from Aristotle at the drop of a hat.

In other circles, conservative criticism has denounced modern
philosophies of education for their theory of interest and need,
and for the concept of education planned for individual students.
Once James' proposition has been stated that knowledge is
created by the individual, and that therefore teaching and learning must concern themselves first of all with the processes of
intellectual growth and maturing, the conservatives rise in a
body to accuse the modernists of creating a self-centered universe, and a society of ignorant individualists. Actually, the proposal of the modern educator is that we accept the realities of
learning, and that we stop behaving as if the motivation and
emotional response of the student were irrelevant to the total
body of knowledge and values which he learns to use in his
life. The conservatives assume that to take account of the interests and needs of the student, as he himself realizes them, is to
pander to his weaknesses and to encourage him to indulge in
indolent studies, chosen for convenience.

The proposal is quite the reverse. The proposal is that the
teacher acquire a vivid sense of the personal reality in which
each of his students is involved. This reality is composed partly
of the folklore of the student's society, partly of the moral values
of his family and community life, partly of a body of knowledge
he has already assembled from many sources in his personal
history, and partly of the intellectual habits he has learned from
his school years. Until the teacher learns who his students are,
what they already know, what they have already studied, how
their minds work, what their attitudes are, he is not ready to
begin planning for their education. Unless he learns these
things, he may plan an education which would be perfectly ade-

quate for an abstract universal student body to whom a set of common principles, ideas, values, and items of information are to be given, but which does not touch in any serious educational way the particular students with whom the teacher has to deal.

Higher education has also been heavily criticized for its relativism, secularism, materialism, and absorption in the sciences at the expense of moral and spiritual values. These weaknesses, combined with the splintering of the student's knowledge due to the elective system, are said to be the cause of the disintegration of the college curriculum and the breakdown of classical values. The recommendations for reform involve greater control of the curriculum and of the students.

The blame for disintegration is attached to the bad effects of trying to educate too many people who aren't worthy of it, or to the loss of religious faith, or to the impact of science, or to the influence of John Dewey, or to a general loss of moral conviction. But is this really true? There is more evidence of religious faith and of moral dogmatism, and less evidence of an understanding of science or of Dewey's philosophy in the colleges, than at any other time during the past twenty-five years. A variety of solutions for the defects of the college curriculum have been suggested, most of them reducing themselves to a redistribution of academic credit for a different and required set of courses. It seems not to have occurred to the conservative critics that although it is true that the world has become more secular (as well as more religious), that science has increased in importance (along with politics), that moral values have changed a good deal (along with an increase in the power of the organized churches), and that John Dewey has actually had a wide influence, the trouble with American higher education is in (a) the absurd credit and lecture system of dispensing academic subject matter, (b) the huge number of students in each class, (c) the ridiculous number of subjects given to students to study at one time, (d) the neglect of students by their teachers, (e) the lack of intellectual challenge to the student in the courses offered, (f) the similarity, in content and in attitude, of the last year of high school and the first year of college, and (g) the lack of a spirited and provocative philosophy in the educators themselves.

There is absolutely no doubt that the elective system as it was allowed to deteriorate under the methods of mass education was a foolish and ineffective instrument for educating young people. It could work well only if faculty members knew their students well enough to advise them intelligently about their courses, and the students cared enough about their education to take their own choices seriously. In addition, to work at all well, it required a total curriculum in which each course offered was not sharply defined as a narrow area of subject matter, but had, along with some breadth of content, a point of view which helped the student to relate it to the other parts of his education. In a great many cases none of these conditions was present, and therefore in a great many cases the education of the student had no center and no intelligible pattern.

On the other hand, it is also true that the system by which freshmen and sophomore students begin to specialize in a given subject to the exclusion of most other subjects is another evil brought about by the older pattern of higher education, of which the elective system is only one part. The philosophy of education on which the elective system rests is sound; it assumes that not every student is educable in the same terms and by the same courses, and it tries to take account of individual differences. Very little serious effort has been made during recent college reforms to make the elective system work as it was intended—as a system of planned choices in which the advice and guidance of the teaching faculty is as much a part of the educational program as the subjects themselves.

The twin evils of the scattered courses chosen at random and the specialized courses ordered in sequence produced an education for students which was both too narrow and too general. It lacked design. Students had no common ground on which they could meet unless it were a narrow strip of intellectual territory to which certain specialist students were confined. The obvious remedy for what was clearly an educational disease was to prevent the scattering of indiscriminate choices among subjects, and to loosen the grip of the specialized subjects. Most educators have agreed that this could best be done by arranging a program to be required of all students which would give them a core of common studies in each of the four major areas of human knowledge.

The pattern which has been followed throughout the country is one comparable in many ways to that recommended by the Harvard Committee on General Education—two years with general courses to be chosen from each of the four major fields, the natural sciences, social sciences, the humanities, and the arts. But the weakness in the total effort of reform in the colleges lies in the fact that the changes themselves were more administrative in character than philosophical and did not touch the underlying educational problems. The philosophy on which the changes rest was insufficiently analyzed. Its assumptions were considered to be self-evident.

Only rarely has there been sharp philosophical analysis of these "self-evident" principles, either by philosophers or by educators. For this reason, the seriousness and the thoughtful approach taken by the Harvard Committee to the philosophy underlying its educational plan commanded respect and agreement among educators in colleges everywhere in the country. The report of the Harvard Committee indicated that philosophical questions had detained the Committee members for serious discussion, but that the discussion had ended too soon.

The conclusion reached was that of Plato, that education was for the "rational guidance of all human activity," that the acquisition of knowledge leads to virtue, that a knowledge of what has been considered by the classical tradition to be good will lead to a commitment to the good, "... the tradition which has come down to us regarding the nature of man and the good society must inevitably provide our standard of the good."[6]

The further question as to which parts of the tradition which has come down to us about the nature of man and of the good society should provide our standards was not raised. Marx had a theory of human nature and of the good society. His views are part of the tradition which has come down to us. Plato also had a theory, of man and of society, which makes of the one a quaint organization of passions held in check by a Reason, and of the other a tightly organized class society of slaves and free men. Which of these can we say gives us the standard for the good? Is not a study of tradition merely the beginning of the task of finding standards? Are we to take standards as given when in fact the whole process of education must be devoted to the task of finding them in our own experience?

Or, consider another piece of unfinished philosophical business. The report takes the conventional view of the role of science—that it has to do with the accumulation of facts, whereas the classical tradition gives us the ideals and values which science should serve. "... science has implemented the humanism which classicism and Christianity have proclaimed. ..."[7] But is this true? Science itself is a philosophy, and creates its own values. Certainly the classical tradition and the Judaic and

----

[6] *General Education in a Free Society*, Report of the Harvard University Committee on General Education (Harvard University Press, Cambridge, Massachusetts, 1945), pp. 50-51.

[7] *General Education in a Free Society*, *loc. cit.*

Christian views of life have had a deep and wide effect on the philosophy of the Western world. But has Eastern philosophy nothing to tell us? Is science merely an instrument by which traditional Western values are put into practice? There are many philosophers and scientists who would disagree, and there are many difficulties in the way of such a description of science. Descartes was a mathematician and a scientist, yet he changed a great many of the ideas and values which came down to him from his tradition. Newton was also a scientist. He developed a system of nature which changed the religious thinking and the classical philosophies of the seventeenth and eighteenth centuries, and paved the way for the Deists and for the Freethinkers of the nineteenth century. The classical conception of man is that he is a rational animal. But a large section of scientific and social evidence from the nineteenth and twentieth century indicates that he is an irrational animal whose ideas about what is rational and what is irrational are conditioned heavily by the perspective of his time, his society, his nervous system, his personal relations, and his sex experience.

In other words, science and the scientist have not merely reported phenomena to be added to traditional lore and to be put at the service of classical notions of the good life and the good society. The scientists have themselves been philosophers, and their discoveries have challenged the traditional ways of thinking. In this sense, science cannot be separated from morality, from philosophy, from art. At the deepest level of inquiry, pure science—that is to say, abstract speculation on the basis of scientific knowledge—joins with philosophy, with ethics, with art, as a work of the imagination and a conception of the universe and its ways.

These and other philosophical questions are the proper concern of faculty members, whether or not they teach philosophy.

and whether or not they serve on committees for planning new college programs. We can only regret that the philosophers themselves have not joined in the discussion of educational principle, and have not used the problems of educational reform as a place to test their own philosophies. The common assumption which has been made, by the Harvard Committee and by so many others, is that the principle by which we can unify an education is the unity of a common knowledge. An additional assumption is made that a knowledge of the Western heritage will give students a sense of values.

There is no doubt that this provides a unity for the curriculum, but there is much less evidence that it provides a unity in the student's own education. By appealing to the unity of knowledge, the educational planners in the colleges are in fact saying that the present departmental system or divisional system by which knowledge is divided will now be united. But in many institutions we have already had just such a distribution of courses in four major areas throughout the first two years, and the unity is merely apparent, not actual. Most students in college can move through hundreds of pages of required reading, and can perform the examinations moderately well. But in doing so, they reach a goal outside the unity and the knowledge itself—that of taking a college degree. The thinking, acting, conscious self is likely to remain untouched in the process. It is with the transformation of the self that all education must be concerned, a transformation which enables the individual to see himself more clearly and to recognize the nature of the world surrounding him. In other words, the purpose in liberal education is, again, to enable the student to form a philosophy.

There is evidence that this is not achieved by establishing an external pattern of unified knowledge, if this is taken to mean that subjects chosen from four major fields are to be required of all students. We will still be left without a philosophy, since philosophy itself becomes a subject, studied for the sake of covering that area of the curriculum. The educational problem of moral and intellectual values is not to be solved by the arrangement of a unified curriculum, although that is certainly one way of trying to solve it. The comments of a student, in answer to a questionnaire in a recent review of school and college teaching, puts the problem in its real form.

My belief is that one of the principal causes of academic difficulty is not intellectual incapacity, but lack of real interest in the material presented for consumption, for which the student is only partially responsible and for which the instructor may be even less so. But because of the limitations imposed by schedules and time limitations of every sort, the instructor is obliged to present much more material to his students than they can profitably assimilate. Aware of this, he is constantly driving for simplification, for "essences" and for "main ideas." This, to be sure, can be stimulating. But most of his students, consciously or not, will be dissatisfied because there do not seem to be any problems to work out. All the interest is simplified out of the material, and the course becomes just another collection of facts for the notebook; and no fact, idea, or theory is interesting unless its acquisition has cost something.[8]

To be generally or liberally educated it is not necessary to have worked only with general ideas, or to have taken courses known as general education. Conversely, intensive study in a special subject with enlightened teaching need not make a narrow education. We look toward qualities of mind and character rather than toward possession of general information, and although a full stock of information is necessary in order to exercise critical thinking, the exact amount and kind of information

[8] *General Education in School and College,* A Committee Report by members of the faculties of Andover, Exeter, Lawrenceville, Harvard, Princeton and Yale (Harvard University Press, Cambridge, Massachusetts, 1952), p. 134.

is not to be predicted ahead of time or out of relation to the individual who studies the liberal arts. If students are to develop a philosophy, each student must be his own philosopher. If this is the case, our problem has only begun when we mark out the areas of human knowledge from which the materials of study should be drawn.

V

The unity which everyone seeks in education has been more difficult to find than it need be because philosophers and educators have persisted in looking in the wrong place. They have been looking through the subject matter of human knowledge for the most appropriate content when they should have been looking at the students who need the education. The educational unity comes through an act of unification by each student who learns. The subject and the content of knowledge are the means by which the student makes his own intellectual design. In a real sense, each course and each subject is the material for a philosophy, and is part of the formation of a philosophy. Otherwise it is not part of a liberal education. The question of what should be included in a college curriculum can be answered only after we know what will actually enable a particular group of students to become liberally educated.

In practice this does not mean that the great writers in the Western tradition are set aside in favor of Book-of-the-Month-Club selections, or that students are encouraged to paddle in the shallow water of popular psychology and books on how to make science easy. In practice it means that the teachers choose books, methods, experiences, ideas, course material, laboratory experiments, and subjects for discussion which are suited to the way their students can understand and profit by them. The aim is to commit the students to an investigation of their own ideas, to raise the level of their intellectual standards, to make them think about what they themselves actually believe.

What ideas, subjects, and books should be included in a beginning course in philosophy? Plato? If so, which *Dialogues?* Hegel? Emerson? St. Thomas? Whitehead? Hume? Communism? Fascism? Freud? Or should we begin with the pre-Socratics and take one philosopher after another until we reach Heidegger? Should it be a history of philosophy? Or a study of the problems of social philosophy? Or aesthetics? Logic? Metaphysics? Should it all be done by lectures? Discussion? Essay writing? Term papers? Should we use a textbook? The original texts? If so, how much of them? One chapter? Five? The entire works?

No one can answer these questions unless he knows from experience with students the way in which they can best learn and the things which are most important for them to learn. Students sometimes have particular interests, others have general interests without a focus, others have read a great deal of philosophy, others have little interest at all and a low intellectual temperature. Most students, no matter what their interests, have not yet learned to distinguish the important from the unimportant, or to put together a scale of values by which their own interests and ideas can be measured. It is here that the construction of a course, from no matter what materials, and the teaching of the course itself, gives the teacher his true mission. It is not a question of whether the student of philosophy is entranced by Kierkegaard, moved by Nietzsche, bored by Dewey, or excited by Descartes. These emotional (and intellectual) factors are subordinate to a total aim on the part of the teacher. The aim is to move the student's thinking toward some ideas of his own which can give his thoughts the beginning of an order which may later harden into belief. The order will not be final, nor will it be an order which the teacher establishes for him.

If the education is working satisfactorily, the philosophers, the subjects, the teacher, the discussion, the reading, the college itself, will all be part of a process by which the student is maturing in his ability to comprehend and to use the ideas he has learned. If any serious learning is to take place, the ideas from the philosophers must be those which the student can understand, not because they are simple and easy (there is no simple philosophical ideal), but because at a particular stage in his development, with the capacity for understanding peculiar to that stage, these are the ideas and issues with which he can most adequately and successfully begin. To construct a good course, in philosophy or in any other field, requires from five to ten years of experiment by the teacher. Once constructed, it will continue to change.

The philosophers who have meant most to this century in American education are those who cared about teaching, who wrote about it, who talked to and with their students and their colleagues. Bertrand Russell said not long ago that Whitehead was "extraordinarily perfect as a teacher. He took a personal interest in those with whom he had to deal and knew both their strong and their weak points. He would elicit from a pupil the best of which a pupil was capable. He was never repressive, or sarcastic, or superior, or any of the things that inferior teachers like to be. I think that in all the abler young men with whom he came in contact he inspired . . . a very real and lasting affection."[9]

This could also be said of William James, and of John Dewey. It is possible to feel in the written work of James, Whitehead, and Dewey the warmth of feeling toward students and toward all those who take the trouble to read and to understand. This is one of the reasons why the educational thinking of these men has had such a wide influence. It is not only that James, White-

[9] Bertrand Russell, *The Listener,* published by the British Broadcasting Corporation, London, July 10, 1952.

head, and Dewey have advocated a philosophy of education which has influenced educational thinking by the sheer power of the ideas. There are contrary ideas just as powerful. But as teachers, both in university classrooms and in their written work, they have shown a continuous concern for the students themselves and a depth of interest in eliciting from a pupil the best of which the pupil was capable.

What has made John Dewey's educational ideas so particularly strong and influential has been the fact that they came out of his experience as a teacher and a student, and were based on the practical experiments which he himself had made. His remarks about education coincide with the teacher's own experience, and convey the fact that they were made by a man who could write about teaching because he knew what it meant to be a teacher. Most people found Dewey's classroom teaching dull, have reported that he thought out loud in a monotonous voice, that he occasionally lost track of the students who were listening to him. But the honesty, range, depth, and humility of a philosopher who cared that people understand the connection between his ideas and their own lives was apparent in everything he did, through his books, his reviews, his lectures, his private conversations.

This too can be said of James and Whitehead. Dewey, James, and Whitehead thought their way into the consciousness of those who are learning, and could see educational problems intuitively and immediately from the point of view of the learner. They worked from there to the demands which such knowledge of the learner placed upon the art of the teacher. This was the beginning of a revolution in education, in the reversal of roles between demands placed unthinkingly upon students by teachers, and demands placed thoughtfully upon teachers because of the nature of the student and of learning itself. This is simultaneously an educational and a moral point of view, the morality of liberalism in the sympathy, affection, and understanding it insists upon if there is to be a liberation of human talents.

This is also the reason why Dewey's philosophy has incurred the enmity of all dogmatists, political, theological, or philosophical, and why in many circles today his philosophy and his ideas on education are bitterly attacked and grotesquely distorted. It is obvious, as many have said, that in a period of deep anxiety about the security of the United States and of democratic values anxiety can be relieved most immediately by clear, simple, dogmatic answers to the questions which are worrying people. These answers are bound to be more reassuring, if they can be believed, than answers which claim only that they are the best to be found with the material at hand. It is also clear that when men are certain that they know the truth, when the truth they find is said to be inherent and perpetual in human nature, society, and the universe, they are likely to insist that their truth be taught firmly to each generation of young people by a discipline imposed and not sought.

In such circumstances, a liberal and empirical attitude toward education is dangerous to the accomplishment of the educational goal, and to such men, the open universe of James' and Dewey's pragmatism is dangerous and upsetting. Those who are alarmed about the risk of not having all the certainty they crave must know that we cannot have that much certainty and still have as much intellectual freedom as we need. A free society must so respect the capacity of men and women to reach truth, to test it by their own experience, and to hold it firmly until further notice, that it is willing to run the risks of error in freedom in order to enjoy its advantages.

But the moral demands of a philosophy of liberalism are clear-cut. Liberalism insists on the use of intelligence and reason to deal with human problems and rejects the idea that the reason is entirely a creature of its own psychological and social origins.

It insists that individual conscience is the ultimate test of morality. It insists that the effect on individual human welfare is the ultimate test for a political or social philosophy.

A liberal education is one in which these moral values are taught, both explicitly in the curriculum and implicitly in the whole life of the college. In fact, the existence of the college of liberal arts is itself a confirmation of the values it teaches. Inside the college there may be many who deny the idea that the individual conscience is the ultimate test of morality, or that the reason is a free agent capable of transcending its own local conditions. But the fact that individual beliefs about the foundations of reason and society exist in great variety in the college community without the coercion of a single dogma means that the individual conscience and reason are in fact allowed to be the test of all values.

The philosopher as a teacher in the college of liberal arts has a responsibility toward his students which he has not yet begun to meet. His task is not only to review critically what is known, and to lay before the student the materials of learning. It is to present a point of view in which he believes and which can serve his students as a place for their own thinking to begin. Every teacher has a duty toward himself and toward his students to be his own philosopher. The scientist, whether he teaches biology, chemistry, or anthropology, must have some notion of the meaning of science, about its relation to society, to the rest of knowledge, and to liberal values. The student needs to learn from it, and he cannot do so unless the scientist himself gives evidence of a point of view in his classes.

If the study of science as a body of knowledge and as a method is completely separated from the study of its implications for other knowledge and its place in society and history, it becomes a technical subject. Science will not serve the function of providing a general education for those who study it unless its general meanings are extracted along with the information about its phenomena. This must be done for undergraduates by the course in science, and not by a separate subject which is then to be labeled the Meaning of Science, or The Philosophy of Science. It is unwise to set aside a course in the philosophy of science in the hope that the need on the part of the undergraduates for an understanding of science will be met there. It will not. Those who need it will not be studying it, since it will already have been transformed into a course for specialists in philosophy by its designation of a special area of that field, whereas the need for an understanding of science exists for every student in every science class. This kind of education in science need not be carried on at the expense of laboratory experiment or the discipline of specific knowledge, and would suffer badly if it were. It needs the materials of science itself as a basis for its general conclusions.

The need for understanding of implication is not confined to science classes. Every subject in the curriculum, including philosophy itself, will be technical in character unless there is some relation made explicit between what is taught and the meaning of what is taught for other parts of human knowledge and human life. I have been told that this would mean the disappearance of departments of philosophy and therefore the disappearance of philosophy itself from the liberal arts curriculum, since it is said that philosophy would then be taught by those who knew little about it to students who would then feel that their education in philosophy was complete. On the contrary, this is the way in which strong philosophical interests develop, and the way in which students and teacher are impelled to go more deeply into issues which they have only begun to realize are important. The real problem is to make room in a crowded schedule to allow the natural interests space to grow, and to find teachers who have an interest in the examination of serious philosophical questions in the context of their own special field. But here again, once a curriculum is planned to deal with such questions in every field, and teachers accept an approach which can enlarge the scope of their own learning in this direction, the reform of teaching is carried out by the day-to-day necessity of dealing with students in these terms.

It is first necessary for the teacher to think his way toward his own philosophy of education as a teacher, and to go beyond the conventional academic philosophies now accepted. The consequences of applying the philosophy of the teacher, rather than asking the teacher to apply a "philosophy of education," will direct the attention of colleges back to creative thought and away from the formalism of the traditional curriculum.

Chapter Five

ON THE EDUCATION OF WOMEN

It has been said many times recently that women should have a special kind of college education because they are women and are likely to become wives and mothers. It has been said further that an education for women which sharpens intellectual curiosity and quickens the imagination is either a waste of time or a source of frustration, since the role of women as wives and mothers will prevent them from enjoying any of their intellectual or cultural interests. A college education in the liberal arts is said to be either unnecessary or potentially harmful.

I find this attitude insulting, both to women and to education. It implies that the role of women in society is fixed and subservient, and that education is merely an instrument for training women, and men, to keep busy doing the specific things society expects of them. Education is for emancipating the intelligence, for enlarging possibilities, for providing a richer variety of experiences in life, for discovery. This is why men and women need to go to college. If there were any other institution in society which could do this better, it should be done there.

But if, during two, three, or four years of college, women are to be educated in the skills of domestic science, motherhood, wifehood, and child rearing, they are already being assigned to the role prepared for them by the social order, in terms of social policy, in terms of the needs and wishes of men, and not in terms of their own fulfillment. They are taught, merely by the existence of a specialized curriculum, that theirs is a special role, demanding special attitudes. If the same reasoning were applied to the education of men, the curriculum of liberal arts would consist of courses in how to dictate letters, how to get promoted, how to read a commuters' time-table, and how to be a father without spending too much time at it.

I have become aware at first hand of the deadly emotional strain which dealing with children for long periods puts on a man or a woman, and I yield to no one in my respect for the strength and resiliency with which the modern woman handles a very difficult role in which she is asked to be mistress, wife, mother, and social secretary to men who are distracted, busy, and quite often unbearable. I have felt the special kind of numbness which sets in after you have talked to no one but two- and three-year-olds for two days. This is something which has to be experienced to be believed. But I doubt that much can be done about overcoming that numbness in later life by anything added to the curriculum of a college. The only thing which will overcome it is the old-fashioned remedy of maids, baby sitters, a cook, or a grant from a research foundation for child study. For most young college graduates, none of this is very likely. In any case, the problem lies in the attitude which men and women take to children and the family. If they are prepared to enjoy children and family life, they are likely to do so and to learn a very great deal from the experience. The college has a role to play in inducing the attitude.

The most that can be done in college to prepare for the consequences of living for long periods with children and husbands is to become as intellectually and emotionally mature as the curriculum or the college will allow, and to become more and more resourceful about organizing one's own life. No amount of talk about marriage, human relations, the family, the biology of sex, or the psychology of children and husbands, will do very much good until the individual develops a maturity and a capacity for responding to situations and to other people in an open, generous, and understanding way. Nothing very helpful can happen until the individual woman student learns to see life as something which extends beyond the circle of her own private interests. Nor will all the education that is available be of much use to women in their married lives unless men are sympathetically conscious of their problems, and anxious to do something about them.

What is needed is the radical reform of colleges, for men and for women, in order to bring to the center of the educational program a serious concern for the intellectual and emotional maturity of each student. This is not so much a matter of a conflict between liberal and technical subjects, a choice between child study and mathematics, community relations and modern poetry, family relations and physics, but a matter of learning through the liberal arts to use the capacities one can discover in oneself. Until this kind of learning begins, the student has no way of knowing what subjects should be studied or what role one should be preparing to play in society.

Men and women are in college to discover within themselves what they can do and what they want to do. The child-study curriculum of a liberal arts college should not be a training program for child care, or a first course in academic psychology. It should be a way in which students can learn to understand themselves, to understand children, to see emotions and ideas at work in their spontaneous forms, to understand the rest of the people who inhabit the world. The insights into children's behavior from psychology and from the whole range of the social sciences are just as important for men as for women. If liberal education is to help with the problem of living in a modern family in a modern world, it will have to do something about the college man, and stop acting as if the whole of family responsibility lies with wives and mothers.

What is wrong with a great deal of higher education for men and for women in America is that it is simply boring, and irrelevant to the use and enjoyment of life. In an effort to put together a common cultural heritage for every student, higher education has developed a standard program of texts and courses to be given to everyone in college, on the assumption that students are identical in interest and in need.

But the cultural heritage is an attitude to culture, an attitude not always communicated by the transmission of the materials of culture. For this reason, we often hear it said that so many of the women of the last generation who did not go to college because it was not thought to be a good idea by their families are much more interesting, informed, and intellectually alive than many of those who have received a college education. The reason that conventional education does not frustrate men as well as women after college is that most American college men do not take academic study seriously, and a great majority think of academic study and a liberal arts degree as something which one goes through in order to take a better job than would be possible otherwise. I believe that there is more serious intellectual and social interest in the content of a liberal education on the part of women college students, partly because they are not so closely confined to subjects and activities which will enhance their business careers after graduation.

Helen Lynd has said that the mistake of the women's colleges is not so much their imitation of men's college curricula, although that is certainly one of the difficulties, but that a great deal of women's college education has tended to accept the standards of external and competitive success as a substitute for deep personal satisfaction in work accomplished. The colleges have, in the past, encouraged women to compete with men instead of fulfilling their own lives in their own ways.

This mistake about competition has been made equally in the men's and the women's colleges. It simply cuts more deeply in the case of women, who are in a very difficult position to make up their minds as to what they want from life. Do they want the satisfaction of being loved by their husbands, their children, their friends, and by society, for the work they do at home and in their communities, or do they want the respect of business colleagues, the prestige of professional and business connections, money and independent social position? Or both? What sacrifices are involved if either, or both, are attempted?

I believe that men have this deeper conflict, that is, the conflict between wanting to be loved and wanting to be successful. For men, the conflict is not so apparent, since most of the time they are willing to concentrate on being successful, and simply to take for granted the assumption that if they are successful they will be loved, by their wives, by their children, friends, employers, and by American society. The conflict in modern life is one of values. It takes place between those values resting on money, power, social position, and material possessions, and those resting on personal fulfillment, emotional richness, and the achievement of social usefulness. The conflict raises questions about personal values which each must answer for himself before he can decide on his own place in the modern world.

The educated person, man or woman, is a person who has begun to think of these questions, and is on the way to solving them. Unless there is some solution, there can be no relief from the confusions, uncertainties, and frustrations of modern life. This is true equally for men and for women. In a competitive society where the material rewards go to overwork, overambition, self-assertiveness, and the uglier human virtues, young people are brought up under a system of conditional love. *If* you do well in school your mother and father will be pleased, *if* you work hard at something your father approves you will be praised, *if* you behave according to a particular moral code you will be considered a credit to the family, *if* you win prizes you are a better man than the one who does not compete. The liberal arts release the individual into a world of noncompetition, where values are to be gained, not in order to show superiority to others, but to attain a broader, more satisfying outlook on life, an outlook which accepts other people in their own terms and does not classify all human beings into categories of high, low, rich, poor, important, unimportant, useful or not useful to oneself.

II

Suppose we are blunt about it. During the next generation, most college-educated women will marry. According to the statistics, most will have two or more children. The children will be born into a social context which is seething with problems and potential difficulties for the parents. Most of the women who come from college will have no one to help them with the domestic work. They will have to get along with an occasional baby sitter, will spend a great deal of time in simple manual tasks which anyone, with or without an education, can do, yet no one else but the particular wife and mother can actually do for these children at this time, and which are necessary if there is to be a character to the home or to the family. The alternative is to live in a big city, have no children, begin a business or professional career, and meet one's husband for dinner, breakfast, and some evenings.

The women who are in college to prepare for careers as doctors, lawyers, teachers, businesswomen, or other professions are a special minority with a different set of problems. Professional women may or may not marry. The chief college population is of women who will marry. Many of them marry before graduation. The statistics show that most women who graduate from college have part-time or full-time jobs at some time during the five years after graduation. About thirty per cent of all college women have part-time jobs which they keep while married. In other words, if education for women is to be planned in terms of the roles they will fill, the motherhood and wifehood curriculum must be supplemented by the business curriculum. What then happens to the liberal arts? And what is the point of having a liberal arts college at all, if nothing is to happen there but training women for particular projects?

When the president of a women's college meets with the graduates of his college in 1953, questions about the content of education for women invariably come up. I remember vividly one question from a Sarah Lawrence graduate which implied that, in her view, all education for women should be built around the problems of the family, marriage, the community, and child study. I asked in reply, How many children do you have? Six, was the answer. How do you think you are getting along with them? Since it was a public meeting with a husband present, perhaps the only answer could be a positive one, but the very well, thank you, was delivered emphatically. What was your main interest at Sarah Lawrence? Sculpture, was the answer. By the time we had finished discussing the use of sculpture as preparation for marriage, it was generally agreed that (a) it is important to work in the creative arts in college, (b) that it would have been a pity to have spent the time in college concentrating on getting ready to have six children later on, and (c) that one good way of learning to be a wife and a mother is to be one.

The same meeting was graced by the presence of another

graduate who as chairman of the local chapter of Planned Parenthood had honored her community work in this field by having triplets. Her chief interest in college was in politics and literature. I then asked the general question, Since you had an open choice in the curriculum of the College, how much time at Sarah Lawrence did you spend in preparation for marriage and the family, in those courses offered? How much time do you think even the most persuasive of faculty advisers could have induced you to spend in these studies even if more courses of that character had been added to the liberal arts program? In the discussion which followed, the only positive suggestion which was made in favor of a curriculum devoted to marriage and the family came from a graduate who, although admitting that she would not have approved it at the time she was in college, suggested that for their own good the present students should be required to prepare themselves by such studies. The reply to that on behalf of the College was that whenever we find someone who wants or needs to be required to do things, we require them.

I have found that most people who have in mind particular requirements for all college students are safely out of the way at the time they make their suggestions, and that the suggestions made are for the benefit of others. I have also found that students now in college rebel strongly against the idea that they should be treated as special female educational problems, or should be asked to prepare themselves in technical or aesthetic skills for marriage at the expense of other studies. Those who carry on their studies in the area of child psychology, the sociology of the family, community relations, and allied fields usually do so because of the educational value to themselves, and only secondarily, if at all, because of a specific role they expect to play as wives and mothers.

The reforms needed in the American college, for men and for

women, should give each person a greater chance to develop interests and talents which can be enjoyed and used in later life. For four years, at an important time in a woman's life, there is an opportunity in college for each woman to enlarge the scope of her intelligence, to increase her insight into human affairs, to learn to know the range of interests and values which lie in American society, and to come to a clearer understanding of herself in relation to other people and her world. Without the chance to use these four years for learning more about the extent and achievements of the human mind, and for learning how to use talents which might lie undiscovered for the rest of her life, women are spiritually and culturally deprived. To advocate either a straightforward academic program which trains all women as if they were going to be graduate students forever, or, on the other hand, to turn the curriculum over to a disguised and enlarged program of domestic science, is to miss the central point of liberal education.

A genuinely liberal education is an education in attitudes, and a way of refining the sensibilities and the powers of discrimination and independent thought. It is in no conflict with vocational education, since all men and women need to bring these qualities to their occupations. The kind of wife and mother who will make the greatest contribution to her children, to her family, and to the society in which she lives is one who has learned how to use her intelligence and her personal talents in the enrichment of her own life and in the service of other people. In our haste to put education to work on all the problems of the family and the home, we should not forget that young people marry each other not because they have read each other's college transcript, or because each has been assured that the other's college preparation for marriage has been academically correct, but for a variety of reasons, most of which are only accidentally related to education.

It should also be remembered that what holds people together in a happy marriage is love, affection, and a mutual respect, a respect which rests upon the personal resources of each partner to the marriage. It is unreasonable to expect that an education which took little pains to develop the intellectual and personal resources of a young woman would do the cause of motherhood and marriage much justice. It is all very well to approach society with the technical equipment of motherhood and wifehood, but it is necessary to marry and to stay married in order to enjoy it.

Contemporary young women believe in their own independence and the importance of developing their own interests. They see a variety of roles which they may play in the future and are not prepared to restrict themselves to a single one. The years after graduation from college have a rhythm of their own— the first five years may mean a job or marriage, the next ten to fifteen years usually mean marriage and a family, the next ten to twenty years are a time for renewed independence and freedom from the severity of the earlier family responsibility. The young women in college today are familiar with that rhythm and reject the idea of disappearing into an intellectual vacuum either in college or in marriage, and have strong views about women who, at the age of forty-five, are intellectually poverty-stricken and socially impotent because they have thought only of their family responsibilities during the preceding twenty years.

III

It is only a short time since people have come to realize that there is anything which education in school or college can do to develop the complete range of women's talent, and it is only a short time since the ideal education for American women resembled that of the European girls' boarding school. Gogol in

Dead Souls has given us an accurate description of the ideal.

Madame Manilov had had a good education. And a good education, as we all know, is received in a boarding school; and in boarding schools, as we all know, three principal subjects lay the foundation of all human virtues: the French language, indispensable for the happiness of family life; the pianoforte, to furnish moments of agreeable relaxation to husbands; and finally domestic training, in particular, i.e., the knitting of purses and other surprises. It is true that there are all sorts of improvements and changes of method, especially in these latter days; everything depends on the good sense and capacity of the lady principals of these establishments. In some boarding schools, for instance, it is usual to put the pianoforte first, then French, and then domestic training. While in others, domestic training, that is, the knitting of "surprises," takes the foremost place, then comes French, and only then the pianoforte. There are all sorts of variations.[1]

The examples of history cause some of us to step gingerly and with some suspicion when newer versions of genteel education for women are suggested, especially when men suggest them.

This is not to say that the curriculum must be constructed as if women did not exist, or as if there were no differences in educational need and social role between men and women. It is precisely because there *are* differences, not simply between men and women, but between individual men and individual women, that college education is in need of reform. In the case of women college students, their choice of college courses, or of the colleges they wish to attend, has to do with the fulfillment of their own plans for the future. If, as is often the case, the individual student has no concrete plan other than to obtain a college education and to enjoy the benefits, privileges and satisfactions of the liberal arts, possibly to take a job, eventually to marry, the

---

[1] Nikolai Gogol, *Dead Souls*, Alfred A. Knopf, N.Y., 1923, Vol I, p. 38 cited by Earl McGrath, *General Education in Transition*.

responsibility of the college is to use its educational resources of all kinds to enhance the student's total development. I do not think that this can be done in the same way for every student, each of whose future is at the time of college unforeseen, and only relatively foreseeable.

The college of liberal arts should therefore make no standard requirements of subjects for all its students. Some women, in choosing college work, or in choosing the career they wish to adopt, will choose to work more, for example, in biology than in physics, perhaps because in biology there is more interesting material relating to the problems of growth than exists in the other sciences, or because there are more opportunities for women to work part-time or full-time in the field of biology than there are in the field of physics or chemistry.

But a course in physics, if it is adapted to the student who will not go into a career in the field, will try to present a view of the physical universe and an understanding of modern science rather than preparing the woman student or the college man for advanced work in physics. Similarly, women will choose to work in psychology, child study, literature, history, anthropology, philosophy, international affairs, the dance, theatre, painting, sculpture, writing. These studies should be related to the knowledge and capacity of the American young woman as she is, rather than to the kind of stereotype she is expected to become.

The choices between one course and another will not be made whimsically or lightly if the college is aware of the fact that in making choices among courses the student is actually choosing to become one kind of person rather than another. The student does not know this when she first comes to college; she will learn it as she works with her teachers. Courses of study will be chosen because of the ends they will serve in the student's life. The student is confronted with choices among values and goals in the process of choosing among courses. When such decisions are put in the hands of students and they must justify their own choices—to themselves, with reference to their own image of themselves in the present and in the future, and to their teachers, who can give advice and guidance in the choosing—the link between education and personal life is made naturally and unavoidably. The student who chooses to work in philosophy, science, and psychology during a given year of college attendance is then doing so because in her own opinion and that of her teachers the interrelation of these three fields is the best educational means by which her present development can go forward to its next stage.

During the period in which women had to fight for their own emancipation, for the vote, for equal professional opportunities, for personal independence, an attitude grew up which was reflected and stimulated by education in the colleges for women, and which was part of an effort to assert the intellectual equality of women with men. The first battle of the war between the sexes was won, at some cost to the emotional security of those who fought it and those who shared in the fruits of victory. It was often difficult to distinguish between those who were intelligently dedicated to the emancipation of women and those who simply adopted the major defects of competitive masculinity while rejecting the major feminine virtues. In many cases, the struggle for personal independence was won by turning oneself into a masculine woman and playing a man's role in a man's world.

The present situation of the educated woman is partly the result of the victories of the feminist movement. The issue simply is, who will take care of the family and the home now that women are to some degree emancipated. There are radicals whom I have met on the left wing of the new feminist movement who give the impression that men should be ashamed of themselves for allowing their wives to suffer birth pangs in the first place, and that if they were real men, they would have the babies themselves. On the other hand, I have met reactionaries on the men's side who still hold that we should go back to the arrangement by which women had babies, looked after the house, got the dinner, and minded their own business.

The conflict is a real one. The effects have been felt in the field of social relations, in the divorce rate, in alcoholism, and in education. There is no doubt that the problems of the educated woman exist today with particular severity, and conflicts arise which a college education may deepen and extend rather than cure. The conflict did not exist in an earlier generation simply because the idea of woman's equality in a free society was so impossibly far from realization. The distress now comes, just as it has come in the past for other groups not granted full social equality, when an ideal of success becomes in some degree attainable, yet the conditions necessary for attaining the ideal have not yet arrived. Women can see the opportunity for a fuller life than they could have had in an earlier generation, yet society is not quite ready to allow them to enjoy it.

According to the report of June 1951 of the Women's Bureau of the U.S. Department of Labor, 19,000,000 women were employed in industry, thirty per cent of the total working force, and of these, more than half were married. More than one quarter of the women in industry in 1950 had children under eighteen, and 1,500,000 had children who were under school age. This represents a major change in American social structure and social habit. Its implications for the future of college education for women are not entirely clear. But we can be sure that the increase in financial and social independence will have a profound effect on the role of women and the image they have of themselves. This will have its own effect on women's education.

More and more women from this working force will realize, as have so many non-college men whose sons are now in college, that the crucial difference between an expanding career and a static one is the matter of a college education. This is a reason for the enormous increase in college attendance by men, many of whom were veterans who had not considered going to college until they learned of its advantages in the military services. The addition of a larger number of women to the working force will mean a big increase in the number of mothers whose daughters will be sent to college. These students will not think of college as a preparation for marriage, but as a move ahead in the social order and a chance to be educated for a better career than the one their mothers had. A whole new social and economic group will be added to the women student body, along with larger numbers of the groups already there.

The question is, what do we do about it now in colleges for women? In these colleges, the administrators and teachers have been studying the matter for a good many years. The members of college alumnae associations have been doing surveys of women's education based on the programs of their own colleges. The members of the American Association of University Women have just completed an intensive study of women's education with the help of trained research workers and systematic questionnaires. The coeducational colleges as well as the women's colleges have carried on research in the educational needs of modern women. Sociologists, psychiatrists, journalists, husbands, and anthropologists have written on the subject. College graduates throughout the whole country have criticized and analyzed their own education.

Leaving aside those who place so much faith in their four years of college that they blame the colleges for everything which happened subsequently, the major criticism from women graduates has been that the colleges did not prepare them for the kind of life they found themselves leading, and that the educational programs were out of touch with contemporary society and its problems. A great many criticisms had to do with the completely academic way in which the colleges do their work.

There has never been a time when there was more activity for the improvement and reform of women's education. A great many improvements have already been made. There is now a greater flexibility in the admission and graduation requirements of professional and liberal arts programs. The students are given more help by faculty advisers and counselors. The idea that a college has responsibility for the personal, social, and emotional life of the student as well as for her intellectual development, and that all these are interconnected, has been recognized in more and more ways, all the way from the addition of more adequate medical and psychiatric services, to the reorganization of the old-fashioned dean's office into something less disciplinary and more useful to the students.

New curricula have been built, in child development, community relations, sociology, social work, field work, and marriage and family courses with a full-bodied intellectual content combined with an opportunity for practical experience with children, adults, social agencies, and community problems. There are new plans now in operation for combining serious study in the social sciences, literature, natural science, the arts, and the humanities with preparation for teaching in elementary and secondary schools. In many ways, the wish for a closer relation between the academic life of the colleges and the lives of college graduates is being met by educational planning.

IV

There has certainly been need for drastic reform. What can we say that college education for women has accomplished in the past? I do not mean the public successes, the cases in which talented women have been given a chance to prepare for public service and have received public recognition. Apart from the reports and the research which exist on the subject, I believe we can mark off three general types of women college graduates.

The first stereotype is that of the coed. She is the general representative of all college women in the popular mind. She appears in short stories, in movies, in *Life* magazine, in soap operas. She is the product of the big coeducational universities where most college women are educated, and where she has been thrown into the social and academic life of men, with a dash of home economics, teacher's certificate requirements, and a separate gymnasium in honor of her womanhood. She is collegiate, a sorority girl, educated in large part outside the classroom. While in college her success is measured, not in academic terms, but by the number of men who ask the pleasure of her company at dances, football games, and dates of all kinds. She is gay, happy, extroverted, healthy, very active, restless, anxious to be doing what everybody else is doing and very anxious about the possibility of being left behind. College for her is a continuation of high school, she wants people to know that she graduated from college, her intellectual interests are underdeveloped, her social life is the main aspect of her college career.

The second type of college woman can be described as the Helen Hokinson girl, educated usually in the women's colleges, where she studied a comparatively masculine curriculum and did well. She was a member of the glee club or the French club, had dates with young men from other colleges, after graduation married within her own social group, usually a man she met while in college. She has raised a family, helped her husband, and later in life spends her time in women's clubs, at forums about women, circulating libraries, garden clubs, beauty parlors, dog shows, amateur theatricals. She says things like, "I am worried enough as it is without Whittaker Chambers," or,

"The taxis are pretending they do not see me." The late Miss Hokinson, who during her life had some interesting things to say about the education of women, commented, "They want to learn; they buy the best books. The fact that they are intelligent, educated women, seeing and commenting on things they do not fully understand, is what makes them humorous."

If Miss Hokinson was right, and I am inclined to agree with her, this means that the education of these women in college was a failure. The Hokinson girls are, within a limited framework, intelligent, educated women, but the area of their experience has been close and narrow. They have been sheltered from the real issues and hard facts of the contemporary world. This is the source of their immaturity. The educational failure lies in an academic curriculum which isolated them for four years from contemporary reality.

The third type can easily be recognized as more desirable and, I hope, more numerous. Through her education this college graduate has learned how to live in her world. She makes up her own mind about ideas, politics, books, people, children, the school board, and husbands. She may be boisterous or shy, pretty or plain, lonely or gregarious, introverted or extroverted, a dancer or a scholar, a housewife or a doctor, or something of each, and she may know a great deal about science or about poetry. She may like skiing or knitting, tennis or sculpture, but she has a sense that her life and her education are something to be enjoyed, and to be used, and something which demands commitments and loyalties. She has been educated, not in subjects, not in standard texts, not in marriage, but in developing a sensitive and flexible character, and a way of facing reality, whether it is a reality of home and her children, or the reality of a profession, with a trust in herself and a respect for necessity. She does what she has to do with grace, and what she wants to do with pleasure.

When the problem of deciding between a home and a career emerges, she does not blame her college for having made her interested in too many things. She does not blame her husband for having presented her with children. She may spend a modest amount of time in her own interests. She may have a part-time job; she may write, or do stenography, or paint; but whatever she does, she has learned to organize her life and has learned to do it with a degree of maturity and self-reliance. She makes a major contribution to America's cultural and social life, and forms part of the liberalizing force this country needs in the face of the social and political pressures which are driving it toward a philosophy of materialism.

It is the task of colleges to organize their educational resources in such a way that the personal development of the woman student can take place with the minimum of interference and the maximum of personal satisfaction. Colleges for women have in the past been guilty of setting goals of intellectual fulfillment and social roles which in fact their students are unable to reach, with the result that the role of wife, mother, and member of family communities has been presented as an unattractive alternative, to be taken only if everything else fails. This has involved a stress on the values of success in a professional or business world, and has resulted often in feelings of guilt on the part of graduates who are reluctant to admit to their former teachers that they are simply married, raising a family, and, as many of them say, becoming intellectually stagnant.

There are some women college graduates who genuinely feel that they have let their colleges down by not using in a career the valuable education they have had in college, and feel that the time and expense involved in their education has been wasted. This is sometimes the result of exposure to teachers who are themselves vividly and wholeheartedly involved in a full intellectual life, and who tend to look upon women and men who are not themselves active in these ways as second-rate cultural citizens. At other times it results again from the academic nature of the college program, with its courses in subjects which are in the curriculum, not in response to the needs and interest of students, but as part of a body of knowledge which is said to make up the educated person's intellectual armory. In this case, since the academic program is complete in itself, and consists of a sequence of courses leading to further study or to competence in an academic field, the graduate may in all honesty feel that the educational time has been wasted, due to the fact that at the time she was involved in it she found herself dealing with subjects of no intrinsic interest, a situation which continued after graduation. The solution is to reverse the traditional procedure of educational planning, and to release the student from the necessity of mastering subjects of no personal relevance, enjoyment, or usefulness, and to plan an education which deals with the individual student.

The reason for starting a college in the first place is to educate individual students. All the rest of the apparatus of education exists for that person and her contemporaries in a college community. Unless the individual student becomes active in the process of educating herself, nothing that the college can do will have much effect.

As for the curriculum, we do not know what subjects to teach, how to teach them, or how to organize the college until we know something about the individuals we are called upon to teach. Who are they and what do they know? What do they want? What do we think they should want? What do their parents expect of them? Do they know why they are in college? Are they able to read and understand Marcel Proust? Melville? Plato? Schopenhauer? What is the kind and extent of their intelligence? Can they speak a foreign language? Do they want to? Do we think they should? If so, what language? Do they

intend to marry after college? How much experience have they
had in working at a job? How many of them are from foreign
countries? How well do they understand English? Have they
been overprotected? Do they intend to enter medicine? Law?
Teaching? Are they stubborn? Rigid? Scattered? Snobbish?
Well-balanced? Prejudiced? Agreeable? Docile? Bigoted?
Rebellious?

Depending on the answers to these and other questions, we
become ready to make educational plans. We then know what
things we can do for these students, at this time in their lives,
with ourselves as teachers.

There is an equal responsibility in the hands of the student.
She is a person with certain goals, usually vague and general,
certain ambitions, sometimes extreme, and an assortment of
talents, illusions, strengths and weaknesses. Until she learns to
face the reality of her own self and her own possibilities, she
will be unable to make true use of her college education. She
will be unable to establish honest goals for her life which she
can reach and which will satisfy her. Under the influence of
literary or social stereotypes, the late-adolescent American girl
gains an image of herself which is often unreal, and which is
often allowed to continue unchecked in her college career. She
thinks of herself as a person who will become an actress, pub-
lisher, fashion editor, author, public figure, and has not learned
what this means in talent, training, and work. Or she has an
image of herself as a charming and brilliant hostess, mother of
four beautiful children who are soundless, happy, and automatically clean, married to a college man who is handsome,
successful, well-traveled, and continually able to sweep her off
her feet.

I do not mean that we should make certain that every college
woman is informed by the college that she is in for a bad time,
or that she should be told that college women cannot become

publishers, actresses, or television producers, since this is untrue. But I believe that the college has a responsibility to discover the real facts about its students and to help the student discover the real facts about herself. The role of mother, wife, and citizen is an attractive one, and as natural and as full of prestige as some of the more exotic roles the immature imagination may devise. But if the student does not face the question for herself as to what kind of person she is and wishes to become and what she wishes to do with her life, she will place the burden of that choice upon her college. Her misunderstanding will be revealed only in later life when she writes bitter reports in the alumnae survey to the effect that the college did not prepare her for anything. Since she is married and has children, she therefore assumes that in default of making her into something she considers to be more exciting, the college should have prepared her for that.

But the college of liberal arts does not prepare or train individuals in that sense, as if students were raw material to be shaped into correct models of an ideal woman. The matter should be put the other way around. The individuals must prepare themselves for a future which the college helps them to face. The college exists as a series of opportunities for the student to educate herself under the influence of good teachers.

On the other hand, I believe that the world has simply moved past the traditional liberal arts college and left it behind with a set of educational ideas more suited to an earlier age with a different student body. The traditional program of liberal arts is an accretion of practices, ideas, and educational propositions assumed to be self-evident. The program is based on certain conventional, and usually unexamined, preconceptions about human nature and human society, about young people and what they can and should do, and what the people responsible for teaching them would like them to become. A great many traditional pro-

grams of liberal arts are simply the result of the slow accumulation of course after course over a long period of years, and
there has been no change in conception or content because no
one especially wanted to change, or because any change that
anyone wanted was put down by those in the institution who,
either through inertia or honest conviction, wanted everything
to remain as it was. I believe that the reason so many colleges
have stayed close to traditional practices is because no one has
questioned the practices seriously or because the college has
not taken a good, straight look at what the students are actually
learning, or because no one has thought of any reason why
there should be change.

To put it another way, there has been little serious discussion
of the basic issues of contemporary culture. When such discussion takes place, even the most conservative and traditional
programs become partly reformed. If the colleges lean heavily
on tradition, and build upon old ideas, without thorough and
sympathetic consideration of new ideas, we are bound to be left
with a large and unnecessary gap between the contemporary
needs of the present generation of students and the actual program of education which we offer. If we do not consider the
capacities, needs, attitudes, expectations, of the individual student, we are likely to leave an even wider gap between what
is important for young people to know and what we actually
teach them.

This cultural lag is typical of most educational programs, as
Whitehead pointed out so sharply in his famous essay on *The
Aims of Education.* "Except at rare intervals of intellectual ferment," said Whitehead, "education in the past has been radically
infected with inert ideas. That is the reason why uneducated
clever women, who have seen much of the world, are in middle
life so much the most cultured part of the community. They have
been saved from this horrible burden of inert ideas. Every intel-

lectual revolution which has ever stirred humanity into greatness
has been a passionate protest against inert ideas. Then, alas, with
pathetic ignorance of human psychology, it has proceeded by
some educational scheme to bind humanity afresh with inert
ideas of its own fashioning."[2]

The experimental colleges, having made passionate protests
against inert ideas, have then made educational schemes which
used the best ideas to be found in modern thinking and in the
history of education. Their efforts have been to bring to the
lives of each generation of college students an education suited
to their situation in modern society. By examining critically the
values and ideas of that society, they have tried to remove the
cultural lag, and to bring into play as quickly as possible, new
knowledge and fresh insight from the resources of contemporary
thought. In doing so, they have not advocated that we perch
on the narrow ledge of a contemporary parochial society, ignore
the cultural tradition on which it rests, and dismiss all ideas
more than twenty-four hours old as archaic. They have advocated the removal of inert ideas, new or old, from the planning
and the content of modern education, and their replacement by
ideas which, after a fair trial, have been shown to be more valuable in their educational effects.

It may be that the only theory of education we need is a
theory of human nature, one which asserts its complexity, its
variety, its malleability, its potential, and its complicated powers
of emotional and intellectual energy. An educational program
then can be built to enable these varieties of energy and talents
to find their own ways of fulfillment. There is something too
mechanical and arbitrary about deciding on the proper mode of
fulfillment for all human beings—a role, a style of life appropri-

[2] Alfred North Whitehead, *The Aims of Education* (Macmillan Company, New York, 1929), p. 2.

ate for all men and all women—and then constructing a college education to fit.

Again, this puts education the wrong way around. The future life of the college student should emerge from the discoveries and life of the student while she is in college. The student should live her way into graduation and into postgraduate life without a series of sharp dislocating experiences which mark one year, one course, one idea, one self, one ambition, from another. The student is a different person in her beginning year of college than in her second, third, or fourth, and the rate and direction of the changes which occur from year to year are significant points of reference for educational planning by her teachers.

Previous generations of college women thought of a college education as a mandatory four-year program. The decision as to whether or not to go to college included the decision to go for four years. If the student did not complete the college degree, she faced the disapproval of her family and of the college, and the one, two, or three years of education were said to have been wasted. Accordingly, marriage or a career was always deferred until after graduation.

There has been marked change in this attitude for two reasons. A sharp increase in the number of marriages among college students while in college was felt during the war and during the postwar years, with the result that a completely different attitude exists on the college campuses toward waiting until graduation before marriage and toward withdrawing from college after having begun. The other reason is that for women, going to college is no longer an unusual venture, to be undertaken only by those intending to have a career, or by those with specific scholastic talents which were to be developed further, but is considered more often as a continuation of the general education of young women, with the possibility of a professional career not yet fully considered or decided.

This has meant a serious change in the attitude of women students toward education and toward marriage. There were many young men and women who, during the immediate post-war years, had their own homes and families in trailer camps, student housing projects, Quonset huts, and dormitories while both partners to the marriage were studying in colleges and universities. It was not uncommon for men to take turns doing the household work and taking care of the children while the college women went about their college careers. This is a change in the family habits of college men and women which has lasted through the 1940's and is typical of the 1950's. Where there are no children, the arrangements are of course simplified. But the attitude of the college women to their own careers and to their marriages has permanently changed. The characteristic attitude is one which no longer separates the possibility of a part-time or full-time professional career from the career of marriage, and places in the hands of the husband some degree of responsibility for keeping a home. If the necessity of taking care of children makes it impossible for the college woman to continue with an independent career, the career is often postponed, and not given up.

In this situation, many young women consider one, two, or three years of college education adequate to the aims they have in mind, and are likely to be impatient with a college curriculum which makes sense only if one continues for the complete four years. We now have a different situation which suggests even more strongly than before that education for women should be planned to take account of the individual student and to take her development from year to year as a general process of growth, exploration, and development. The direction of the development, as far as the curriculum is concerned, must depend on the changes which have occurred as she is going along. In practical terms this means once more that education for women must be planned on an individual basis, that subjects to be selected for study must be chosen in the light of her plans and her situation from year to year. Otherwise, the educational program is quite likely to be inappropriate for that thirty to forty per cent of college women who leave before graduation, and for that sixty to seventy per cent who are attending college in order to discover what they can do and what they might become.

What is to be said then about the question of curriculum? Should it be a curriculum which differs in its content from that offered to men? If so, in what respects?

If colleges are interested in dealing with individual students, the answer is simple and direct. There *are* differences in curriculum, both in the content of individual courses, and in the general program offered. But these differences are not entirely due to the fact that the curriculum is arranged for a population of women students who are therefore thought to have different intellectual and educational needs. To a great extent the differences are due to the greater freedom for experiment which women's colleges possess because they need not adjust their educational program to the demands made on the men's colleges for an education which will fit men for a vocation or a profession. For example in several of the women's colleges there are broad programs in the creative arts, painting, theatre, dance, sculpture, music, not only because such programs are educationally desirable but because there is much less of the vocational pressure which exists in most men's colleges to study only those subjects which are related to a position in business later on.

On the other hand, we discovered at Sarah Lawrence College, during a four-year experiment from 1946 to 1950 with a group of men students who came to the College under the Veterans' Administration program, that the same curriculum and courses

192 *On Education and Freedom*

planned for women students were adaptable without change to the work of the men students. The men simply joined the existing classes, worked with the same faculty, put together individual programs on the basis of our regular system. In their case, the distribution of work was more in the direction of the social sciences, the natural sciences, and psychology, less in the areas of child study, languages, literature, the creative arts, since their plans for a career limited the variety of choice among courses which is usual among our women students. But the content of individual courses was not altered by their presence, nor the total curricular offering, nor the way the community life was organized, nor the educational methods. Approximately half of the men worked in one of the creative arts, usually music or theatre. All the men in the group who graduated went on to positions in business or the professions, the largest percentage into teaching.

The chief differences between the curriculum needed in the education of women and that of men lies in the emphasis on certain areas of study. In the case of women, there should be more opportunity for work in the field of child study, community relations, marriage and the family, more varied programs of study in literature, writing, philosophy. The use of materials in the field of social science can be drawn from sources more directly related to women's life and thought. This would mean, for example, the study of economics from the point of view of the consumer rather than the producer, the study of the sociology of the family rather than the sociology of prisons. These are shifts in emphasis which naturally arise in educational planning for women. The field work and research carried out by students also differs to some extent from field work which would be offered to men, more emphasis on work with child clinics, social agencies, galleries, hospitals, community centers, housing projects than on other forms of experience.

But here again, it is a matter of emphasis rather than one of constructing a different curriculum. The addition of men to the Sarah Lawrence student body, if it had continued, would have meant changes in emphasis among certain courses, possibly the addition of others, but not in the sense of constructing a new program for the College. The college which develops its curriculum around the students themselves is bound to take account of differences of all kinds in the educational requirements of young people. But the degree to which young men and young women share intellectual and social needs in common is so great that, when put to the test, the curriculum itself is one which both may share with equal benefit.

V

The degree to which men and women share emotional needs in common is equally great, but seldom recognized. Suppose we take again the familiar theme of the preparation of women for the psychological problems involved in giving up their own interests and independence in order to have children and a family life. Should we try to adjust young women to accept a kind of life limited by the demands which a masculine society puts upon them for work in the home, and to accept a separate sphere for the life of their husbands, with consequent division of labor and responsibility? Are their emotional needs to be satisfied entirely by the decisions the husband makes as to what time and energy he can afford to give to their interests? Are we to accept the pattern of social structure set by the corporations about which we read, where the executive management considers the psychological adjustment of wives to the demands of the corporation to be a primary factor in the employment and promotion of a young executive? Is the care and affection needed by children, by husbands, by wives, by families, to be the sole responsibility of the wife and mother? Is the emotional need of children for a father to be satisfied only by the mother and the school teacher?

If the answer to all these questions is yes, then education for women should be psychologically and practically organized so that the college provides a means by which women can learn of their fate before it overtakes them, can build up their own defenses against having any interests and needs of their own, can learn to submerge themselves, to become docile in their political and social beliefs so that there will never be an awkwardness when an executive of the husband's company comes to dinner, or whenever a serious question is asked in the company of other adults. It will be clear that my own answer to these questions is No.

I have talked with women college graduates about the content of their education and their preparation for future careers. Some of them have said, sadly, that the increase in their knowledge and understanding of children and adults through college studies has placed a double burden upon them in their marriage. Not only are they learning to see the extent of their responsibilities in the care and upbringing of children and the extensive emotional demands which children place upon a mother who recognizes their need for love and affection, but they also learn that in order for children to have the kind of family life they need, women very often must educate their husbands to a sensitive point of view about children simply for the sake of the children, leaving aside the interests and needs of the wife. Why should this educational responsibility be placed on the shoulders of college women? Is it not the primary responsibility of all colleges, whether for men or for coeducation, to teach young men the facts of family life, the responsibilities of the citizen, not only for his place in the community and the society which supports him, but for the home from which personal and social values develop in children? Is it not of at least equal importance that young men as well as young women come to understand the need for generous, kind, and sympathetic attitudes in personal relations, whether with their wives, with their children, or with anyone else?

Too often, in the discussion of education for women, these elements in the psychological situation of married life and family responsibility are treated as if the family were not an organic entity in which the role of the father and husband is crucial. Too often it is also assumed that women in their college education are isolated from the company of men and do not learn to understand men or to be understood by them unless they are taught to do so in an academic curriculum. From my experience in a college for women, I can testify that any notion of such isolation is false. The fact that approximately twenty per cent of the graduates of our college are married before graduation is an indication that their lives are not lacking in some measure of acquaintance with men of their own age. From my experience with the men and women students themselves, I believe that there is a great deal of understanding and respect on both sides. As for the coeducational institutions, there is such a degree of hand-holding, pin-wearing, dating, dancing, and general activity between the sexes that in many instances education cannot break through the social barrier which is put in its way by these habits of late adolescents as they go about making their efforts to understand each other.

One of the reasons why there has been so much discussion about the possibility of a separate "women's education" for women is that there are in fact separate women's colleges, sometimes independent institutions, at other times separate units within large universities. This is to some extent an historical accident, which met the problem of the exclusion of women from men's colleges. But once the accident occurred, the women's college movement has continued under its own initiative, and does provide a form of education different from the coeducational institutions. It is probable that separate colleges for women will exist in the future. In the case of those men's colleges which have become coeducational, the transition was relatively simple. There existed a shortage of educational opportunities for women who wished to go to college and the colleges simply announced that women would be admitted. In the case of colleges for women, even if the colleges thought it desirable for educational reasons to change their admissions policy, an announcement to the effect that men would be admitted would not provoke an equivalent response.

In any case, there are certain advantages shared by students of a women's college which are not available to women students in coeducational institutions, and which to a great extent balance some obvious disadvantages. In most coeducational institutions the opportunities for experience in student leadership are limited to men. Women are very rarely elected to student office. Their campus lives are much more limited by university rules. The competitive necessities of the campus social life are a constant source of distraction and anxiety. The pressures toward conformity in social and intellectual habit are very strong, and there is in general less opportunity for individual development or the indulgence in individual (and therefore strange and bohemian) tastes in ideas and interests. The students in the college for women do gain a real sense of companionship in a noncompetitive way with other women of their own age, and, freed from the social demands of the college week, can take a serious and sustained interest in the curriculum and the community life. They also learn in a great many different ways the responsibilities of student leadership, through a complete range of campus organizations in which they work and gain experience in co-operation to carry out useful projects. They also have unlimited opportunity to learn how to get along with other women.

The most important advantage, however, remains in the opportunity for educational experiment and the wider opportunities for the enjoyment of the liberal arts. We have found at Sarah Lawrence College, as I am sure many other colleges have found, that once the curriculum is planned for individual students, the fact that the students are women means that both students and faculty plan their college work with some difference in the choice of materials for study. But this is a natural outcome of planning for individual differences. A course might be planned differently if it were one which either included men, or was exclusively for men.

One of the experiments carried on at Sarah Lawrence College for sixteen years has to do with exploratory courses designed for freshmen. There is no syllabus or subject matter established in advance, although each teacher who offers an exploratory course has had a great deal of experience with freshman students and a wide knowledge of material in his own field and those fields related to it. The purpose of the course is to give to beginning college students a sense of the interrelation of a variety of forms of knowledge, and a working ability to read in original sources, to carry on independent work, and to organize materials competently. The course is also designed to introduce the student to several of the conventional academic subjects in ways which can show the problems such subjects involve, and to enable the student to discover whether or not this would be a profitable area in which the student should work in the future. The inclusion of several subjects demonstrates in reality the interconnection of various forms of knowledge. The fact that the students with whom the college teacher is dealing are women makes a difference in the choice of the materials selected.

One of these exploratory courses may serve as an example of one way of planning an education for women. [3] The course is announced as an exploratory course in the field of psychology, and is taught by a psychologist. Among the materials used are books, magazines, and pamphlets from the fields of literature, biology, sociology, anthropology, and psychology. Plays and novels are included. In addition, there are case studies from psychiatric and social work agencies drawn from the actual records, field trips to family and children's case work agencies, juvenile court, children's institutions, and hospitals. The methods of teaching include conferences and discussion with leaders in specialized fields, such as delinquency and unemployment, meetings and conferences of psychiatric, social work, and child study groups, observation of the behavior of young children in the Sarah Lawrence nursery school, one two-hour class meeting each week, and a series of special class meetings for a period of the college year with another member of the faculty, a biologist, to deal with material on heredity, the nervous system, and the function of glands, with a weekly half-hour conference with each student by the faculty member teaching the course.

[3] Further examples may be found in a series of five volumes of Sarah Lawrence educational studies:

LITERATURE FOR INDIVIDUAL EDUCATION, *Esther Raushenbush*. Columbia University Press. $2.75. Sarah Lawrence College Publications, No. 1, 1942.

PSYCHOLOGY FOR INDIVIDUAL EDUCATION, *Lois B. Murphy, Eugene Lerner, Jane Judge, Madeleine Grant*. Edited by *Esther Raushenbush*. Columbia University Press. $2.75. Sarah Lawrence College Publications, No. 2, 1942.

TEACHING THE INDIVIDUAL, *Ruth Munroe*. Columbia University Press. $3.00. Sarah Lawrence College Publications, No. 3, 1942.

EMOTIONAL FACTORS IN LEARNING, *Lois Barclay Murphy* and *Henry Ladd*. Columbia University Press. $3.50. Sarah Lawrence College Publications, No. 4, 1944.

FIELD WORK IN COLLEGE EDUCATION, *Helen Merrell Lynd*. Columbia University Press. $2.75. Sarah Lawrence College Publications, No. 5, 1945.

Since the student spends one-third of her college week in one course, it is possible to assign a generous proportion of reading for each week of the class work. A sample reading list for the first weeks of one year's class is: selected parts of Ruth Benedict's *Patterns of Culture*, William Burnham's *The Normal Mind*, Edmund Conklin's *Principles of Adolescent Psychology*, Floyd Dell's *Moon-Calf*, James Farrell's *Studs Lonigan*, Ernest Groves' and Phyllis Blanchard's *Introduction to Mental Hygiene*, Hollingsworth's *The Psychology of the Adolescent*, Margaret Mead's *Growing Up in New Guinea*, George Moore's *Confessions of a Young Man*, Marjorie Rawlings, *The Yearling*, Elsie Smithies' *Case Studies of Normal Adolescent Girls*. The discussion of the questions raised by the authors in this list might occupy several class periods, and certain of the questions might occupy most of the discussion time, depending on the direction given to the discussion by the teacher. The list of reading forms a body of material designed not to give the student information on which examination questions are to be asked, but to give a spread of knowledge from many quarters, all of it dealing, in one way or another, with the problems of the late adolescent. The fact that this course is planned for young women has shifted the emphasis in the choice of material to certain works which are more likely to be informative and helpful to young women than others chosen for a group of men or for a mixed group. The list changes from year to year as new material becomes available, or as other works are found to be more successful.

The aim is not to introduce the student to famous works, or to the best novels or to psychological monographs, but to bring material to the students which they are capable of using immediately in preparation for other material still to be selected as the work of the year develops.

By the close of the year, freshman students are able to read and discuss intelligently original monographs in the journals of psychology, anthropology, and sociology, have read a number of original works by the founders of modern psychology and sociology, and have read and discussed a variety of works of literature. There is no intention to turn literature into a series of psychological problems, or to apply psychological theories to literary characters. The aim of the student is to understand and appreciate the literary and psychological insight of contemporary writers. The reading and discussion are carried on in the context of practical experience with social and personal problems of the community, and the student is better able to relate the materials of study to the real situations out of which the material itself has come. The variety of the reading provides a marked advantage over other kinds of courses with a more restricted syllabus, and is successful in its application only when the teacher takes great pains to give each student the help she needs in bringing together the variety into central points of focus.

Education for women, if it is to help young women to find themselves and their role in life, must necessarily shift its emphasis in this way to those matters which are of serious importance and interest to women themselves. The matters are no less important to men, but the content of this kind of course, had it been planned for a group of men students, would have contained other materials in place of some of those selected in this instance. The regular program for a year of work would include two courses in addition to the one I have described, chosen with the help of a faculty member from fields other than psychology. This might involve one course in the creative arts or in literature, another in natural science, philosophy, religion, or a foreign language. But the decision as to which particular group of three courses would provide the best education for the student during a given year is made by the student and her teachers together, and is made in terms of the talents and resources she brings to her education, and the way in which she can learn to use the resources of the college for her own future. The education of women and of men, if it is to develop individual talent, must take account of individual students. I believe that it is only by understanding this kind of individual planning that we can deal directly with the problems and needs of modern women.

V I

It is impossible to have two kinds of liberal arts which separate themselves according to sex—Literature for Wives and Mothers, Introduction to Physical Science for Young Mothers. Nor is it possible to maintain a level of cultural achievement in this country if the arts are not taught widely, or if their teaching is restricted to the education of men who will seldom use them in their daily lives. There is room for every kind of education, and we have more varieties than were ever dreamed of in the fantasy of any educator in his wildest moments. There is certainly room for the special education of women for marriage and motherhood, where women are to be found who wish to undergo it, and where educators are to be found who wish to plan it. But the function of the college of liberal arts is to help men and women achieve the ability to think and to act intelligently, among other things, and this imposes some restriction on the kind of curriculum appropriate to such colleges.

The college women of this country serve as a cultural influence of the first order of importance, and constitute a liberalizing influence on political and social opinion which is often underrated and seldom understood. Their influence is felt in every community, and works through the family, the school, the library, the social agency, the professions, the women's organizations. To the degree that college women are intellectually emancipated and freed from the necessity of conforming to the political and social ideas of the business community, they act as independent critics and sensitive observers of public policy and cultural trends. They are not subject to the same degree of pressure to conform as the husband whose position may be affected by the expression of dissident views on public policy. No one who has worked with such organizations as the Association of University Women, the League of Women Voters, or Parent-Teacher Associations, can fail to be impressed by the good sense, liberal spirit, or strength of purpose shown by the women graduates of colleges. Editors of women's magazines know that to write down or to write illiberally to a readership of women, whether in style, content, or subject, in the fashion of the popular magazines for men and for mixed readership, is to cultivate a loss of circulation.

As for the status of the individual woman who wishes and deserves a college education, it should be remembered that in the United States we are committed to the goal of giving everyone a chance to achieve the most of which the individual is capable. In this principle there is no distinction of sexes. Men and women live and work together closely, they have interests which they share in common—interest in children, books, vacations, politics, business, people, goals, ideas. If they are to be companions and friends in addition to being provider and housekeeper, husband and wife, they need an education in the liberal arts, whether it is received in college or elsewhere. It would be wrong to set different limits to personal achievement between men and women by whatever educational programs we devise for each. This would foster conflict where we need understanding and mutual respect. Or it would, in the case of the home-and-mother theory of women's education, inflict the standards and values of the extroverted masculine world not only on women and the family, but on society in general.

The particular questions to be raised about the education of women raise all the other questions of modern life. They cannot be answered by assigning women to a role decided upon by a combination of cultural habit and masculine prejudice. We have to remember that there is no ultimate purpose in liberal education beyond that of learning to live a complete life to the limit of its personal, social, spiritual, and physical dimension. Education, for women and for men, is good or bad as it contributes to that ultimate purpose.

Chapter Six

LIFE, ART, AND THE HUMANITIES

Our ideas—that is, culture. The present crisis is less a crisis of culture than of the position we have given to culture. We have set it before and above life, when it ought to be behind and below life—because it is a reaction to life. We must now stop putting the cart before the horse.

—ORTEGA Y GASSET

THERE is a section of the college curriculum generally known as the humanities, and it is generally considered that within this section college students learn values, whereas in other parts of the curriculum, such as the social and natural sciences, students learn facts. This is obviously nonsense, but it persists under very respectable auspices. It is the contemporary version of the genteel tradition, which, some time ago in cultural history, for social and metaphysical convenience, divided the world into two, putting abstract thought, philosophizing, fine art, policy making, and not working with your hands in a separate realm referred to as Mind, Spirit, or the higher values, and reserved a lower realm for matters of fact, science, manual labor, sex, practical politics and simple pleasures to be referred to as Body, Matter, or Sense Experience, which ordinary people have. In colleges, the higher things are bundled up into the humanities, while the rest of the curriculum and a substantial part of the extracurriculum take care of the lower.

Once the humanities have been isolated in this way, it usually follows that for students they become emotionally sterile. The study of higher things as such is often tedious, and a good deal of time and energy goes into arguments about why they are higher, when it is a fact that if the student cannot feel their value for himself, no amount of explaining will help him very much. All knowledge is saturated with values, high and low. The primary subject matter of each teacher lies in the values he holds. The outcome of education in the liberal arts lies in the values the student holds. The separation of knowledge into the accumulation of fact and the interpretation of fact, as if they were two separate processes, makes philosophical studies empty and scientific studies barren.

American education is plagued by a variety of such separations, and is overridden by classification and analysis. It continually draws up pairs of opposites where in fact they do not exist—science versus art, fact versus value, classic versus modern, method versus content, student versus teacher—and then lines up on one side or the other for interminable arguments. If an educator proposes that we pay more attention to the present, either because it is said to contain all there is, or for some other equally good reason, he is accused of wilfully neglecting the past. If he draws attention to the importance of method, on the grounds that until you know how to go about learning and looking for truth, you cannot be sure about what it is you are finding, he is disregarding content. If he says education is for the student, on the simple grounds that it is, he is disregarding the teacher, the tradition of scholarship, discipline, the warnings of the older generation, and the future of higher learning in America.

But more than this, American education is notorious for separating and classifying knowledge into special pieces of subject matter. In certain areas of information, this is useful and necessary. But a particular subject matter, it must be remembered, is a word used to describe the information and knowledge after it has been collected, and after it has exhibited certain characteristics which mark it off from other forms of knowledge. It is not very long ago that philosophy contained in its subject matter the whole of natural and social science, psychology, ethics, a large part of religion, and the whole of the humanities. As segments have been classified and expanded, they have given the appearance to the unwary of being independent parts of knowledge, each comprising a special area with its own discipline and its own content, when they are simply divisions made for practical convenience between one general kind of phenomena and another. The same practical convenience is served under the general name *humanities,* by separating literature and philosophy from science, ethics from psychology, the fine arts from the vocational arts, poetry from history, so that one can consider them separately for purposes of study.

But this is not to say that there can actually be a separation. The total body of knowledge is not a system of classified information but an organic system of interrelated ideas, facts, values, theories, and general information, some of it useful, some of it useless, some of it interesting, some not. The task of the college is to teach the student how to select from the enormous body of knowledge the most important things for his own life and the life of his time. There is no standard way in which this can be done for everyone, and there is no standard course or program which can give the student a sense of values. The total sum of values each person holds is made by whatever integration he achieves within himself. The integration comes from within, and no amount of integrating and correlating of subjects in external ways will achieve a genuine integration unless the student himself is affected totally both in intellect and emotion.

Yet I believe that unconsciously most educators assume that it can. The structure of most college curricula indicates that the assumption is acted out. The divisions are set down—the natural sciences, the social sciences, the arts, and the humanities. The values come in the humanities.

What is a value and what are the humanities?

A value is a name for something which people value. It is a name for an act of choice. People value freedom because of the richness it can bring to their lives, and freedom is therefore said to be a value. If it brings no richness they do not value it. It is an idea on which people act, or a principle on which they judge how to act. Instead of asking, What are values? as if values were forms or things in a separate realm, we should ask, What do people value? Then the active, immediate, and personal quality comes out. The purpose of education is certainly to teach values, but when this phrase is reduced to something more specific, the purpose is to teach students to prefer one thing to another and to acquire a set of ideas and principles which they believe and on which they can act. This is what is meant by their values.

The word humanities is an educational term used as a general name for the work of philosophers, poets, or other writers, art objects of all kinds, including musical compositions, paintings, sculpture, and architecture, and the histories and commentaries written by critics on such documents and art objects. Educational programs in the humanities are usually surveys of the documents, art works, and commentaries. A number of the more famous documents and objects are read, looked at, or listened to, as many as can be managed in one term, one year, two years, depending on how long it is considered desirable to deal with values at a particular institution. The works are usually read, or observed, in the order in which they were first published or made. Medical and engineering students partic-ularly are often required to take three credits' worth of survey-ing these works during their first two years of college as a means of bringing the higher values into the professions.

What does it mean to say that the humanities deal with values, whereas the sciences and the rest of the curriculum deal with facts? It means simply that the philosophers, poets, writers, and artists are less concerned to convey exact information than they are to express their judgments and standards about what is good and bad, true and false, beautiful and ugly. Such judgments may be expressed directly by the statements of philosophers and other writers, or indirectly in the work of the artist. There are values of equal size and significance in psychology, anthro-pology, or physics, waiting to be extracted by critical thinking. The trouble is that courses in the humanities do not communi-cate the ideas and values which the writers and artists had in mind, but usually convey information. The distinction in this case is that the information being conveyed is about art objects, artists, writers, philosophers, and their values.

Accordingly, the purpose of teaching the liberal arts is lost. This purpose, I take it, is to deepen the response of the student to certain experiences in human life which teachers, scholars, artists, painters, sculptors, architects, writers, scientists, or phi-losophers and others have found to be of a richer and more satisfying kind than those to which the student has become ac-customed. There is a difference between watching a B movie and listening to a Beethoven quartet as far as the quality of experi-ence is concerned. But the student, in order to enjoy a deeper level of experience, must learn to do so. For some students, the learning has already taken place by experiences outside his col-lege education or before it began. For most, it has not. In teach-ing the liberal arts we want to deepen the level of the student's awareness of the world around him, to teach him to be more sensitive to its character and subtleties, and to find in it sources of emotional and intellectual satisfaction which are usually shut away from him by his lack of experience.

I I

Most students when they first come to college have not gone beyond school habits of gathering, recording, transcribing, and remembering the segments of knowledge with which their education has dealt. They have not yet learned to see the relations between different kinds of knowledge. They lack the experience of enjoying the work of philosophers, poets, artists, and dramatists. Therefore, the aim of the teacher is not only to give the student more opportunity to gather more information, but to enable him to find through his own experience the excitement, enjoyment, and understanding which come from knowing the arts at first hand.

Educators, for the most part, do not include this aim in their educational planning. All the discussion is about the content of courses, little of it is about the student's experience. Learning to *know* philosophy or to *know* art is itself a creative process, and unless the student becomes enmeshed in an interest in ideas and in art, he cannot actually be affected by the values with which the philosopher or the artist is concerned. Instead, he tends to treat the works of the humanists and the artists as more material to be covered, passed, and dismissed.

To be successful in teaching the arts, the teacher must have some effect upon the student's emotional life, his personal attitudes, and upon his capacity to respond freshly to new experiences. For this reason a teacher must ask himself, What will the study of these works of art provide for these particular students

in their present state of development, or, What kind of experience with poetry, drama, the creative and performing arts will
have the deepest effect upon their personal lives?

Usually the student's emotional and personal life is considered
to be the concern of the psychologist, the psychiatrist, the coun-
selor, or the personnel worker. The business of the academic
teacher is said to be with the materials of learning and the training of the intellect. This again is a dangerous separation of two
parts of human life which, if once cut off from each other by
educational philosophy and institutional practices, seldom
come back together again. The student's motivation, interest,
and enjoyment in what he learns is the force which drives him
toward obtaining knowledge and appreciating values. Those
who teach philosophy, literature, theatre, history, music, dance,
are dealing with the intellectual and emotional content of human experience. This may certainly be called a body of knowledge, and may certainly be classified under various headings,
the most general of which can be called the Humanities. But
the significant fact within this body of knowledge and collection
of objects is that they furnish a set of experiences which can
influence the student to see life differently.

Some students respond more readily to one form of knowledge
than to another. Some students react immediately and warmly
to literary works—the novel and the play in particular. Most find
a more compelling interest in contemporary works than in the
classical texts. The reason is that the experience which most
students bring to the study of literature is limited and contemporary. They have not yet developed the imagination and the
ability to project themselves into the experience of persons who
are unlike themselves. If the purpose in teaching is to deepen the
response of the student to literature, philosophy, and the arts,
and to enable him to learn something about the deeper levels of
human experience, then the choice of literary, philosophic, or

aesthetic documents is made, not because the works are classics of Western civilization, but because of the degree and kind of response of which the students are capable. Stephen Spender makes this point in relation to teaching poetry: "All poetry may do," says Spender, "as an incidental effect of its use of language, is to provide the reader with an experience which will affect him according to the laws of his own nature."[1]

No matter how much enthusiasm we may have for a specific work of art, there is a limit to the extent to which we can communicate to the student the values we find in it, and a limit to the number of ideas we can stimulate in the student's own life. The limits are set, not by us, but by the readiness and the capacity of the student himself. This is the problem—how to get the student ready to receive the values in the work itself, and how to help him match in his experience some of the importance we have found. At the crucial point, that is, when the student is left alone with the work, as E. M. Forster points out in another connection, we can only withdraw in the hope that he will see what we want him to see.

The task of the teacher in the humanities is to find the poems, novels, plays, paintings, music, philosophies, ideas, which can affect the student and integrate his present values with those of the artists and thinkers. Many of the works of literature now given to students in college are in the curriculum simply by cultural habit. The curriculum of the humanities has accordingly become listless and limp.

I am not suggesting that college students should confine themselves to contemporary literature, philosophy, and art, or that they should be introduced to bad literature simply because they have not learned to choose between good and bad, or that

[1] Stephen Spender, "On Teaching Modern Poetry," pp. 96-110 in *Essays in Teaching*, edited by Harold Taylor (Harper and Brothers, New York), p. 101.

the works of art in the classical tradition are aesthetically less valid than contemporary work. I mean what Ortega y Gasset means when he says, "There is but one way to save a classic, to give up revering him and use him for our own salvation—that is, to lay aside his classicism, to bring him close to us, to make him contemporary, to set his pulse going again with an injection of blood from our own veins, whose ingredients are *our* passions . . . and our problems."[2]

But the student, as a beginner in learning, must go through some preliminary stages before he is ready to understand and enjoy all works of art. He may never learn to enjoy *all* works of art in any case, since as his experience grows his taste will be formed and he will have his own enjoyment in his own particular categories. One of the best ways for the teacher to help the process of understanding and enjoyment to begin is to present his students with those contemporary works which relate themselves to a world with which the student is already familiar. Another way of beginning lies with translated works from the Greek theatre or from the literature of seventeenth-century France or from nineteenth-century Germany. It is impossible to say that there is only one way of beginning or one kind of content or one way of teaching. There is only the teacher and the student, and only one aim, to teach in such a way that the student becomes involved in the ideas, values, and emotions of the writers and artists.

III

It is very hard to achieve this aim through a prescribed curriculum in the humanities. One of the most damaging results of the prescribed curriculum is its effect on the teacher. Often the

2 José Ortega y Gasset, "In Search of Goethe from Within," *Partisan Review*, Vol. XVI, No. 12, December, 1949, p. 1186.

effect goes unnoticed by the teacher himself because he has become accustomed to fitting himself into a department, a division, a syllabus, or a course, rather than thinking of the course he is to teach as the means he can take to teach the students what he knows. The course is the art form through which his gifts and talents are realized. It is in fact only a certain number of hours in a schedule. The question for the teacher should be, How can I use these hours of the student's time and experience to convey to him what I know?

Instead, unconscious of his lost opportunity, he takes the assigned anthology, the source-book, and the selected works in their prescribed order, and dogtrots his dutiful way through fifteen weeks of academic subject matter, with occasional bursts of speed and excitement when ideas or books in which he is interested turn up in the sequence. All ideas and all books are somehow reduced to a common level of significance. They all suffer together the handicap of having been classified as equally great.

An even worse result is accomplished in the case of other teachers, usually the younger ones, who have a private scorn for the whole syllabus on the grounds of its inhibiting character. When faced with a conventional set of prescriptions, the teacher openly shows his cynicism, and with a wearied air which indicates that he is only doing this pot-boiler work of warming over the classics in order to make a living, permanently damages the latent interest among students for the works of art. The art has been laid out before them at the wrong time in the wrong way.

It is very difficult, for a teacher or a student, to be intelligently interested in all the famous works of the past, nor is there any drastic need that he should be. The definition of a well-educated person is not one who has read the right books. He is one who knows how to think, how to read, and how to choose books and ideas for himself. He is a man who knows for himself when a book or an idea is great. Young people in college need to know what there is to be found, not to know a little about everything which has been found. They also need to come to the great works in their own way and at the right time in the development of their own sensibility. If we could use at a better time only the thousands of wasted hours which have been squandered on the plays of Shakespeare with students who were not yet ready to understand him, we would save enough time to teach a whole new educational program.

I believe it is wrong to make a closed syllabus into which the teacher must fit. I know of programs of the kind entitled *Contemporary Civilization* at Columbia College where the enthusiasm and quality of the teaching and the interesting selection of the works to be studied overcome many of the difficulties inherent in the prearranged course. But a syllabus, by its nature, is an artificial device to give form and structure to teaching. At its best, it provides a good structure within which the students and the teacher can move. At its worst it can destroy the interest of students in works of art. In general it has the effect of making a standard educational pattern which can be transferred from one institution to another and one student to another without touching the real problems of education.

The syllabus should be the outcome of choices made by each teacher as to the best means of educating his students. The works of art, the order in which they are to be placed, the way in which they are to be presented, are all matters for which he must take responsibility himself. Otherwise, he is seldom compelled to think as a teacher or an educational planner about the development of his students, and the planning is done for him either by the editor of an anthology or by a curriculum committee assigned to that duty. If for no other reason than the sake of his own intellectual development the teacher should choose the content of his own courses. The content will change from year to year as the teacher's own interests change and as his experience with students makes him aware of the adequacy of his previous choices. In the best situation for the teacher and for the student, the course consists of work in the books, ideas, and problems in which the teacher is most interested and about which both he and his students have a serious concern to learn.

I believe that the pattern of formal education must follow the natural pattern of human development. It must accommodate itself to the reality of the human nature it is trying to educate. When it fails to do so it becomes educationally impotent. By accommodation I do not mean adjustment to shallow preferences, to adolescent social customs, to easy habits of sloth, or to philistinism in the young. I mean that in the case of the arts, there are certain truths about the way in which the arts become important to those who are learning to know them, and there are certain values which are to be found in some ways and not in others. Everyone accepts these truths and values when the discussion is not about education, but denies them as soon as questions are asked about what to do with a college curriculum.

One of these truths is that the most engrossing way to read is to refuse to have anything to do with prescribed lists, and to read from one thing to the next. There is something about a prescribed list of books, either inside or outside an educational institution, which puts the curse of duty on them and which imposes an artificial constraint on the reader. The mere idea that they have been prescribed means that they are out to prove or to represent something, or to have a calculated effect of some kind. This is what spoils so much of the reading students do in college. They are not reading because they have come to the writer by themselves but because he was assigned. They must read with an idea to answering questions to someone other than themselves. Or they read with a view to having something to say in a discussion group. This distracts them from the very things which are important about the reading itself.

The ideal way to teach would be through independent reading supervised by an individual tutor. The student might begin with Virginia Woolf and read straight through her novels and her criticism, perhaps being drawn on to read E. M. Forster because of Mrs. Woolf's references to him, or to read Bennett and Galsworthy to discover what it was Mrs. Woolf meant by her rejection of them. The student, after reading *To the Lighthouse*, might go to Sir Leslie Stephen to see what kind of father he really was and what kind of man in what kind of age could become so rational as to become unpleasant. From there, to the *History of English Thought in the Eighteenth Century*, to those parts of it which seem appropriate, taking a side-track to the letters of David Hume, or Locke's *Enquiry*, or to Addison, or Swift. The reading would have an organic development and not a linear one. Periods would merge with each other, the sense of one generation following another would assert itself. The student would feel the continuity in history as a natural result of the reading, and would be aided to feel that sense of the past which is so necessary a part of one's ability to sense the present. The choices of books, paintings, music, plays, sculpture would become part of a continuing interest in knowing more about the lives and minds of those in the tradition of the liberal arts. The teacher's role would be one of helping with the choices, trying out the student's ideas, giving him a chance to test beginning thoughts against more mature ones, suggesting those works of art for further study which seem most likely to be significant and useful in the accomplishment of the student's education.

Another student, whose interests were less literary and more developed in the direction of philosophy, might begin with Kierkegaard simply because he is so often mentioned in contemporary literature, go back to Luther, to Calvin, or to St. Augustine, or forward to Bergson, or James, or Kafka, or around the nineteenth century, to Freud, to Marx, to Nietzsche, to Darwin, in order to assess the intellectual character of a single period. This, at least, is the natural way of learning, and the way in which the mature scholar with wide interests normally reads. He does not refuse to consider contemporary work because he has not yet read everything in the past, nor, on the other hand, does he consider a work less valid because it has been crusted with layers of comment about its place in the classics of intellectual history. He often finds that to read exhaustively and thoroughly in a single writer is the best way to achieve the depth of insight into the value of humanism which we wish our students to have. Most students are not ready to deal so completely with one writer, but most can gain a better sense of the meaning of literature and the humanities by working very thoroughly in a few writers and artists rather than by trying to locate the entire Western tradition through a schematic presentation.

I believe most scholars and humanists would agree that if it were possible to conduct education in this way, we should do so. We have tried, as far as possible, to do so at Sarah Lawrence College, and have resisted all impulses to become larger or to try to teach more students with the same number of teachers, or to allow the curriculum to become structured in departments. divisions, required courses, or prearranged syllabi. A preconstructed course to be administered to all students is certainly the most convenient form of education to provide. Its educational effect on the teacher as well as on the student, however, is to draw attention away from the values in the arts and toward the accomplishment of educational requirements.

Unfortunately, even if educational philosophy were to take a turn in the direction of naturalism and the more creative ways of learning and teaching, there are too few teachers to allow sufficient time and effort to be spared for individual students. But this is not the chief difficulty. In many colleges, the ratio of students to teachers is a good one. It is the use of the teachers' time which needs altering, along with the prevailing academic attitude to the liberal arts.

No matter what the number of students in a class, it is possible to plan a course in literature which follows a natural pattern of individual reading. To do so it is only necessary to break away from the conventions of the curriculum and to plan the course as a process of development taking place in each student, with choices of the content made as if there were only one student in the class, a student who, by necessity, had to act as the general type of all his classmates.

The liberal arts exist to be enjoyed and to give a new dimension to the lives of those who know them and practice them. They are sources of aesthetic satisfaction among many other sources, and are the result of creative work by talented people, some of them geniuses, who worked in particular ways in particular periods of history for their own purposes and for the enlightenment and enjoyment of the people who were alive at the time. We want young people to take an open-hearted attitude toward all good writing, great authors, music, the theatre, religions, philosophy. We want them not only to know something about a painting they see, but to feel something when they look at it. We want them to construct some sort of judgment of their own to distinguish between first-rate and second-rate work in any field, whether or not they like it. I do not believe that we can give them this education in feeling, in attitude, or in values by dealing entirely with their intellects, or simply by reading and analyzing assigned books, or by analyzing the objects of art. These are parts of an education, but are not at the center of it.

To be educated in the arts, the student must practice them. He needs to play and compose music, not read about the lives of composers and analyze their scores. He needs to paint, to sculpt, to write, to philosophize, to act, to read, to discuss his own ideas with his friends, to understand their work, to live in a community where the arts are a normal part of conversation and of everyday life.

IV

At the present time, the creative arts are to be found, in one condition or another, on most college campuses. But they are usually outside the curriculum, or harnessed to a professional school where the opposite defect of professionalism and technical study make them almost useless as an element in the liberal education of students. Music students in the universities are as grudging about spending time outside the practice room or away from their technical subjects as are the professional students who often think of the arts as frills or women's work. Painting and sculpture are considered valid subjects for practical work only when they are part of a training program for teachers. College theatres, which are often mentioned hopefully as a factor in the revival of the dramatic arts in this country, are not centers of creative work, nor are they recognized as part of the liberal arts curriculum. They are often commercial enterprises which pay their own way by producing second-hand Broadway plays and are consequently as conservative and aesthetically backward as Broadway itself. Sometimes the theatre is an extracurricular project of the students, or it is an adjunct of speech departments, where, hidden away among diagrams of the throat and phonetic charts, there is an occasional creative artist who encourages his students to write, to act, and to produce new work. The dance is regarded as a branch of physical fitness rather than an art form, and is placed in the middle of the physical education department.

It is very seldom that the college theatre does more than to provide training in the techniques of the theatre arts for the students, many of whom have talent, but who seldom gain from their college experience a love of the arts themselves. Instead they think constantly of whether or not they will ever become successful in the professional theatre. While students are busy learning theatre technique in one part of the campus, the great plays are segregated elsewhere as documents for reading and discussion in humanities programs, new and experimental plays remain unwritten, and the student mind is exercised in class-rooms.

Aside from the educational loss in humanities programs by the neglect of theatre, music, dance, the visual arts, and the creative arts in general, there is a personal loss to college students in their lack of opportunity for experience in creative work. It would not be appropriate to look to these students for new work of importance, nor would it be the intention of a college to teach them to be professionals in the various media. But they need a chance to experiment in the media of the arts in order to understand the arts themselves. The results of the experiments—the poems, stories, paintings, music, plays, or choreography—are not designed to capture an audience or to contribute to the monuments of Western culture. They are stages in the development of students, and their importance can be measured only as they contribute to the refinement of sensibility and the increase in human insight.

The creative arts are those most directly related to personal expression, and, therefore, to personal development. The emotional aspects of learning are more directly and immediately involved. The demands for intellectual discipline and self-understanding come out of the work itself. In teaching literature, the actual changes we see in students as they progress from one stage to the next have to do with whether or not they learn to read critically, talk well in discussion or conversation, show an understanding of ideas and of the implications of the action and human character presented in the work, are able to write papers, do research, handle a bibliography, or answer accurately on examination. As far as the personal development of the student is concerned, the teacher of literature contributes a number of important elements. What he does when he is successful is to teach the student how to get the most from a book, how to understand himself and human nature, and how to think maturely about a variety of human situations where ethical, moral, social, or political issues are involved. A taste for good literature comes from this interest in the play of human character in particular situations or in the ideas and images of a poem, not from the exclusive study of literary form, social setting, historical significance, or anything else of an external kind.

The teacher of literature, if he is seriously interested in his students, will wish them to be intellectually astute and well informed, but he will also show a continuing concern for their emotional and personal growth. By this I mean simply that he cares about the attitude they take to the books they are reading, is happy about their enthusiasms, regrets their failure to react to work which he admires, wishes to make certain that they see all that there is to be seen, and cares whether or not they attack their work with the attitude of a serious student, and if not, that they learn how to do so before he is too far along with his teaching. Literature exists, and the teacher of literature exists, to open up new areas of experience in the lives of those who read. The teacher helps to open up these areas of experience, to sharpen perception of what is there to be read and noticed, to make clearer the insight of the writer. In this sense he is a true literary critic, not one who classifies and arranges, puts the author in his place, analyzes his form, and drains his blood away, but one who points to the ways in which the reader can receive the most the writer has to give.

The teaching of values is a normal outcome of this process. The values themselves will be learned through that continual rearrangement of the student's ideas and preferences which comes when students have an opportunity to test their own values and opinions honestly and openly by comparing them with those of an older, wiser, and more experienced person who is sensitive to the need for such comparisons. Literature provides the occasion and the medium through which these values are tested and revised.

In education through the literary arts, there are three principal components in the act of learning—the writer, the student, the teacher. They are in the midst of a creative process. The writer has seen one or another part of life in a certain way. With the talent he can command, he writes about it, discovering a literary form which will convey his total meaning. The teacher, by choosing a particular work for his students to read has made the claim that this work has significance for them. As a creative artist in the medium of education, the teacher invents a style of his own to convey to his students the meaning he finds in the work. He looks for a way to involve his students with the ideas and values which compose the work itself. The student enters this process, bringing whatever he can to it, and if the process is successful, he projects himself into the life and mind of the writer, and learns from the writer and the teacher something more than was possible before, something more than he could find by himself. This is an act which links together the consciousness of the student with that of the writer. The teacher provides the means by which the link is made.

In the case of the creative arts, theatre, music, dance, writing, or painting, the student is himself involved in the same process of expression which the writer or the artist carries on in his work, and comes closer to the consciousness of the great writers and artists by the mere fact that he is put in a role comparable with theirs. In the theatre, when students learn to act, to write, to direct, to study plays, a great deal of their education involves the direct exposure (and covering up) of their own individuality. They are put to the test of values by the situations in which they find themselves. By the nature of the work they are doing they must say what they think, what they are, and what is their taste. When the student deals with the regular academic system of textbooks and lectures, it is possible for him to remain withdrawn, uncommitted, and noncommittal.

The main virtue of the creative arts in education lies in the wide variety of experiences they give to the student. The teacher aids the formation of standards of value, not simply of an aesthetic kind, but of the whole scale of concerns found in the work of artists, playwrights, poets, novelists, and philosophers. A demand is placed upon a person who expresses himself merely by the fact that he is expressing something. This can mean the beginning of a process of self-criticism and self-understanding. Until the student finds for himself some mode of criticism by which he can judge the quality of his own expression and of his own preferences, he will be unable to find ways of approaching the work of others. He does learn to judge himself by first learning how others have judged themselves, but a more direct route to achieving a set of personal standards is through experience with expression.

V

These are parts of education which have to do with personal development, or, to use the familiar educational word again, values. They are essential parts of the coming of age of American students who have not had a wide experience in aesthetic or philosophical matters. But they are ignored in planning courses in the arts. What is emphasized instead is the formal arrangement of reading lists, lectures, slides, reproductions, and text-books. Most courses in the humanities show the marks of this emphasis, and most of the reform of the college curriculum over the past ten years has been of this kind.

The most complete and rigorous application of this theory of the arts is the four-year curriculum drawn from a selected reading list of approximately one hundred books at St. John's College, Annapolis. When first instituted at St. John's College more than ten years ago, the idea of the definitive reading list was widely promoted through the use of radio broadcasts, magazine articles, and public statements by Mr. Mortimer Adler, Mr. Robert Hutchins, Mr. Stringfellow Barr, Mr. Scott Buchanan, Mr. Mark Van Doren, and others, but since that time it has ceased to provoke much serious educational comment. However, it did represent, in an extreme form, an attitude to education which has found acceptance in the programs of humanities of the large universities. The two most influential models for the courses themselves are those developed at the College of the University of Chicago, and in the general education program at Harvard College. Each shows an academic weight sufficient, if not to crush the life out of the arts, to flatten them considerably.

The philosophy, proposals, and practices of the Chicago plan are the most formal and conservative of any of the current programs and have had a wide effect on educational planning. They are described in an article by Mr. Russell B. Thomas,[3] and in *The Idea and Practice of General Education; an Account of the*

[3] Russell B. Thomas, "The Humanities Program in the College of the University of Chicago," pp. 194-206 in *Humanities in General Education,* edited by Earl McGrath (W. C. Brown and Co., Dubuque, Iowa, 1949), p. 196.

College of the University of Chicago.[4] The clue to the philosophy on which the program is planned is to be found in two statements by Mr. Thomas:

Another [i.e., the Chicago] approach to the humanities concerns itself with the products of man's arts as kinds of constructed things . . . [5]

and

These values [i.e., the values derived from the study of the humanities] lie in the recognition of works of art as complete in themselves and capable of giving appropriate kinds of pleasures. Unless such disciplines are taught, the study of the poetic arts tends to drift into a confused discussion that fails to distinguish among several kinds of values.[6]

Elsewhere, Mr. Clarence Faust, former Dean of Humanities at the University of Chicago, refers to the subject matter of the humanities, which are "products of man's creative activities in art, literature, and philosophy,"[7] and which can be dealt with in three different ways, as events, with antecedents and consequences, as symbols, referring to a truth or a philosophy within them, or as artistic structures, to be studied by examining the literary materials and technical devices of the writer.

The didactic element in this philosophy can be seen in the choice of its terms—"kinds of constructed things," "products" "capable of giving appropriate kinds of pleasures," distinctions "among several kinds of values," works of art considered as

[4] *The Idea and Practice of General Education; an Account of the College of the University of Chicago*, by present and former members of the faculty (University of Chicago Press, Chicago, 1950).

[5] Thomas, *op. cit.*, p. 197.

[6] *Ibid.*, p. 197.

[7] *Fifty-first Yearbook*, Part I, "General Education," National Society for the Study of Education (The University of Chicago Press, Chicago, 1952), pp. 104-06 *et seq.*

"events," "symbols," "structures." These are static concepts useful for classifying ideas in a proper order, but what have they
to do with the spirit of humanism, the artists, or aesthetic enjoyment? The arts are to be enjoyed. To teach the arts is to show
students how to enjoy them and to learn from them, not to take
students through a museum and point out the labels on the
objects. What pleasures are appropriate for us to have from
reading Gide? Nietzsche? Faulkner? Hume? Schopenhauer?
Rabelais? Who knows, and who should tell us? Is Plato's *Republic* a constructed thing, an event, a symbol? It is all of these,
but these are the least things about it. The work had to be written in a certain way in order for the writer to convey what he
wished of Socrates and Greek life and thought, but this is merely
the form Plato gave to the life and thought he wished to contain
in words. It is the life which we want to know, the flow of the
ideas and the values themselves in the reality experienced by
Socrates and the others. The construction is the means through
which we can get to the experience inside.

Scholars or students who are interested in the construction can
look at it, those interested in its antecedents and consequences
can look at them, and those who would like to relate its symbols
to its inner meaning can do so. But the student or the person who
wishes to learn what Plato had to give to his own world and to
ours, must come into direct relation with Plato and with Socrates,
must project himself into their ideas and look at life in their
terms.

For the student, this may be quite confusing, but is not some
confusion educationally desirable? The aim is to start the student
toward a discovery of values which he can honestly hold because
he feels them to be good, because he commits himself to them.
The beginning of a commitment lies in an interest in ideas themselves. Nothing which a teacher or a curriculum does should
stand between the work of the writer and the student himself.

No program of the humanities planned by collecting together famous objects and books, and centering the education of the student on the discussion of the history, form, and cultural content of these monuments to creative art, is likely to incite the student to a concern for values. What is more likely is that the student will learn how to talk about values knowingly in academic language, will take over the judgments placed upon the objects by tradition and the educational program, and will learn to place every new object of art in a system of aesthetic categories. It is left for other auspices to give him the experience of art itself.

This is the treatment America gives to the arts. Outside the universities they are commercialized. Inside, the same defeat of art is accomplished by domestication. The predominant attitude to the arts in our universities is one of duty, good form, humility, respect, veneration, and the university voice is a cultivated monotone which deliberately excludes even academic excitement. The wit is long-winded, full of literary anecdote, the mood is tolerant, satisfied, liberal, gently smiling at the irony of youth and its misused vigor. As a result, the young literary gentlemen learn to smile their tolerant smiles, to be amused by Mr. Eliot's ironies, to note continually the capacity of the human race for error, ignorance, and bad form, and to consider excess enthusiasm, whether for football, politics, America, or literature, to be either unwise, youthful, or downright vulgar. What this china shop needs is a large number of active bulls.

We have all the conditions for a new burst of cultural development. We have put more than two and a half million college students into institutions which at least cannot deny an interest in cultural and humanist values. A large number of these young people are in touch with serious cultural ideas for the first time. No one who has seen at first hand the variety and scope of creative work in the arts done by students, farmers, local residents, housewives and others grouped around the central facilities of the state universities of the Midwest can fail to be exhilarated with the possibilities of the future. These are cultural centers where music festivals are annually held, with productions of new work by teachers, students, and visiting artists, where there are dozens of symphony orchestras composed of students and amateurs, where two thousand students begin the study of painting in one institution alone, where first-rate chamber music groups play regular concert series as part of university annual schedules, where university radio stations produce statewide educational programs of high quality for thousands of citizens who listen to them regularly.

I remember seeing young men and women from the small towns of the Midwest coming to their universities at the age of eighteen with barely enough money for one semester, with nothing more than a skirt and sweater, or two pairs of trousers and a T shirt, without having read a contemporary poet, without having seen a good moving picture, read a philosopher, or seen a play. Within a year or two, some of them had written for the newspapers, had written stories, had formed philosophy clubs, acted in their own plays, produced their own radio programs, played in an orchestra, had begun to paint, had written poetry. Often they were contemporary non-objective painters before they were anything else. Some of them could not draw. But they learned, and they learned to know the value of the arts.

They were not only responding to the opportunities given in their new environment, but were finding new forms of aesthetic expression of their own, and were responding directly to the educational experiences which were possible only through the media of the arts. Vast areas of the curriculum remained closed to them, and wide stretches of literature, philosophy, and the humanities remained barren ground over which they ran as quickly as they could. But in those places in the university which were outside the curriculum and which gave them a chance to work in the creative arts they learned, and they went from that kind of learning to the sources of inspiration for it in the works of the great humanists. There had been nothing comparable to that demonstration of student interest in the arts in any part of Europe I had known. This was new, lusty, invigorating, and promising.

I believe that the future of the arts in America lies with these young people and their teachers. The creative artist who teaches need not fear that his art will be lost or his talent dulled in this environment. On the contrary, if his spirit is humble before the possibility of talent which can come from these new sources, he will find an encouragement and a support for his work which he may not find elsewhere. The young are ready to make the effort to understand, are ready to share in the experience of the creative artist if he brings his work and his ideas to them in a spirit of mutual interest in the development of new work and the enjoyment of the old.

In the past, our best writers and artists have tried to stay away from the academies, with very good reason. They did not wish to be put into situations in which their own work would be diminished by the grinding and turning of academic machines. But we now have ways of freeing them to work in the atmosphere of eager aesthetic interest and in the company of young people who respond quickly and readily. The educational foundations, in search of ways of enlivening the humanities, can look to the creative arts for their answers, and away from those busy men who would put all ideas into encyclopedic form, order the world of aesthetic excitement into filing cabinets and synopticons, and think their way back to a medievalism so abstract that it touches at no point the daily experience of those who live in the contemporary world.

V I

Why then have the programs in American higher education gone in a different direction? I believe they have done so partly from academic habit, partly under the influence of European models, and particularly because of the recent influence and leadership of the programs in the humanities developed at the College of the University of Chicago and at Harvard University. At a critical time in the reform of liberal education and in the midst of a renewed search for unity in general education, these two institutions provided a reasoned, carefully planned set of answers to questions which most educators were asking.

Consider the Chicago program in some of its details. It draws upon the history of Western culture for the most important "constructed things." Its philosophy is severely intellectualist, with moral overtones of puritanism. Those who teach in the College are serious, gifted, led by a learned and intelligent dean, and bound together by common interest in making a new program of general education. The liberal arts college is said to have the specific function of training the mind to know certain ideas and facts and to know them well. The College faculty are efficient and capable in the organization of knowledge into a tightly knit curriculum, so that it can be taught, learned, and examined with precision and thoroughness. The philosophy holds that every young person who can show that he has the intelligence to absorb it should be given the same basic general education in the social sciences, the humanities, the arts, and the natural sciences. It holds further that a liberal education in the humanities is composed of the materials of knowledge, properly administered, and it lies within the competence and the responsibility of the College faculty to decide, by discussion among themselves, which poems, novels, ideas, methods, and art works should be presented to American college students and designated as the best in the Western tradition.

The philosophy of education underlying the program is applied with a logical rigor unusual in most colleges. If the intellect is everywhere the same, and the unity of knowledge is clearly understood to be a set of materials chosen from all other material as the most significant content of a liberal education, the business of the college is therefore entirely with the intellect and its appropriately chosen objects. The emotional, personal, and social areas of student life are not the concern of the college, since this is the job of the Y.M.C.A., the athletic clubs, the Boy Scouts, the extracurriculum, the family, and the personnel services or administrative part of the educational institution. Serious intellectual effort is the one thing which is required of everyone, and, once undertaken successfully through the work of a required curriculum, gives the individual the equipment of the educated man. The program is clear-cut, completely planned, rational.

If, again, the intellect is everywhere the same, intellectual ability can be measured by tests. If there is a clear definition of the content and knowledge required for a liberal education, this too can be tested. Once administered, the tests indicate the presence or absence of intellect and information, and if the presence is detected in a thirteen-year-old, the thirteen-year-old should be in college with his older colleagues, regardless of any personal factors in his total development. Only those young people who show the precise qualities of intellect and information measured by tests and scholastic records should be allowed to attend a college of liberal arts. Those with more amiable if less formidable minds should go directly into business or into a vocation without wasting the time of the college faculty and administration.

It follows, therefore, that there is no good reason to think about individual differences among students once they are admitted, neither their interests, their needs, their aims, nor particular intellectual character, since intellect is distributed to each, and it would be as foolish to consider what forms of knowledge or education they consider to be important as it would be to ask a three-year-old child its views on the relative nutritional values of cod-liver oil and all-day suckers. It is logical, too, that attendance at classes should not be compulsory, since if the student can manage to cover the same ground without the aid of a teacher, and pass the tests with adequate skill, there is no reason why he should be forced into the company of other students and teachers simply to do in public and on a schedule what he can do better in private at his own leisure. It is possible to receive a higher degree under this system, as was demonstrated not long ago, by not attending the college or university at all, but by passing the tests.

The humanities section of the curriculum contains a good sampling of works of art whose reputation is beyond reproach. It is administered on a weekly basis with a syllabus so exact that at any point in a given week all the classes are discussing the same work. Since the works are chosen by the faculty consulting together as to the best and most representative samples of the style, art, form or period in history, the syllabus may change slightly from year to year. However, the changes are not due to the success or failure of the current syllabus in educating students in the values of the arts, but are made to match the views of the faculty as to what is best among representative works of art.

The appeal which this scheme has made to the educational planners at other universities with similar problems of curric-

ulum in the humanities lies in its clear, logical, and unequivocal
answer to educational questions. It has three virtues which
make it attractive as a model: it provides a clear syllabus of
representative work; it is comparatively easy to administer; at
Chicago it succeeds in developing students who can argue, and
who take intellectual matters seriously. At other institutions
with similar programs where the faculty planning is not as co-
hesive and the teaching less forceful, the students plow through
the material, look at the slides, listen to the music, do whatever
they are asked to do, and graduate without having increased in
sensibility or taste. The curse of the humanities in the large universities is that when they are reduced to units of subject matter,
and covered by examinations they leave the nerve center of
student appreciation untouched.

VII

The Harvard plan rests on a philosophy less severe in its syllabus, more flexible in its choice of material, and more sensitive
to the actual learning of the students. It is assumed that all students need to know something about the history of civilization,
Western civilization in particular, so that the cultural heritage
will be transmitted from generation to generation, and the contemporary student will be given an intellectual center around
which ideas and values of the contemporary world may be
grouped. An indication of the style and tone of the thinking can
be seen in the course description of the Humanities One section
of the Harvard program in general education. It reads:

The authors with which this course deals will be read and discussed
as sources of our common ideas and as great examples of ways of
thinking and feeling current among us. The intention is to examine
their essential thought as the core of the Western tradition, the
tradition through which we still comprehend man and society. No
attempt will be made to give a complete picture of any of the authors.

We are at once in a more relaxed environment than that of Chicago, ends *are* left hanging loose, the Western tradition is represented by ways of thinking and feeling rather than by a syllabus. Since there is more than one course available to the beginning student it is clear that no narrowly specified body of knowledge is regarded as the exact content of a liberal education. The humanities program was developed through the work of the faculty committee which prepared the report *General Education in a Free Society*. In its analysis of educational philosophies, the report makes a distinction between facts and values, and conceives the function of the humanities to be that of communicating the values of the Western tradition. Other colleges which accepted the reasoning of the Harvard program have followed suit.

What is meant by general education at Harvard refers to the distribution of knowledge into the conventional four divisions, and the need for nonspecialized subject matter in each of the courses within those divisions. The purpose of this education is stated to be nonvocational, for cultivating a sense of values, the development of clear thinking, an understanding of the physical and social world, and an appreciation of the traditions of Western civilization. The report states that our values rest on and emerge from the Western tradition and that therefore the study of the great works of that tradition will lead to an appreciation of Western values.

But the educational means of cultivating a sense of values seems to come down to preventing students from choosing wildly among any number of Harvard courses, and limiting their choices to a few from each of the four major divisions. That this should have been the major outcome of two years of careful study by a number of intelligent people indicates the limits of cloistered discussion for achieving educational reform. It has been obvious for many years that an elective system which

runs unplanned and without a great deal of faculty help to individual students will have no educational center unless the
student is lucky enough to find one by himself. But it is less
obvious that genuine reform is accomplished by changing the
content of some of the courses offered and eliminating some of
the extra choices, while keeping intact the lecture system, adding more students to the lecture classes, removing tutorial
methods, and preserving the apparatus of credits, examinations,
and educational obstacles of which the elective system was
only a part.

At a time when a more liberal and creative philosophy of
education advanced by Harvard might have started a series
of lively experiments in the arts throughout the whole system
of higher education, the Harvard committee simply proposed
that the system be kept pretty much as it had always been, with
a minor alteration in arithmetic and a loosening in the joints of
the regular departmental courses. This seemed to sanction similar conservatism on the part of other college faculties around
the country, a sanction which the academic profession did not
need. It pushed universities deeper into the regular grooves of
educational habit, and at the same time produced the illusion
that the institutions had suffered a change.

What was really important about the changes accomplished
by Harvard was the serious and critical study given to existing
courses by a number of first-rate teachers who had been carefully chosen and who were asked to develop a new content for
courses of general interest to students. Freed from the inhibi-
tions of departmental limits, and enriched by the scholarship
of interesting minds, the new courses were of a kind best calculated to involve the students in an understanding of important
ideas in the Western tradition. Students in the humanities were
now allowed to go more deeply into a few representative topics
rather than being called upon to survey a long series of topics

drawn from a narrow field of knowledge. The evolution of the
new courses into new forms was assured by a process of review,
correction and further change. As before, the Harvard students,
through their council, examined the courses, interviewed a cross
section of the student body, and made recommendations both
to the college and to the other students. In the meantime, a
new faculty committee assigned to report on the program recommended after two years of study that much more attention
be paid to the students themselves, whose need for smaller
classes, discussion, tutors, and all the other things which bring
life to ideas, was clear from the beginning.

This marks a sharp difference between the Harvard and the
Chicago plans. Not only do the students have an important
part to play in an empirical, evolutionary method of dealing
with reform, but the faculty members themselves have a chance
to experiment with individual courses. At Chicago, the individual faculty member and the individual student are instruments of the curriculum. The added virtue of the Harvard
approach lies in the flexibility with which it is administered
and the open-ended quality to the planning.

The weakness is that everything is still a matter of subjects.
The creative arts are subjects, taught as the history and criticism
of a series of works and objects. The theatre remains outside the
liberal arts. Music is designated as something which students
can play if they have the time for it, but not as part of their education. Nor does there seem to be any relation between the
planning and what the psychologists have to say about learning and education, or what the facts show about how values
are actually learned. It is ironic that a short time after the pub-
lication of the program for general education, a book written by
a committee composed largely of Harvard psychologists, entitled *The Place of Psychology in an Ideal University*, provided conclusions which, if the authority of its psychological

evidence were taken seriously, would have destroyed most of the educational assumptions made by the Harvard Committee on General Education.

The double impact of the Harvard and Chicago plans has been to push educational reform, in the humanities and elsewhere, in a conservative direction. Except in the case of the work in social science in the Chicago scheme, neither plan calls for a sharp look at the structure of contemporary society, nor for the consideration of those value questions which are at the center of contemporary moral conflict. Neither plan suggests that the question of values in one's own life is the central educational question to be asked, and that every part of the curriculum must provide its own humanism, its own philosophy, and its own method of affecting the feelings and attitudes of the students in college. Until this humanism permeates the entire curriculum and is carried in the intellectual atmosphere of a college community, we cannot hope to accomplish our ends by concentrating the means within a program of humanities.

William Faulkner said in his Stockholm speech, on the occasion of the Nobel Prize-giving, that the writer must teach himself, if he has forgotten them, the universal truths lacking which any story is ephemeral and doomed—love, honor, pity, pride, compassion, sacrifice. "Until he does so, he labors under a curse. He writes not of love but of lust, of defeats in which nobody loses anything of value, of victories without hope and, worst of all, without pity and compassion. His griefs grieve on no universal bones, leaving no scars. He writes not of the heart but of the glands."

The student needs to be taught these truths, and the truths can be learned, among other ways, from the great writers and creative artists who are perhaps the greatest universal teachers. Sometimes they are learned by soldiers in combat, although not always nor necessarily. At other times they are learned through the teaching in family life, or through personal experience with religion, or experience with principled and honorable people. Such experience is not simply a matter of reading books, in or out of college, and there are highly educated people who are inhumane. It is a matter of choosing to live in certain ways because those ways are found in experience to constitute a higher form of life, to be preferred because of the ideals they help to satisfy. The good teacher is one who, by his influence on the student, can show him how to gain the experience of these ideals, through appreciation of the work of great artists and thinkers, and through the appreciation of great acts of human conduct. We need teachers who themselves understand the truths. They will make their own curriculum of humanism.

Chapter Seven

COMMUNISM AND THE AMERICAN COLLEGES

COMMUNISM is a word now used in the United States to express anxiety rather than to define social doctrine. Yet for the United States, the most important thing about communism is that it is a social doctrine and should be known as such. Otherwise we will not be able to understand it, to distinguish between those who are its exponents and those who oppose it, or to cope with its operations abroad and within the United States. We will not gain the necessary understanding as long as our national policy is simply to fear it, condemn it, and attack it. We need to treat communism as a body of fact and doctrine with its own history, we need to analyze the roots of its power, to distinguish between its claims for humanity and its acts against human beings, to determine the conditions of its success or failure, and to become clear as to what we should do about the problems to which the communists bring their own solutions.

The colleges and universities are the centers of organized thinking, where all political questions and systems can be studied in theory and in fact, and where questions about the politics of communism can be answered without rancor or distortion. Within the colleges and universities, where the duty and function of the scholar is to cherish the facts and to be scrupulous in judging them, we have the nerve center of the country's political and social intelligence. It is there that we can find relief from confusion and the security of informed opinion.

Outside the colleges there is an extraordinary amount of confusion about the threat of the Soviet Union to the position of the United States in world affairs and the internal threat of communism and the Communist Party to the political welfare of the country. In the one case, the threat is serious and has alarmed many countries other than our own. In the other, the threat has been strongly met and thoroughly bottled up.

Yet the confusion persists. In some cases the confusion is deliberately created by those who wish to make it serve their own ends. In many others it is a confusion resulting from the unreasoned application of political and social emotions to a complicated subject.

The role of the colleges with regard to communism is to dispel the confusion, to reach for the truth, and to clear up the rumors and misinformation which are now distracting the public mind. They are doing their best to fulfill this role. As far as their resources make possible, they have taken care to provide their students with an education in democracy. Students cannot be indoctrinated with liberal or democratic ideas, they must learn to value them through the exercise of their own intelligence and through the example of democratic principle in operation.

To indoctrinate means to present one set of ideas to the exclusion of others, or so to arrange a variety of points of view about controversial issues that only one point of view is allowed credence. This is the method taken by political opportunists to extend their power. The policies of the American colleges are opposed to indoctrination and to any form of scholarship, teaching, or research which would distort the objectivity of tested knowledge. These policies serve the public interest by acting as a safeguard against the corruption of political truth by those who seek political power. They do so particularly in the case of communism and the issues it raises.

By reason of the fact that these issues are so controversial and so easily distorted by fear and anger, it is crucial to the welfare of the country that the colleges and universities remain free to judge the issues in rational terms, without the pressures of political bullying or public antipathy. It is crucial to the cultural and political security of the United States that the informed intelligence of university scholars, teachers, and administrators be free to deal with communism and communists in their own ways. The question of what should be taught and who is fit to teach is the affair of the colleges and universities. It is too important a matter to be left to the politicians.

II

The preservation of intellectual freedom in the colleges and universities is therefore the primary duty and responsibility of boards of trustees and educators. It is primary because it is the basis for so many other freedoms in our society. Once it has been damaged, either by the failure of boards of trustees to act on its behalf, or by the failure of nerve on the part of educators under pressure, it is not merely education which suffers, but society itself.

The principle of academic freedom was not invented by college presidents, political radicals, or by a confusion of liberals. It has been built, slowly and carefully, at great cost to many individuals, over the past three thousand years, by thoughtful and conscientious men and women who saw that in the protection of scholarship and learning from interference by the State, by the Church, and, more recently, by political, social, and economic groups, civilization was in fact protecting itself and insuring its own continuance. The premise from which the scholars and teachers have argued is that truth can emerge only from the clash of ideas and opinions. It cannot be determined finally by one person or by one group of persons. The alternative is a passive acceptance of the truth asserted by those who have the power to force an acceptance. In the present situation in the United States, this would mean that we would have to force the American scholar to accept a standard political and philosophical dogma to be used by him in meeting the communist dogma head-on.

Democracy and the concept of intellectual freedom both rest on a principle different from that of communism. Soviet-Marxism-Stalinism is a monolithic intellectual and political position, with an absolute goal, and shifting means to achieve it. Democracy is a pluralistic philosophy, with many goals, all leading to the good of the individual. Our greatest strength as a country lies in the fact that we have diversity of opinion and diversity of people. We can absorb and use ideas of all kinds, provided we keep ourselves in a situation in which every idea can have public expression. What has given this country's thought its vitality in the past is the continual struggle of men and women to gain acceptance for their own views, and the continual push of a variety of minority opinions. What marks our history from that of other countries is the way in which we have been able to avoid an orthodoxy, to remain open-minded and flexible, to absorb radical ideas into the flow of social process, and to put them to work when they were needed.

We have made certain gains, and have established an attitude and a national sentiment against the restriction of personal freedom in ideas and action. It should not surprise us that a struggle which is as old as the history of civilization is still going on, or that in a time of international tension a relatively small number of bigoted individuals and organizations are capable of stirring up anxiety and distrust in the general public against the scholar, the teacher, the writer, the artist, and against all those whose primary concern is with ideas and values. But unless the educators and the citizens fight to keep them, the gains already won will be lost by default.

The attacks on intellectual freedom, for the press, for education, for the theatre, books, radio, television, government service, are becoming more and more frequent, more and more bold, and, it must be admitted, more and more successful. When not successful in securing the dismissal of honest and loyal faculty members, school superintendents, government employees, writers, actors, entertainers, and others, they have been successful in producing a timidity, in some cases amounting to paralysis, in social thought and creative work. Deeper than this is the more dangerous effect on the national life of creating so great a fear of subversion by communists that we have become rigid, paranoiac, dogmatic, and overaggressive. The more we frighten ourselves with our own political investigations, the less we count on reason, information, and cool judgment to settle our national policies.

The preservation of freedom in the colleges and universities has its own necessities and its own rules which have been worked out by generations of scholars and teachers. Their classic expression holds that no teacher can be dismissed for holding opinions or belonging to organizations which are contrary to the orthodox, provided he carries on his work as a teacher without allowing his opinions to distort the process of his students' education. Faculty members can be dismissed in a democracy, where all political opinions are to be tolerated, and in a university, where all ideas are to be discussed, for incompetence, neglect of duty, physical or mental incapacity, dishonesty or immorality, and conviction of a felony involving moral turpitude. To allow other causes would be to leave the individual teacher vulnerable to a wide variety of pressures, and would, in fact, make original thinking on controversial subjects either impossible or covert.

Academic freedom as it is generally understood by people outside the universities is a much more limiting concept. Judging from public statements made by those who are hostile toward the freedom enjoyed by the colleges and universities, many people are willing to grant freedom to those who have mild things to say, but not to anyone who holds beliefs contrary to the current orthodoxy in political, economic, religious, or social affairs. Similarly, many people are not willing to grant the teacher the right to belong to an association or to sponsor organizations which advocate ideas and courses of action antithetical to those held currently by the United States government, aside from whether or not the teacher belongs to communist organizations.

To the outsider, the issue is a simple one. Does the teacher belong to organizations listed as subversive by the Attorney General, or has he ever belonged to them? Is he sympathetic to communism? Does he write books against the capitalist system? Or does he write and speak in favor of the Chinese communists? Is he antireligious? If you do not want communists in the universities, fire them when you find them, hunt them out if they talk and act like communists, rule them out before they apply. The matter seems very much simpler to those outside the university and college than to those inside. There are some who refer to academic freedom as a shield behind which communists and subversives hide to conduct their indoctrination of students with communism. It is a shield. It protects not subversives, but men and women who, in the judgment of the colleges, have something of importance to say to other scholars and to American students.

There are further arguments made against the principle of academic freedom by those who genuinely fear the indoctrination of youth with subversive ideas, and who feel that young people in college are too immature to be able to deal with radical thinking. This is an anxiety which can be understood, and one which some parents have about every aspect of the education of their children. It is very easy to extend this anxiety beyond one's own children to the whole of American youth, and to see in the free play of all ideas a threat to the faith of college students in democratic values. The anxiety usually disappears on closer acquaintance with college students and the colleges they attend.

American colleges do teach the facts of communism to their students in those courses where the subject is relevant. There are occasional faculty members who have at one time been members of the Communist Party or have once belonged to organizations now listed as subversive by the Attorney General of the United States, although more often these are not the persons who are teaching courses in which communism is part of the subject matter. There are occasional faculty members who disapprove completely of United States foreign policy, others who reject the economics of capitalism, others who have sympathized with certain policies of the Soviet Union, although they do not usually press their views upon students or colleagues. A handful of faculty members at present teaching in American colleges have refused to reveal their political beliefs and associations when accused of being communists or pro-communists.

But this does not mean that the American student is in danger of indoctrination by subversive ideas. Faculty members, like everyone else, do have political ideas and associations, mostly conservative in character. But they are not at liberty to use their classrooms or faculty position to distort the truth, even if they wished to do so. The policy in teaching politics, economics, international affairs, American history, and the social sciences in general, is to present information from textbooks and standard authorities in the field of the subjects taught.

Although I believe that this procedure is wrong-headed—the use of standard textbooks rather than original documents, the absence of personal interpretation of controversial issues, the consequent neutered effect which such teaching methods produce both in the teacher and the student—it is nevertheless standard policy. If anything, the academic programs have been remiss in not stating favorably points of view other than the American in matters of world politics and in not presenting views critical of the *status quo* in domestic affairs.

In their regular course of studies the students learn very quickly to detect points of view where they exist. In fact they look for them eagerly and welcome them as a refreshing change from the academic flatness with which most of their subject matter is conveyed to them.

A college teacher who attempted to slant the facts toward a biased interpretation of the material available to the students would very quickly be criticized by the students themselves. A faculty member who assigned a reading list which was weighted toward one point of view to the exclusion of others would very soon be criticized heavily by his colleagues and by his students. As for teaching which is so skillful that the students and colleagues of the teacher would not be able to detect communist bias, antidemocratic prejudice, or dishonesty where it was present and active, this is of course a possibility, although fairly remote. Certainly if a college teacher genuinely believes in the validity of Marxist philosophy and looks at political and social events with the intellectual habits of a Marxist, he may put the events in his own perspective. There is no reason why this cannot be helpful to the education of college students since it is a point of view which they seldom hear expressed. What we object to is the concealment of a Marxist point of view by those who hold it, and any effort by a teacher to present such views as those of a non-Marxist. In the organization of most colleges, such a concealment would be extremely difficult. Most students, in addition to most faculty members, are able to identify the political attitudes of college professors, as well as many other attitudes they convey, to a high degree of accuracy.

We must face the fact that all education involves risks and that nothing short of threats, orders, and intimidation can prevent human beings from thinking and acting in their own ways. If we reach the point in our colleges at which we must ask students to analyze smirks, smiles, gestures, intonations, and double meanings in order to insure their own protection from intellectual harm, we have declared a complete loss of faith not only in our teachers but in the American student.

When college students have a chance to learn, to listen, to think, and to talk freely, they may very likely come across ideas which are more daring than those of their parents and of the general public. They should do so. There is no reason why they should agree with the older generation. They may be attracted to new ideas and use them as a part of the formation of a new point of view. But the possibility of students being corrupted or rendered disloyal to their country by such freedom is remote. "It is only when the freedom to express beliefs is limited," stated the student council of an American college last year, "that the danger of indoctrination is present."

I am referring of course to those universities and colleges where a serious interest is taken by the faculty in teaching and in the curriculum. If there are institutions in which biased teaching goes on undetected, and in which the regular administrative officers and faculty committees are unaware of the quality and content of the individual courses, this is not merely a political matter. It is a failure in educational quality in that institution.

III

In all the present tension, controversy and concern over communism in the colleges, there are too few people who stop to take an unhurried look at the facts of education itself. The most recent survey we have of the politics of the country's college graduates [1] covers a period in their education when the country was much less antagonistic to communism than is presently the case; most of those surveyed (86%) had taken their degrees since 1920, and a large majority (66%) since 1930.

The study was made of 9,064 men and women graduates of all ages from 1,037 colleges of all types throughout the country. The results show that the largest percentage of college graduates, 38%, are Republicans; the second largest, 35%, are Independents; the third, 26%, are Democrats; and $\frac{1}{2}$ of 1% are in all the other parties combined, including the Communist, Farmer-Labor, Socialist, Liberal, American Labor, Prohibition, and others. The statistics also show that most college students retain the political affiliations of their parents. Only 6% of the entire group have ever held an elective office.

Those who are familiar with the political education of college students will confirm the fact that the weakness in that phase of student development does not lie in the influence either of communist teachers or communism, but in the lack of practical concern by college-educated men and women for political issues, and the lack of their involvement in local or national political activities after graduation. One of the reasons for this is that faculty members are for the most part disinterested in

[1] Ernest Havemann and Patricia Salter West, *They Went to College* (Harcourt, Brace and Company, 1952), pp. 108-125.

politics and inactive in political affairs. Their political and personal outlook is only in rare instances unconventional or radical. What is lacking in the political education of most college students is the excitement of real controversy about real issues, and the occasions on which their conventional or uninformed assumptions about politics can be challenged by a fresh point of view. We need not worry that college students are being challenged to turn to communism by their teachers, nor that they are being secretly persuaded in that direction. The difficulty is that too often they are not being challenged at all.

I do not believe that most Americans outside the colleges realize the virtues which attach themselves to the American college student—his tolerance, his genuine interest in ideas, the freshness, honesty, and fearlessness with which he asks questions. He has a natural confidence in his own ability to judge the ideas of his teachers in his own terms. The students apply the same standards to teachers which they apply to everyone else, and do not hold college professors at an intellectual distance. What does he know? How important is it? What can he do? What does he think? How good is he at his job? Does he have anything important to say?

Both consciously and unconsciously the students assert their own right to judge the truth, the value, and the significance of what is said and done in their education. It has not occurred to most of them to think that they have to believe what they are told. They act with a high degree of responsibility and good sense when given the opportunity to take responsibility.

An educational philosophy which encourages students to face real issues of controversy and to make up their own minds as to where the truth lies is a stronger instrument for the development of democratic citizens who can put communism in its proper perspective than a timid philosophy which seeks to withhold ideas on the grounds that they might be dangerously used. If college students seize upon ideas which we wish they would ignore and carry them further than we think they should, we can assume that further thought and experience will provide its own correction. In any case, it is at least possible that we may be wrong and that the young may see farther and deeper than we do.

Because of the attacks on colleges for "harboring subversives" and "teaching communism," the educational philosophy of colleges and universities has in many instances become more cautious and less independently democratic. Often the right of student organizations to exist on college campuses is challenged by outside groups, and colleges are attacked for allowing "radical," "pro-communist," "progressive," or "pacifist" speakers to appear before students. In many cases administrative action has been taken under political pressure from boards of regents or private organizations against student and faculty groups and against speakers who have been invited to appear before college audiences. Such action is not only timid and weak on the part of those who take it, but is educationally unsound if the aim of college education is to develop democratic citizens. In some institutions, it has become the practice of students to test out the degree and kind of freedom which their colleges will allow by inviting Howard Fast, who seems to be the only advocate of communism now capable of speaking about it, to speak on their campuses. Mr. Fast has in fact served this purpose on several recent occasions and has produced some interesting controversies, but has added little else to the enlightenment of the students.

It is true that in the past, student organizations in which the communists had an interest have been formed on a national as well as a local basis, and most educators can testify that efforts have been made by representatives of the Communist Party, working through these organizations, to interest students in their doctrines and to influence them to accept communist ideas. At various times the Young Communist League, the American Youth Congress, its successor, American Youth for Democracy, the Young Progressives of America, and, more recently, the Labor Youth League, have shown the hand of the Communist Party in manipulating the organizations. What has usually happened on college campuses has been that students interested in political reform of all kinds have joined whatever political organization was active at a given time, and after signing petitions, organizing meetings, listening to speakers, and involving themselves in discussions, have left the organizations when it became clear that they were being directed by political technicians outside the campus toward political ends quite different from those stated in the prospectus. The few students who remained in such organizations after their sponsorship had been clearly revealed presented an educational problem for their universities, and one which was not always solved satisfactorily.

American student organizations are capable of mature and adult political behavior which could serve as a model for some of their elders. The National Student Association, with very little help from educators or faculty members, has not only organized itself into a strong national organization but has handled its political affairs with skill and wisdom. The Association has rejected collaboration with communist organizations, including the communist-sponsored International Union of Students, whenever it became clear that the organizations were instruments of propaganda rather than democratic student movements. They have also prevented infiltration of their organization by communist groups, and have done so by educational means, without damaging their own positive liberal policies.

At the present time, the only student organizations of a national kind active on the college campuses are the Students for Democratic Action, who specifically exclude communists from membership, the National Student Association, the International Relations Clubs, sponsored by the Carnegie Endowment for International Peace, which conducts an information program in the field of international affairs, and the World Student Service Fund, which has no political program.

I V

The fact is that in American colleges communists are either banned or overwhelmingly contained. It may be that the colleges themselves have been remiss in not making these facts and their educational policies better known to the general public. One difficulty is of course that plain statements of fact about the proper functioning of educational institutions are not in themselves of wide interest to the general public, and lack the dramatic appeal of accusations made against colleges by those who prefer for whatever reason to ignore both the facts and the philosophy of liberal education. Another difficulty is that when such accusations are made, the colleges are put in a defensive position where their statements must unavoidably be protestations of innocence against charges involving a totally different conception of social philosophy and democratic values. It is a very much more complicated and involved task to make clear the philosophy by which policies of academic freedom are administered than to repeat the hollow statement, The colleges are full of communists and communist sympathizers. When the statement is made, it is unsatisfactory to the public for the colleges simply to reply, No they are not, and what do you mean by a sympathizer?

At the present time, the threats to the freedom of the colleges are of three kinds. The first, and perhaps the least harmful, is from journalists, writers, and commentators with a doctrinaire turn of mind who argue that all education should be controlled by an authority and should teach religious, political, social, and economic doctrines prescribed by the Church and State or by themselves. This, they argue, would take care of communism, neglecting to state that it would also take care of democracy. The reason these suggestions are less harmful than others is that the tradition of the country is so thoroughly against the imposition of a single doctrine that the argument itself breaks down when confronted with the question of which church or state doctrine should be imposed. The answer of the colleges to this kind of criticism is to ignore it and to continue to follow democratic educational policies.

The second kind of attack is more harmful because it works by publicity and distortion to undermine public confidence in educators, teachers, students, and democratic education. Its standard procedure is to issue newspaper releases or magazine articles accusing college teachers or public school teachers of being communists or pro-communists. The accusations are based on information about the former affiliation of faculty members with organizations now listed as subversive by the Attorney General and other reports which can be obtained by writing to the Committee on Un-American Activities or to the equivalent committees of the various State Legislatures, and on excerpts taken from speeches, articles, and books, and clippings from newspapers, particularly *The Daily Worker,* all arranged in such a way that individuals can be accused of thinking, speaking, and writing in a way labeled by the accusers as collectivist, pro-Soviet, progressive, subversive, anti-American, pro-communist, or communist. Through newspaper publicity, the college or school system is called upon for investigation, or is called upon to dismiss the accused persons, or to dismiss the president, dean, or school authority who is responsible for their membership in the faculty.

The college in this situation is faced with a dilemma. If it ignores the accusations, which are usually so garbled and distorted as to be beneath the notice of any serious person, some members of the public, the alumni of the college, members of the community, friends, and others interested in college education who hear only the words communist and subversion may begin to feel that perhaps there *is* something wrong with the educational program or with the integrity of the faculty, otherwise the college would say something in reply. On the other hand, if the college treats the charges seriously, if it replies by defending the individuals attacked, or discusses their merits publicly, it is lending the weight of its public reputation to organizations, individuals and points of view which otherwise would receive little public attention. It may also find itself providing fresh material for an extended public controversy, which then serves the purposes of the attacker. Again, the difficulty is produced by the fact that what is at issue is a totally different philosophy of education, and a totally different set of standards by which intellectual honesty, teaching ability and political integrity are judged. The attack itself has no serious educational purpose, except the negative one of inhibiting political thought, and in each case seems designed to attract attention to the accuser and to advance his public career or his financial welfare.[2]

-----

[2] In a situation of this kind, in which various individuals and groups, including the American Legion, Louis Budenz, Alfred Kohlberg, Rabbi Benjamin Schultz, *Counterattack,* Allen Zoll's *Reducators,* and the Hearst press, impugned the political integrity of three faculty members at Sarah Lawrence College, the Board of Trustees of the College made public its statement of educational policy, and made no other comment. The statement reads in part:

An educational institution must teach its students to think for themselves by giving them the knowledge on which to base judgments. The teaching faculty of Sarah Lawrence College is responsible for the
(*footnote continued on next page*)

The only answer the colleges can give to these attacks is to state the educational policies in which they believe, support them in action, and exercise their right as independent institutions of education to conduct their own affairs regardless of the pressures of hostile organizations. Those who wish to make the informed criticism of educational policy which all colleges need and welcome will choose an appropriate way to make it and will not try, by the pressure of distorted publicity, to cast doubt on the integrity of an educational institution. To yield to such pres-

---

development in students of intellectual independence and maturity. In carrying out this responsibility faculty members are expected to deal candidly and honestly with controversial questions. Teachers who meet the test of candor, honesty, and scholarly integrity may not be deprived of any rights they hold as citizens of this country, including the right to belong to any legal political organization of their own choosing.

It is a principle accepted by the Faculty, the President, and Trustees alike that there is to be no indoctrination of students with a political, philosophical or religious dogma. No person, therefore, who takes his intellectual orders from an outside authority, whether communist or any other, could be given or could retain the responsibility of membership in the Sarah Lawrence faculty.

It is an essential part of good educational policy that a college ask for no orthodoxy in its teachers as to religion, politics, or philosophical theory. If it were otherwise, teaching would be done not by the faculty but by the governing board of the institution. The teacher would be a mouthpiece for the preconceived philosophy of the institution rather than a seeker for the truth about problems in his field of learning.

It is in this refusal to exact an oath or to cross-examine the teacher as to political belief or to spy upon his political activities that the educator differs from the outsider who wishes to investigate college faculties. The latter fails to understand the necessity that the teacher be free to have and to express his own ideas, and that the teacher is not a person hired to follow certain rules and to advocate certain economic or political dogmas.

sures would simply mean that education would become as devoid of intellectual vitality, independence and social content as the television, radio and moving picture industries have become under similar circumstances.

The third kind of threat to the freedom of the colleges is the most serious, since it involves a direct challenge to the independence of private and public education from political control by the government. It is the political investigation of college faculties by committees of Congress. The design of the American system of higher education is one which establishes boards of trustees or boards of regents to stand between the State and the citizen and to make certain that there is no political interference with educational policies as the result of control by the State. When Congress acts through legislation and when the executive branch acts to carry out the laws, it is acting on behalf of the citizens. But the citizens, in order to know which government acts are judicious and in the interests of the country, must learn to think for themselves and must have the opportunities of education in order to do so. Therefore, it would be fatal to the development of informed and objective opinion by the citizens if it became possible for a government to force the educational system or the educators, by whatever means, into a pattern of political or educational philosophy which it insisted, no matter how sincerely, should be the orthodoxy which the citizens should accept.

The existence of independent institutions of education, and in particular the institutions of higher learning, guarantees that the citizens may have the means and the opportunity to form enlightened judgment about the wisdom of their government, whether in matters of foreign policy, domestic affairs, or the best means of dealing with communism. The American citizen's hatred of totalitarian government stems from the fact that such governments tell the people what to think and what to do, and make the citizen the servant of the State with no opportunity either to learn or to act in any way except the one dictated by the State. In this country, the government is the servant of the citizens. The citizens therefore need their own independent institutions of education in order to determine the truth about the best courses of action which their government should take.

We are coming dangerously close to direct political control of education by the State when committees of state legislatures and committees of Congress can secure the dismissal of individual teachers on political grounds, not by dealing with the duly constituted authorities responsible for appointment and dismissal—the boards of education, trustees, college presidents, and deans—but by investigating the teachers themselves, the books they write, the ideas they profess, the associations they have had.

What would be the most appropriate action for Congress in determining the influence of communism on the colleges, while preserving the autonomy of the educational system and its freedom from government control? It seems to me that the wisest course of action, and one which would meet adequately and sensibly any possible threat which communism could make, would be to appoint a commission of informed and respected jurists, educators, and laymen to prepare a report for the President, Congress, and the public.

The country would then have an opportunity of knowing the facts about its system of education, and the facts stated would be those obtained by authorities competent to decide the conclusions to which the facts lead. The right of the citizens to conduct their own educational affairs without political interference by the government would then be affirmed. If after such an inquiry the commission called upon help from Congress to deal with the problem of communism, Congress could act in ways suggested by a study of the facts contained in the report. It would then be acting correctly as representatives whose responsibility it is to act on behalf of the citizens.

V

The actual method taken by Congress to meet the problem has of course been quite different. A series of investigations was set in motion, based on the false assumption that American education is in serious danger from a conspiracy conducted by the Communist Party and communists inside the universities and colleges, and that educators themselves are incapable of dealing with it. Congressional committees certainly have the constitutional power to investigate any matter on which factual information is needed as a basis for legislation. But if there are those who are teaching in the colleges and universities who have broken laws or have committed subversive acts, it is not Congress but the law-enforcing agencies of government which should prosecute the offending individuals. The investigations have been in fact trials of individuals and not legislative investigations—trials conducted on the basis of opinions, associations, and beliefs, without benefit of the due process afforded in courts of law.

The method of the committees has been to investigate individual teachers by collecting information about their political views and associations from ex-communists, government agents, and other sources, and summoning them to private and public hearings where they are asked about past or present membership in the Communist Party, about their friends, colleagues, and associates, about their beliefs and opinions, and about organizations to which they have belonged or which they have sponsored. Senator Jenner, Chairman of the Senate Sub-Committee on Internal Security, which has conducted most of the investigation of the colleges, has issued statements to indicate the purpose of his committee and the methods it has chosen to use. One such policy statement reads:

If a totalitarian organization such as the evidence shows to exist in our Nation's schools is allowed to flourish in our institutions of learning, unexposed and unchecked, not only will our youth be infused with seeds of their own and the Nation's destruction, but academic freedom, the right to free enquiry, the right to dissent the development of our culture, and the right to express free ideas and free thoughts will be choked and stifled.[3]

There are a number of assumptions in this statement, most of them wrong. It is true of course that if there were totalitarian organizations flourishing in our Nation's schools unexposed and unchecked, results which everyone would dislike would therefore follow. No evidence in the hands of educators, however, has led them to believe that a totalitarian organization is flourishing, or that organizations which set out to destroy free thought have been going unchecked. President Harry Gideonse of Brooklyn College testified voluntarily before Mr. Jenner's Committee that at one time the Communist Party, a totalitarian organization, flourished in his institution, although he did not testify that it had gone unexposed or unchecked but rather, he testified at some length and in detail that he and others had been constantly at work to expose it and to check it.

Senator Jenner remarked further, during the course of the hearings of his Committee:

Our purpose is to protect and safeguard academic freedom. . . .
Our committee is not concerned with telling the leaders of our

---

[3] p. 413, Subversive Influence in the Educational Process, Hearings before the Sub-Committee to Investigate the Administration of the Internal Security Act and other Internal Security Laws, 83rd Congress, 1st session.

schools and colleges what to teach or how to teach. It is concerned with showing them where this alien conspiracy is hidden, that it is fully armed with every weapon, waiting to attack at every vantage point. It is concerned with helping our academic leaders to meet the threat. There can be no academic freedom until this Soviet Conspiracy is exposed to the light, and the rule of Moscow over its adherents in the education world is broken.[4]

The Committee Report of July 17, 1953, also states: "The sub-committee was called upon to act because of the almost complete inability of the educational authorities to expose the Communist conspiracy with the means available to them."[5]

Who, then, called upon the Sub-Committee to act? Certainly not the educators, not the educated community, not the Congress who simply gave authority to the Sub-Committee to investigate the administration of the Internal Security Act and other internal security laws, and not the Committee on the Judiciary nor the Attorney General, and not the President of the United States, himself so recently a university president. The only conclusion is that the Sub-Committee or its Chairman Mr. Jenner called upon the Sub-Committee to act. This is an important point, in view of the fact that the Sub-Committee statements emphasize the desire of the Committee to help the educators and to support academic freedom. Those educators who have been most interested in protecting intellectual freedom both from communists and from political opportunists of all kinds have been those most critical of the way Congressional committees have chosen to act.

The question then is, has the investigation of colleges conducted by Congressional committees protected democratic education from communism and safeguarded academic freedom?

[4] *Ibid.*, p. 154.
[5] Report of the Sub-Committee to Investigate the Administration of the Internal Security Act, pp. 2-3, July 17, 1953.

Has it helped the country's educational leaders to meet the threat of communism? Has it exposed a flourishing totalitarian organization in the colleges? Have the educational authorities been unable to expose or to check "the Communist conspiracy with the means available to them"?

I do not believe that Congressional committees have protected and safeguarded academic freedom. They have damaged it. Have they exposed a communist conspiracy in the colleges? They have not. They have demonstrated that there are college teachers, many of whom have not been teaching for some years, who by their refusal to testify before a Congressional committee have given reason for believing that they have at one time been members of the Communist Party or have been associated with communists; but they have produced no evidence to show that the college teachers conspired to subvert education or to destroy academic freedom. Have the educational authorities been unable and unwilling to deal with conspiracy toward subversion on their campuses? They have not. They have dealt with communism and communists in a way different from the way recommended by Congressional committees because they wished to preserve the quality of mutual respect and trust in their communities and they wished to encourage political freedom and not to inhibit it. But the way of deciding who is and who is not fit to teach is a task for scholars and teachers, and not for political investigators.

VI

What are the rights of the scholar and the teacher in a free society? Does he have any special privileges? Can he claim the right not to testify to his government?

He has only this special right—that if in the process of his

own thinking he develops basic and radical criticism of the
mores or the structure of the society in which he lives, he is
entitled to the protection of his society for the continuance of
his criticism. As a teacher and a scholar he retains the right of
all citizens to engage in legitimate political activity of his own
choice. No good teacher has ever claimed the right to engage in
subversive activities, although he reserves the right to define
carefully the meaning of subversion. Nor has he claimed more
rights than any other citizen, although he has been more sensitive and informed about the rights of all citizens than is common
among most.

He would agree that no person has a right to teach, nor does
any person have a right to belong to a college faculty unless (a)
there is a need for his particular services in a particular college;
(b) he has the qualifications necessary to meet the need of service to a particular college; (c) he is a good teacher who can
communicate what he knows without damaging the knowledge
in the process; and (d) he commands the respect and confidence
of the accredited faculty bodies and college administrators
whose business it is to judge merit and integrity in teachers.
Once these conditions are met, however, he has the right to be
judged by his colleagues in any question as to whether he should
continue to teach. Neither he nor any of his colleagues is infal-
lible. Like everyone else, scholars are sometimes wrong. They
may mistake a partial truth for a whole truth, a political theory
for a political fact, a political mistake for a moral principle, but
they are subject to the corrections of self-criticism and mutual
criticism, one of the basic skills of their profession. They have
a right to be understood by the public, by college presidents and
by boards of trustees, to be supported by their colleagues, and
to be treated in all university matters not with suspicion and
distrust, but with respect and public confidence.

The Congressional investigations of the colleges have obscured the main fact about intellectual freedom—the fact that a scholar may honestly hold a political philosophy different from orthodox American capitalism and may act politically on his convictions without becoming disloyal to the United States in the process. The distinction between political opinion and political action is one of degree. The scholar who reaches his own political views by weighing the evidence may keep his opinions to himself, he may tell his friends and colleagues, he may tell his students, he may publish his conclusions for the reading public, or he may do all these and also find a means of political action which would help to bring about the political changes he advocates. But the true scholar, when he acts politically, is impelled to do so by the sincerity of his intellectual and political motives, not by the power of a political organization which forces him to think and to act in a preordained way.

Whatever else they have done, the Congressional investigations have forced teachers and educators to face social and educational issues which had previously been ignored. The degree of isolation of university faculty members from the reality of contemporary politics has not been good for the education of college students. The academic conservatism and lack of political awareness on the part of college teachers has meant that all political ideas, communist included, have had much more discussion outside the colleges than inside them. The threat of the investigations to the independence of the colleges has meant that the educators, as well as the general public, have had to devote serious thought and attention to the problems and issues in the struggle between authoritarianism and freedom, communism and democracy, American political power and educational autonomy. There is now a much greater awareness of the necessity for defending intellectual freedom in the colleges from the attacks made upon it.

VII

The fact remains that because of a variety of political causes, of which Congressional investigation is simply one, there is a serious confusion in the public mind about the meaning of the term communism when it is used in public debate.

There is first of all the use of the term *communism* to refer to the philosophy of communism as developed by Marx and Engels and expounded in their texts.

The philosophy has failed to hold American intellectuals in any significant or lasting way principally because the social idealism which led them to support it was betrayed by the uses to which it was put in the Soviet Union and by the American Communist Party. In addition, the oversimplification of all social and political issues to a standard dogma was often false to the facts, and the analysis of society and of capitalism did not fit the social conditions or the democratic evolution of the United States or Great Britain.

A second meaning of communism has to do with the political system developed in the Soviet Union, first through the revolution, then by the Communist Party and its leaders, principally Lenin and Stalin. Many serious Marxists, apart from communists, believe that the Soviet Union under Stalin and now under Malenkov has not followed the philosophy of Marxist communism, but has simply substituted economic and political policies suggested by the original doctrine for the tyranny of the former Russian system, and has organized an efficient police state which will never wither away but can only disappear by internal conflicts or be destroyed in war. Militarism, aggression, nationalism, and nationalist power politics without moral purpose, the mechanical system of control over the mind and the body of every citizen were not Marx's stated intention. The use of coercion as the normal means of political discourse is the mark of a system which many Marxists and others refer to as Stalinism rather than communism.

Thirdly, communism may mean membership in the Communist Party—in the Soviet Union, France, Yugoslavia, China, Italy, England, the United States, or elsewhere. The character, quality, strength, and political action of the Communist Party varies from country to country. In Italy and France many intellectuals are members and there is strong activity on their part. In England there are very few and the Party has no power. In the Far East there are few intellectuals and many peasants, political revolutionaries, and soldiers. In the United States there is practically no serious intellectual activity within the Party, no serious intellectuals among the membership, there are no serious publications for which Communist Party members write, the quality of communist propaganda, journalism, and political action is of a very low order, and the Party is one of the weakest in quality and in political influence of any in the world.

The proper use of the term communist is for those who are officially connected with the Communist Party as members, who attend meetings, and pay dues. It seems to me also correct to classify as a communist a person who accepts completely the philosophy of Marx and the social consequences which flow from it, whether or not he has any interest in the present policies and activities of the Communist Party or the Soviet Union. There is nothing intellectually improper in his doing so, no matter how much the majority of us may disagree with him. In fairness to such a person, however, it would be preferable to refer to him in the United States as a Marxist, since at present any use of the word communist bears too heavy a weight of confusion to be used for a person of intellectual sincerity. On the other hand, it is proper to question the intellectual integrity of a person who approves the philosophy and policies of the Communist Party and the Soviet Union in all particulars, and to refer to such a person as pro-communist, aside from the question of whether or not he is a member of the Communist Party or knows very much about Marxism.

But these legitimate uses of the term communism and communist must be sharply distinguished from a fourth use as an epithet and political weapon to refer to any person with socialist, liberal, or anti-capitalist views on domestic and foreign policy, or those who give an economic interpretation of history, politics, and culture, or those who defend the civil rights of all citizens including communists, or those who oppose the segregation of the Negro, or those who approve membership in the United Nations for Communist China, or those who oppose the Smith Act, or those who are considered insufficiently anti-communist, or those who, without any reason connected with communism, Marx, the Soviet Union, or anything else except a functioning social conscience, joined groups and sponsored organizations with which communists have at one time been affiliated.

It is in this use of the term that the greatest amount of deliberate confusion, personal damage, and social harm has been caused by politicians and Americanist groups. Their political technique is to accuse individuals and institutions of communism and pro-communism without regard to the facts or without regard to the standards of honest discourse. The attacker makes his accusation with the knowledge that when individuals are publicly accused of communism, the general public will treat the subsequent denials as partial admission of guilt, and will assume that there is something wrong with the integrity and loyalty of the person accused. The danger in all accusations of communism made against individuals is that the particular use of the term is not designated. The connotation of disloyalty and subversion which is correct in the case of Communist Party members who have engaged in conspiracy or espionage is attached to individuals whose only political action may have been to state an opinion or to sign a petition.

It is of first importance in considering the individuals who have joined the Communist Party or who have been sympathetic toward it to be clear about the nature and extent of their commitments, and the quality and honesty of their motives. The failure to make such distinctions has resulted in a great deal of the present confusion about the amount of influence communists have exerted in American life and the most effective way of dealing with communism as a national phenomenon. In the end, the only test of political or moral integrity, for communists or for anyone else, lies in the ideas, acts, and expressed opinions of the individual. Patriotism, loyalty, honesty are individual virtues which can be measured only by standards set in moral and constitutional ways. If narrower standards than these are taken, or if distinctions are blurred by the use of general categories of accusation for whole classes of people, we have betrayed the moral principle of individual worth on which the democratic value system has been built.

VIII

It is clear that the policies and acts of the Soviet Union do constitute a serious threat to the maintenance of peace and to the security of the United States. It is also clear that the Communist Party in every country has the potential, and in some countries the present ability to subvert democratic institutions. But in the United States in 1953, of the 60,000,000 votes cast in the most recent election, barely 200,000, or three-tenths of 1%, were cast for any candidates or parties which could properly be labeled left-wing. According to the latest F.B.I. estimates available, there are approximately 25,000 members of the Communist Party in a population of 163,000,000. The political influence of the Party is such as to handicap the success of any candidate or issue to which it gives public or private support. Whatever work the Communist Party is doing underground is having no discernible public effect in its favor. Our counter-espionage agents and the F.B.I. are those designated to deal with communist spies and subversive agents, and can receive little help from members of the general public who attempt to designate other citizens as communists without the resources in information or in talent and experience to do so.

Any person at work in the moving picture industry, in radio, or in television who has been sympathetic to the Communist Party or the Soviet Union, or has been a member of the Party is dismissed from his post unless he can demonstrate a high degree of anti-communist sentiment. There is no pro-communist press except for a small and feeble *Daily Worker,* and I imagine there are very few communists among professional journalists. Every federal law-enforcing agency, every agency of government, every state legislature, the entire range of public officials, labor unions, educators, businessmen, veterans' organizations, and private organizations of all kinds are actively opposing communism. A teacher who argues in favor of Soviet policies or indicates a sympathy for communism to his students, his colleagues, or the general public is vividly outlined against the academic sky as a target for attack. A student whose ideas or acts show support of the Communist Party is immediately subject to hostile criticism. Congressional investigations by three separate committees have combed the teaching profession for present and former Communist Party members. The cultural, political, and social atmosphere is thick with anti-communist sentiment. With the whole country so braced, so prepared, and so on guard through every part of its institutional life, and with educators, parents, and students so acutely sensitive to the danger of communist indoctrination, I do not believe that, short of closing down the colleges altogether, very much more can be done in a negative way to protect American higher education from communism.

It has been no secret to the average citizen for the past 25 years that Communist Party policy has been to recruit members where possible from strategic posts in government, labor unions, the military services, the churches, educational institutions, the entertainment industry, or in any other place where the members might use their influence and position to further communist policies. Communist texts have declared the intention and have exhorted communists to carry it out. But the degree of communist success in influencing policy or in subverting American institutions has been comparatively slight, and at the present time, with the exception of a very few labor unions, is at zero.

This is true of the institutions of education. The recent report of the Senate Sub-Committee on Internal Security, made after several months of investigation, provided little evidence of present organized or unorganized Communist Party activity in the schools and colleges, even though the investigation began with the stated intention of showing that such a conspiracy existed and ended with the assertion that the college conspiracy was proven. The Committee examined privately and publicly a number of present and former teachers, former Communist Party organizers, and some ex-communists who informed the Committee of their work for the communists in the past and gave the names of their associates in that work. A reading of the transcript of the open hearings in which present and former teachers testified reveals no testimony as to how communism has subverted American education during the past, and no testimony to indicate that it exerts any influence at the present time.

The striking fact is that from the entire teaching staff of the country's colleges and universities, two Congressional committees working over a period of more than six months could find only 42 present college teachers[6] who, by their silence under the Fifth Amendment, raised questions about their connection with the Communist Party, and about whom no evidence was produced to indicate that they had subverted the educational institutions in which they were employed. Some of those who refused to talk about their political affiliations to the committees, did so freely to their colleagues in the universities. Of these, some admitted former membership or some connection with the communists, and most denied present attachment. The only sensible conclusion to be drawn from these investigations is to restate what had already been known and often stated by the educators, that the colleges are in no danger from the operations of communists on their faculties, and that the persistent accusations that the colleges are suffering infiltration by the Communist Party are ill-founded.

The committee reports and the testimony itself leads to this conclusion. The aftermath of the testimony leads to further conclusions. Of the 42 present college teachers who declined to answer questions about communism before the two committees, 19 have either been dismissed or suspended, three have resigned, 12 are presently under inquiry by their colleges, two were not reappointed, and six were retained after careful study of their cases by college authorities.[7] This means that even had there been subversion due to the presence of the 42 teachers in the

---

[6] According to an analysis of the hearings of the House of Representatives Committee on Un-American Activities and the Senate Sub-Committee on Internal Security, by Robert M. Hallett, *Christian Science Monitor*, July 21, 1953.

[7] As of August 1953.

colleges and universities, an hypothesis which was not explored by the committees and seems to have been overlooked by most of the educational authorities who dismissed their faculty members, that possibility has been removed by the actions of university officials. It can also be assumed that if either of the two investigating committees had had more and better evidence of the way in which education had been subverted, or the way in which teachers other than those called as witnesses had conspired with and through the Communist Party to subvert educational institutions, this testimony would have been added to the record.

As for the success of communists in the past, if the Congressional investigations are taken as evidence, it is clear that the problem of subversion, apart from the question of how many communists have taught in American colleges, must have been one largely confined to the public schools and municipal colleges of New York City. If the statements made to the Senate Sub-Committee on Internal Security by former communists are accurate, Communist Party units on the metropolitan college campuses in and around 1939 totaled nearly 100. But the fact that education in the schools and colleges of New York City was therefore subverted has still to be proven. It may be that further evidence on this point is available elsewhere, or that further testimony by teachers and administrators would provide clear evidence of the indoctrination of students and the subversion of educational policy. It is certainly to be assumed that where they were present in large numbers in one or another municipal college, communist teachers had influence in support of communist policies and doctrines.

But it is also to be assumed that the influence against communism of the hundreds and thousands of other non-communist and anti-communist teachers in the schools and colleges had at least as compelling an effect on the New York students as any support which a minority of communist teachers could have given to communism.

The communists have been much more highly organized in all their political work than non-communists, and have developed unscrupulous tactics for dominating policy in whatever social institution they are employed. But the limits of influence either in teaching or in educational policy are severely set down in colleges and universities by the standards of academic behavior demanded by the teaching profession of itself. It would be a very serious indictment of any college, its trustees, its president, and its faculty, if within the regular procedures governing faculty appointments and educational policy-making, the individual, communist or non-communist, who attempted to subvert the education of the students within his college could not be prevented from doing so by administrative action.

IX

Why then has the issue of communism in the colleges been of such concern to the public? It is partly due to the fact that the investigations and the attacks on schools and colleges have drawn attention to the issue, and partly because of the extent of anti-communist sentiment in the American public.

The use of narrow and ill-founded standards of political integrity has resulted in a great deal of confusion about non-communists and democratically minded people who are said to be "soft toward communism" when they simply act in their own ways to serve the cause of democracy. Those who have never been attracted by the philosophy or politics of communism and who, on the evidence, do not consider the American Communist Party a present danger to the security of the United States or to its educational institutions are said to be soft toward communism or pro-communist unless they make a sufficient number of anti-communist statements. Others who wish to respect the constitutional rights of communists along with those of every other citizen are said to be confused. The liberal who has never had anything to do with communism or communists, who judges each issue and each individual on the merits of the case, is said to be confused and naïve if his opinions do not coincide with those of the anti-communists.

Those who are hardest, and in some cases most irrational, toward communism are those who were former officials or espionage agents in the Communist Party and who, after leaving it, have carried the dogmatism and bitterness, and in some cases, the dishonesty, of communist attitudes into extremes of anti-communism. They are joined by others whose political and social views are extremely conservative and who oppose with equal bitterness any liberal views on any subject and demand a strict nationalist, isolationist, capitalist, and anti-communist attitude from everyone else on pain of being considered pro-communist and un-American. There are also political opportunists who use the issue of communism and the denunciation of others as a means of advancing their own careers. For psychological, political, or financial reasons, the combined members of these groups have an interest in exaggerating the internal danger of communism to the United States and in thwarting efforts to achieve a rational, objective and considered judgment about social and political facts. Any attempt on the part of scholars, teachers, or citizens interested in civil liberties to put the issue of communism in its correct perspective is considered by such groups to be a sign of softness toward communism itself.

A strong democratic attitude and a strong belief in social justice and individual rights is a more effective antidote to communist influence than the ideology of anti-communism. There are many ways of exerting influence against communism, and there are many different kinds of people who do so. But not all those who exert such influence do so by head-on collision. To assume that ideas are always beaten by frontal assault, or that the only way to lessen the influence of an idea is to treat it as a monstrous danger and then badger other people who refuse to be sufficiently frightened, is to mistake the nature of social influence. An idea can be defeated only by a better one, and if too much attention is given to the evil and danger in ideas contrary to democracy, this itself becomes more fascinating and engrossing than the furtherance of democracy, and provides a form of escape from the reality of those present social issues confronting a democratic government.

The danger in the kind of anti-communist ideology now used by a number of intellectuals, as well as by such groups as the American Legion and right-wing Republicans, is that it places the center of gravity for political virtue in an attitude to communism and not in an attitude to democracy. It tries to combat communism by the methods which communists take to undermine democracy, and in doing so has a damaging effect on democracy itself. It makes alliances and lends its weight to anti-democratic philosophies and practices on the grounds that they serve to defeat communism. Anti-communism then becomes the criterion for judgments of loyalty and integrity. The effect of this attitude is to increase the suspicion that there are communists everywhere and to spread the notion that a person who acts as a democratic citizen and fails to see life in America as a constant struggle between anti-communists and communists is somehow lacking in judgment, moral sense, and perhaps even loyalty.

Another effect is to create the myth that communists in the United States by reason of concealed methods of operation and the strength and vigor of their minds and actions are invincible social giants who have only to write, speak, hold a rally or address a student meeting in order to subvert a democratic state, or at least to influence readers and listeners to believe what they say. As many educators have found, the most direct way of convincing students of the failure of American communists to meet even the most elementary standards of intellectual acuity and moral insight is to have a Communist Party member address students and answer their questions.

This is all very well, say the anti-communists, but what about the concealed communist or the liberal who supports Soviet communism or world communism or who believes that the failure of the Communist Party or of the Soviet Union under Stalin is only a temporary failure due to bad leadership and a misunderstanding of Marx? These individuals are said to be even more dangerous because they are masquerading as liberal democrats when in fact they are crypto-communists. Here again, the concealed communist or the pro-communist can only be as effective as the influence his character and his opinions can exert publicly and privately. He has no magic to transmute opinion. If he supports Mao against Eisenhower, the Soviet Union against the United States, or advises neutralism of moral judgment between the two countries because they are said to be two power systems equated in evil intention, he must take the consequences of his support as far as the reader or the listener is concerned.

His influence is limited by the degree of cogency his arguments reveal, the appeal his statements make to his listeners, or the extent to which he can persuade other people to work with him toward his aims. If he has lost faith in the ability of the democratic system to achieve social justice under capitalism, he cannot be prevented from saying so, nor does it enliven the moral health of the country to spend very much effort in berating him for not having the faith which so many others share.

During the 1930's there were a great many serious people

who pointed out the defects of the American economic system, and a few people expressed doubt and bitterness about the integrity of the democratic system itself. But the strongest condemnation came not from any political arguments, from communists or non-communists, but from the sheer facts of the depression. Many people construed these facts as evidence that the Marxist analysis was correct and that the capitalist system in this country was about to destroy itself at the expense of the American people. The negativism of the Marxist approach can be infectious, and there is no doubt that the economic interpretation of human behavior, whether Marxist or capitalist, does emphasize the selfish and self-interested parts of human motivation or national policy.

At one time a segment of the liberal movement seemed to accept the notion that to praise the United States or to admit openly that one enjoyed the life here and believed in American culture and its future was to appear simple-minded, that the People's Culture Park was a tribute to the new world while Jones Beach was a bourgeois scandal. There were a few liberals who seemed actually disappointed if good acts were committed by the American government or by individuals, while finding it possible to forgive the Soviet Union the most obvious betrayals of humanitarian principle.

Although some of the influence in this direction came from communists who worked intensively at the demonstration of American evil, more of it came as a reaction against something which had gone wrong in American society, and against the America Firsters, Babbittry, the excesses of self-righteous nationalism shown by the patriotic organizations, the Ku Klux Klan, the materialism of a business culture, and against the facts of a difficult economic situation. In any case, whatever degree of influence the communists exerted in making intellectuals lose faith in the resourcefulness of the American system to overcome its difficulties has been dissipated for a long time. The weakness in the American liberal movement at present does not lie in any failure to reject communism or the Communist Party. The situation is quite different. Having rejected communism and the Communist Party, and having rejected laissez-faire capitalism and the right wing of the Republican Party, and having found no political leadership in the Democratic Party, the liberals lack a positive program of ideas and reform linked to a political instrument which could bring it about. The weakness in the literature and philosophy of liberalism lies in the lessening of an active interest in social progress, a timidity about political action, and a tendency to analyze and deplore cultural trends rather than to do something about them.

X

It is very often remarked by conservatives and anti-communists that the liberals of the 1930's and 1940's were the dupes of the communists, since idealistic intellectuals joined communist-sponsored organizations and sometimes the Party itself in order to achieve aims in which the communists claimed to believe but which they did not in fact support. In doing so, it is assumed that the liberals were foolish, woolly-headed, and gullible. This may have been true in some cases, and there is no doubt that the intention of the Communist Party has always been to exploit any individual or group of individuals who could be politically useful to their ends. It is also true that many liberals had a false image of the communists and their Party and thought of them as possessing a combination of idealism and hard-boiled political realism. Without any experience of Party politics and the rough and tumble of political infighting, such liberals were ill-equipped to judge the integrity of communist politics and many of them therefore harbored an illicit admiration for the ruthless use of political power by communists when they saw it in action.

However, from the evidence I have seen, to assume that liberals as a group were merely tools of the Communist Party seems to do less than justice to the intelligence and thoughtfulness of the liberal intellectuals who have engaged in political action during the past twenty-five years. Most of them took political action in the 1930's and 1940's because they felt at the time that it was their duty as citizens and intellectuals to do so, and they signed petitions, sponsored meetings, attended conferences, all of their own choice, and read widely in the field of radical politics as part of the fulfillment of their own sense of responsibility for the social and economic difficulties of their country.

Where communists were also connected with such liberal groups, according to the record, they provided the time, energy, and in some cases, the money to carry out projects sponsored by the liberals. When the communists failed to support liberal ideas, and began projects to aid the Soviet Union, the liberals left the organizations, after having engaged in serious and fruitful political action on behalf of democratic causes. When they did so, the liberals damaged the Communist Party irreparably, by removing its liberal element and exposing the naked power motives at its heart.

Similarly, it is false to consider liberals as a politically united group with identical ideas about social change and social strategy. In the nineteenth century the liberal supported free enterprise. In the twentieth century he supported labor in its underdog phase against free enterprise. Ever since the *Communist Manifesto* there have been anti-communist liberals as well as pro-communist and non-communist liberals. What the liberals hold in common is a commitment to protect the individual, a commitment to the use of reason rather than force, and a belief

in the cluster of values which lie in the ideas of equality, freedom and the brotherhood of man. It is false to locate the American liberal as a political type close to the communist in a line
of political positions which run from fascism on the right wing
to the Communist Party on the left. The political philosophy
of the communist moves away from the liberal and toward the
authoritarian. The radical point in communism is its theory of
the collapse of capitalism, the control of society by the workers and the seizure of control by revolution. In this plan for
society there is no room for deviant thinking. On the other hand,
the radical element in liberalism is its devotion to personal
liberty.

The American communist does not carry into political action
the philosophy of the liberal, nor does the liberal carry communist philosophy into his political acts. In fact, the independent
liberal along with the democratic socialist is the communist's
most dangerous enemy, and nothing is so advantageous to communist success as a solid reactionary opposition. But there is
little indication that most of the liberals who supported the
Communist Party actually believed that it would overthrow the
American government. Most of them believed that uncom-
promising opposition by the Communist Party to the social evils
which they recognized would have serious political influence
on the other parties and the formation of their policies.

Liberalism and communism could work together with practical and logical consistency only as long as the actual democratic values upon which liberalism rests were not distorted,
corrupted or abused by the methods and aims of the Communist Party. The difference between liberalism and communism is
clarified in practical terms when it is noted that upon leaving
the Party the committed communists and the professional Party
workers who occupied key positions have moved, not to a liberal philosophy, but to a dogma of some kind, often to dog-

matic theology or to the secular ideology of an extreme anti-communism, or both. On the other hand, the logical extension of liberalism when it becomes more and more radical is not communism but extreme individualism—the antithesis of authoritarian philosophies.

There is at present a wide variety of periodical literature on the subject of pro- and anti-communism as distinct from the literature about communism itself. Serious judgment about political issues and liberal values is prevented rather than aided by a great deal of this discussion. The discussion takes the form of a dialectical process by which numbers of hyphenated terms are set up for gambits in an intellectual game among those who like to argue in abstract terms.

The material for the game is the content of liberalism. It is played as follows: The anti-communist is first set up as an ideal abstract type against the pro-communist. No further definition of the type is given. Then a system of new categories is set up to distinguish between those who are for or against communism, and those who are for or against the anti-communists and the pro-communists. This yields the more difficult hyphenation of anti-pro-communist and the pro-anti-communists. A category of anti-anti-communists is then designated as soft, dishonest, muddle-headed or dangerous, while the non-communist is considered barely defensible.

To be a non-communist is hardly enough. It is better to be an ex-communist turned anti-communist than never to have been a communist at all, i.e., to have been a non-communist. The latter can hardly be expected to take the correct attitude to communism, anti-communism, ex-communism, or pro-communism. The non-communist is suspect because he runs the risk of suffering the defect of being non-anti-communist, or of being pro-non-communist. I have tried to find my own way through this maze of categories in an effort to check on the correctness of my attitude, and can only conclude that I am a non-anti-pro-non-communist. The key to the puzzle is to start with the term communist and work backward through the hyphens. In the face of all this, I prefer the term independent democrat. Such intellectual parlor games played by men with polemical styles and vast quantities of undirected emotion are entertaining but not useful in advancing understanding. They distract the writer and the reader from considering what the man who is hyphenated says, and draw attention away from what he says to his classification among a variety of loosely defined categories.

XI

Those who have struggled with Communist Party members in teachers' unions, labor unions, or liberal organizations, can testify to the bitterness of the struggle and the sense of frustration which comes from combating dishonest tactics used by Party members. Communists have preyed on the good will of others, have tried to exploit friends for political purposes, have concealed their political intentions and affiliations, and have shown a duplicity of personal and political motive. These are the reasons for the deep anger felt against them in every democratic organization which they have tried to manipulate. Individuals who show dishonest qualities of character in their actions, whether or not they are communists, have no place in a college faculty.

Many of those who assert firmly and often that all communists are dishonest and cannot be free or open-minded and therefore should be excluded from the teaching profession feel no compunction in asking colleges whether or not there are communists on their faculties. If the question were asked, Do you have any intellectually-chained, closed-minded, corrupt, disloyal, and dishonest teachers in your faculty, the college president or dean would feel obliged to say no, and would also say that the regular procedures by which faculty members are judged as to worth would be adequate to detect any such moral reprobates who were present and to see that they were removed.

The trouble is that the question is always put the other way, Do you have Communist Party members in your faculty? Because if you do, they are dishonest, deceitful, traitorous, closed-minded, and so on. Or the question is put, do you believe that Communist Party members should be allowed to teach in American colleges? The simplest and easiest way to answer the question is to say of course not, since this is the answer which is demanded by the question. But it is the wrong question, and has been the source of so much abstract and useless speculation and argument that it has obscured the main issues in the matter of faculty membership in American colleges. There are no abstract communists and no abstract colleges. There are real faculty members teaching real students and being judged for their quality by real deans, college presidents and colleagues.

It is useless to speculate about theoretical situations which do not exist in most colleges and then draw specific conclusions from the speculations. For example, if in answer to the question, Should communists be allowed to teach, a college official says yes, provided they meet every other test which could possibly be given to college teachers, the questioner and the general public assumes that the colleges are therefore filled to the brim with conspirators, and that the person who answers in this fashion is in favor of helping communists by insuring their employment. If the answer is no, the next question is, How do you know there are no communists in your college? What about the pro-communist liberals? What about Professor X who sponsored the Waldorf Conference? Or Professor Y who opposed the Smith Act? Alger Hiss is then mentioned as an example of the way in which a plausible-looking intellectual could be deceiving everyone, and very soon we are in the intellectual abyss where those who speak against the Soviet Union are said to do so on special dispensation from the Communist Party in order to conceal their affiliation.

It is the wrong way to put the question because the question cannot be answered satisfactorily, or even accurately, with a flat statement about all faculty members. General Bedell Smith, in answering a similar question about the United States counter-intelligence personnel, was faced with the same dilemma. If the assumption is that every person is a potential or actual communist, regardless of his opinions or acts, then it must be assumed that short of a constant and continuous loyalty investigation of each faculty member from year to year, there is always a possibility that the most ardent anti-communist or pro-democratic faculty member or government worker or counter-intelligence agent is a communist.

If, as the evidence shows and the courts have held, the Communist Party operates by concealed methods, and the fact of Communist Party membership and activity can only be determined by professional investigators who work full-time in keeping track of the Communist Party, it is literally beyond the power of the college president, his faculty, or his board of trustees, or the United States Congress to know whether individual faculty members are communists.

The question of communist affiliation of a faculty member, in any event, may properly be introduced into college discussion only when there is some indication that he is acting on behalf of the communists rather than on behalf of his college. If, as the evidence also shows, individuals who are in fact working for the Communist Party are often not allowed to become members for tactical reasons, the question of membership itself becomes irrelevant. The educator who announces that no Communist Party members should be or will be allowed to teach has merely stated a view and stated a problem, he has not solved it. No matter what his views, he is thrown back upon the regular methods for determining fitness to teach, and there must be some indication of bad faith or dishonesty to raise the initial question of dishonest or illicit political behavior on the part of a faculty member.

If no such question comes up, there is no point in pursuing in the abstract what would happen in a theoretical college to a hypothetical communist. The real issue is, should colleges be organized on the basis of mutual suspicion among scholars, on the assumption of double motivation, on the hypothesis of a common dishonesty? Or should their basis be one of mutual trust, the assumption of integrity, and the assumption that those who think, talk, act, and teach in an honest fashion are not to be maligned by the implicit accusation involved in continuous political surveillance?

The Senate Sub-Committee on Internal Security, after its period of investigation of the colleges, recommended among other things that a security program similar to those in certain California institutions be organized in each college to work with agencies of the state in checking the political qualifications of all faculty members. The recommendation for the organization of a security agency in the colleges is a logical development of the hypothesis that everyone is a potential communist until he can produce evidence to show that he is not, and from the further principle of judging fitness to teach on a primary question of political views and affiliation rather than on the more basic question of the personal qualities, scholarship and integrity of the individual human being.

This is the assumption made and the method used in the Soviet Union for determining the intellectual qualifications of scholars, artists, scientists, and teachers. It was used in a similar way in Nazi Germany where the students also assisted in watching the faculty for political deviance and reported secretly to Nazi authorities. It is an assumption and a method which does not fit the pattern of a democratic society or its educational system. Once the question of political affiliation, whether Socialist, Democrat, Communist or Republican is made the first question to be asked about the fitness of a teacher to occupy his post, the rest follows. There is no satisfactory solution to the problem of discovering the political affiliation and opinion of teachers, as the Nazis and the communists have both demonstrated, without some form of police action on each college campus. This is not only abhorrent to the American academic community, it betrays a curious lack of faith in the process of intellectual discovery itself, and denies the possibility of reaching truth and valid moral judgment by the methods of free inquiry and the use of enlightened standards of community organization. The attitude to higher learning which it conveys would destroy free scholarship. Its equivalent in private life would be for a husband to hire a private detective the morning after his marriage to check on the loyalty and faithfulness of his wife, and to explain the action by saying that this is the only way real security can be achieved. It is not hard to imagine the quality of relation which this would bring about in the marriage itself, or the equivalent relation in a community of scholars. The attitude of most educators is conveyed by Mr. Conant, former President of Harvard University, who said, "I would not be a party to the appointment of a communist to any position in a school, college or university. There are no known adherents to the Party on our staff and I do not believe there are any disguised communists either. But even if there were, the damage that would be done to the spirit of this University by an investigation by the University aimed at finding a crypto-communist would be far greater than any conceivable harm such a person might do."

Those who apply to the president of a college, or to a dean, or to a departmental chairman for a teaching post, or those who are recommended by colleagues in other parts of the country will be unlikely to list Communist Party membership or lack of it among the qualifications for a post, or to say yes to a question about Party membership if it were asked. Nor is it likely, as Bernard de Voto once pointed out, that a faculty member's Party card will fall out of his pocket in the dean's office. The problem is not with the appointment of a known Communist Party member to a college faculty, since no college authority has any intention of making one. This might mean that the colleges would be deprived of a Picasso, but since there is every chance that by waiting a year or so, Picasso would be able to come as a teacher in his non-communist period, it would be preferable to allow the communists to administer that unpredictable style of genius during the intervening years.

The real problem is whether or not a respected member of a college faculty who holds academic tenure and is found to be or to have been a member of the Communist Party should be dismissed. The fairest answer is that he should not be dismissed because of his political affiliation, but that his case should be judged on its individual merits through the regular faculty procedures with standards applied by a constituted faculty committee.

The member of a college faculty who has been known and trusted as a colleague and teacher for five to twenty-five years does not suddenly change into a different person by reason of the discovery by his university that he has been attached to the Communist Party; unless of course, there is evidence that in concealing his political connection he also concealed political activities of an illegal or subversive kind with respect to his students, his colleagues, or his country. But the assumption is that if the individual teacher merits membership in the faculty by virtue of his personal qualities and the honesty of his scholarship and teaching, and is trusted as such by the grant of tenure before an action of dismissal is taken, the fact of former or present membership must be accompanied by some evidence of the abuse of his post to inject communist policies, to follow a communist line, to act dishonestly on behalf of the party, or to lower the standards of his profession and his institution by his political conduct.

XII

This is said to be an extreme position in the matter of academic freedom, taken by the American Association of University Professors, the American Civil Liberties Union, a minority of liberals, Mr. Robert Hutchins, the late Senator Taft, and some members of the academic profession. It is rejected by the Association of American Universities, whose membership includes more than three hundred college and university presidents, the National Education Association, the Association of American Colleges, and a majority of the American public. It is a difficult one to maintain in the face of the enormous weight of opinion against it, and the comparative ease with which one can say, We will grant academic freedom to all teachers except those who belong to totalitarian groups and who thus commit themselves to following the orders of a national and world conspiracy against the United States and the democratic countries. To grant academic freedom to such individuals is to grant to them the privilege of helping to destroy freedom itself.

This is a compelling and plausible argument, and it is tempting to submit to it. Membership in a totalitarian organization of any kind means that the individual is willing to make some degree of commitment to its aims. No responsible educator or citizen wishes to have young Americans indoctrinated with subversive ideas, and no responsible educator wishes the colleges and universities to aid the Communist Party to accomplish subversive aims. Neither does he wish to have on his faculty or to retain in it anyone who is incapable of trust in fulfilling the aims of democratic education, since faith and trust are the essential ingredients of the true community of scholars.

However, the argument does not exactly fit the situation of the contemporary American college or the requirements the college must have to protect the political freedom of its teachers. It does not fit the situation because the American college is not threatened by the presence of communist teachers in its faculty membership, and although the American college is not obliged by any principle of democracy to protect the freedom of communists to indoctrinate their students, it is obliged to protect the political freedom of all its qualified faculty members by refusing to make political standards the determining factor in their appointment to the college. This puts the principle of freedom first and then applies it to all teachers who are thus protected. The case of the hypothetical communist is the extreme which tests the adequacy of the principle.

Stated simply, my own view is that we do not need a double standard of moral and intellectual judgment for scholars and teachers, one for communists and one for the rest. The standards of the scholarly community which have been developed through years of experience with ideas and with those who profess them are strong enough and precise enough to ensure the integrity of the American colleges and universities from subversion by political intruders. If all communists are as corrupt as they are said to be, they will be kept out of any college where even moderate standards of intellectual integrity, teaching ability, and fair dealing are in effect and are applied by the regular procedures of faculty appointment, retention and dismissal. If the standards are too low to be effective in keeping out corrupt teachers, the solution is not to turn to political investigation of the entire faculty with a new standard, but to make badly needed improvements in the standards and methods by which faculty members are judged, since it is clear that an institution incapable of keeping out one kind of bad teacher would lack the necessary ability to prevent other forms of subversion from different sources.

As soon as we depart from standards applicable to all scholars and teachers in the proper exercise of their duties, we open the door to special criteria of judgment pressed upon us by those who are unfamiliar with the delicate process by which truth is found and intellectual honesty is determined. The work of the teacher and the scholar is to be judged, in the community of scholars, by the quality of his evidence, the sincerity of his convictions, the honesty of his mind, and the wisdom he shows in drawing his conclusions. There are professional standards applicable to scholars and teachers just as there are in the case of lawyers, doctors, architects or engineers.

When political criteria and public pressure of any kind, no matter how sincere and well intended, are applied to this principle, an immediate conflict of judgment occurs. The political pressure seems justified to the public, since it is already prepared to be suspicious of political deviance. The real distinction must be made between those who are political deviants and those who are disloyal to the principles of free inquiry and to their country. Political deviance and disloyalty are two different things and can be distinguished from each other in individual cases only by the use of informed judgment and the laws of evidence.

It is on this question that the most serious issues in the protection of freedom for teachers have turned, and it is because disloyalty and political deviance have become equated that the freedom itself is in serious danger. While the question of whether or not college faculty members are communists continues to fascinate the public and a large segment of the academic community, and while the Congressional investigations divert our attention to the political opinions and activities of teachers five, ten and fifteen years ago, it is forgotten that during the past ten years only two cases of present Communist Party membership have been brought before university authorities for decision. The rest have been cases of teachers accused of being communists in the past, or of being sympathetic to communism, in whatever meaning of the term used, in the present, or of refusing to testify before committees of Congress about communist affiliation.

The two cases in point were those of two members of the faculty of the University of Washington in 1948 and 1949, where the precedent for automatic dismissal of communists was set. The case marked the first time in recent educational history that the test for faculty membership was put solely on political grounds, and that the criteria of personal competence and integrity of scholarship were deliberately excluded from consideration.

The argument made by President Raymond Allen of the University of Washington is the one which has become so familiar and has been used so often since that time, that according to communist doctrine itself, Communist Party membership compels adherence to dogmas which allow no criticism, and means that the individual is under orders to think and act in specified ways, and is thus not a free man and not entitled to the privileges and protection of the academic community. The two faculty members denied that their membership involved submission to intellectual and political orders. But this question, so important to the determination of their fitness to teach and to the establishment of the facts on which a national policy in dealing with communism was to be based, was not decided on those grounds. The case was an extremely important one, partly because the issue had been simmering for so many years beneath the surface of the national life, partly because it came after several years of attacks on the University of Washington for its "liberals," "Reds," "Pinks," and "communist sympathizers" by individuals in the state and by an investigating committee of the state legislature, and mainly because it marked the first public test of the principle of whether individual college faculty members should be judged for their acts, opinions and beliefs or for their political associations.

President Allen made his recommendation for dismissal to the Board of Regents of his University after very long and detailed hearings and discussions of the cases had been carried out by a faculty tenure committee, a majority of which held that under the existing administrative code of the University of Washington, "the simple fact of membership in the Communist Party does not subject the member to removal." President Allen's was an extremely difficult decision, made under formidable psychological and social pressures, and one which no other university president has had to make during the current struggle over academic freedom. On the one hand, if he upheld the scholars' criteria of personal competence and honesty, he would have had to recommend retention of the two communists, since the judgment of their colleagues and students was that in matters of teaching and scholarship, the individuals concerned were fair and objective.

This would have been the signal for renewed action by those who had been attacking the University for its liberalism, and by other pressure groups within the state, all of which might have led to President Allen's forced resignation. On the other, if he dismissed the men on the grounds that they were communists, he would be rejecting the majority recommendation of his faculty, and he would damage the whole fabric of academic security both at his own University and elsewhere, by replacing, at a strategic time in educational history, the principle of individual worth and individual responsibility with the principle of political screening. This would have a damaging effect, not upon communists, who were already marked men and subject to the continual and hostile surveillance afforded to such political affiliates, but on non-communists, former communists, liberals, non-conformists, and radicals.

As the events have shown during the past four years since the case was decided, this is what has actually happened. Faculty members are now being dismissed from universities not because they are members of the Communist Party, but because they have been members in the past, or because they refuse to give political testimony before Congressional committees.

Those dismissed from the University of Washington were men who had been teaching at the University for more than twenty years, during which time their work, in Middle English and philosophy, had been considered satisfactory and reliable. It was revealed only at the hearings and by their own statements that for thirteen years of that satisfactory period of service to the University they had been members of the Communist Party without having subverted the students, alarmed the faculty, or offended the administration by their political point of view or affiliation. These facts directly controverted the logic, if not the persuasiveness, of President Allen's argument, since if it were true that the two faculty members were not free to teach objectively, and were morally incompetent, they should have been dismissed many years before on the grounds of an unfitness which assuredly would have appeared in their daily association with their colleagues and students. The facts seemed to demonstrate either that the University of Washington had no adequate standards for judging its faculty, a fact denied by its distinguished educational record, or that here were two living examples of a species of human being President Allen asserted could not and did not exist. Whatever else one may think of the decision in the case (and there have been many conflicting views expressed about it before, during, and since the case was decided), two faculty members, judged to be able and conscientious by the University of Washington standards, with long years of good service to their University, were dismissed for their membership in a legal political party.

XIII

It is here that we come to the damage caused by the state and federal investigations of the colleges. In effect, the state and Congressional committees have taken over the matter of determining fitness to teach, and in spite of statements to the contrary, are not simply leaving decisions of educational policy in the hands of the local educational authorities. The members of the committees have in their minds necessarily a general image of the correct political orthodoxy which a teacher should represent if he is to be considered a good member of a college faculty. Although not an accurate image of the college teacher, it coincides in a great many ways with the public image of the correct political attitude all Americans should take. The image excludes association with communists of any kind at any time, it excludes all varieties of association with liberal groups with which communists have been involved, and makes suspect anyone with deep convictions of a radical character about politics, whether or not he can be shown to have communist connections.

Departure in small measure from the norm of political orthodoxy is tolerated by committee members, and the limits of tolerance differ from member to member.

But if the witness has associated occasionally or actively with
communists in the past, or continues to think and act in ways
which indicate lack of sympathy with American policies or with
the capitalist system itself, or fails to confess former errors in
having taken left-wing political action in the first place, he is
met with antagonistic questions. The committee conception
of correct political behavior is based on an absolutist and static
view of truth. It is possible for an individual to have acted honestly and honorably in the light of his social convictions in 1938
or 1945 and have no need or desire to recant or feel remorseful
in 1953. Everyone who thinks seriously about politics must
adjust his thinking and acting to new situations, and what may
have been right for a particular person in the context of 1938
or 1945 might be wrong for him in 1953. But in the absence of
other evidence, this cannot be taken to impugn his integrity
either as a citizen or as a scholar when he is confronted with
his political past by a committee of Congress with a different
political point of view.

In other words, it is the image held in the minds of the Congressional committee and its counsel, or a stereotype of what
the American public accepts as correct political behavior, which
shapes the pattern of questions to each witness. The pattern
is designed to show how the college teacher differs from the
stereotype of a loyal American citizen, without giving the
teacher a chance to explain the reasons for his beliefs and his
acts or why he differs from others. It is here that Congressional
investigations begin to exercise power over teachers for political conformity. Not only the teachers who appear before the
committees are affected, but also those who have not been

called—those who have ideas and beliefs which they are unlikely to state publicly to their students or in their publications because of the risk of subsequent action either by Congressional committees or by university disapproval. The students are infected with the same degree of caution.

At this point, the Congressional hearings cease to be investigations of the existence of a conspiracy to subvert American education and become a form of prosecution, with exhibits introduced into the record along with the testimony of other witnesses, and citations in pseudo-legal style. This is particularly true in the case of those who invoke the Fifth Amendment and refuse to testify against themselves, or refuse to say anything at all about the Communist Party when it is referred to in a question. The advice of many sound and non-political lawyers, on the basis of experience with former Congressional hearings of this type is that to answer any questions about communism may lead to perjury charges because of slips of memory or misstatements of fact, or might mean what is called "opening the question," thus forcing the witness to answer all questions asked, whether they are personal or political, on pain of being cited for contempt of Congress.

No matter what any witness replies at a public hearing, he damages himself and damages his relationship to the educational institution with which he is connected, since newspaper publicity, and in some cases television, makes the public to some extent his judge and unavoidably brings pressure on the educational institution to consider his case as one demanding further investigation and possible action leading toward dismissal. If the college teacher answers freely all questions asked, he runs the risk of being misunderstood by the general public and by his college, simply because in the present political climate the attitude to political activity involving the Communist

Party, no matter how long ago the activity occurred, is one which automatically assumes political unreliability and uncertainty of character in the participant.

If the teacher says that under the Constitution he may belong to any political organization which is legal, that he invokes the First Amendment protecting freedom of speech, and that he therefore refuses to answer questions his government has no right to ask, his argument is ruled out by the committee and he may be cited for contempt. On the other hand, if he testifies about his political opinions, affiliations and present or former attitudes to communism, he may create the possibility of perjury charges which have nothing to do with his loyalty, scholarship, politics, connection with communism, or teaching ability. If the teacher, in order to avoid spreading his personal history on the record and running the risks of misunderstanding, perjury, or later prosecution, should choose to invoke his constitutional right not to testify against himself, he will probably be dismissed from his university post, or at the least will be considered a potentially unreliable teacher whose activities must be watched carefully both inside and outside the college.

There are a number of serious students of constitutional law who advise witnesses before Congressional committees to invoke the Fifth Amendment when questions are asked about political affiliation simply because it is impossible to tell what kind of activity may be proscribed as subversive within the near future, and because any sworn testimony before a committee of Congress may be revived at a future time and used against the witness under new legislation, even though it is testimony about acts which were perfectly acceptable at the time they were carried out.

The college presidents themselves are put in a very difficult public position by the proposal to investigate their institutions. To object to the investigations is to convey the impression that the colleges have something to hide, to oppose them seems to indicate a lack of desire to join Congress in preventing communists from infiltrating the colleges. Some people have argued that the colleges should welcome honest investigations as a way of obtaining a clean bill of health and putting an end to accusations made against the colleges. But the nature of the Congressional investigations is such that even if the committees wished to demonstrate the integrity of the colleges, they could not do so. The investigations began, not as a search for facts on which to base legislation, but with the stated assumption that the colleges were threatened by a plot made in the Soviet Union and carried out by communists on college campuses. Failure to find evidence of such a plot and evidence of danger to the colleges would be an admission by the committees that they had been wrong in the first place. The investigations seem to have no terminal point at which a bill of health could be issued. They are geared to public opinion and may continue as long as they provide political advantage to the investigators.

In any case, the Congressional inquiries were not designed to assure public understanding of the colleges. They were not investigations in this sense. The investigation had already been made—by a research staff which put together material from former F.B.I. agents, ex-communists, newspaper clippings, magazine articles, and Congressional committee files. The witness was called to a public session in order to expose beliefs, opinions, and associations which usually involved some aspect of communism or the Communist Party. This would then help to back up the theory of communist conspiracy in the colleges, and add to the general feeling of fear and public uncertainty about the security of the country from communism.

The authority for making decisions about who is or is not a fit member of a college faculty is indirectly shifted from the proper authorities in the college to the Congressional committees by the publicity given to the record of the hearings and the quasi-judicial nature of the record. Faculty members whose work had been satisfactory to the colleges in which they have served and whose teaching, often in fields not concerned with politics, had been considered worthy of respect by colleagues, students and college authorities, have been dismissed because they have invoked the Fifth Amendment before a Congressional committee.

If a college finds that any individual in its teaching faculty has allowed political motives or affiliations to corrupt his conduct as a scholar, a teacher, and as a representative of his institution, it has the responsibility of dismissing or otherwise disciplining the offending person. But the decision must come from judgments made about the individual teacher, as appraised by his faculty colleagues through the regular processes of college appraisal, and not on the grounds of his having exercised a privilege which he inherits from the Constitution as an American citizen. Once the principle of independent decision by educational institutions on matters affecting university appointment is lost, there is no other to take its place and a retreat from all independent principle has begun. It may be true that some communists before the committees have hidden behind the Fifth Amendment, but this does not mean that all those who invoke the Fifth Amendment are communists or that, by reason of their exercise of the privilege, they are dishonest or intellectually weak and incompetent as teachers and scholars.

XIV

In this situation, the colleges and universities themselves have a serious obligation toward their faculty members, an obligation which some have shirked. In certain cases, colleges have made refusal to testify fully before a Congressional committee grounds for automatic dismissal, thereby creating the assumption that educational policy is in the hands of the government and not in the hands of the university or the citizen. Such policy also creates the presumption of guilt of some kind, incompetence, or moral failure, in the absence of any evidence other than the exercise of a constitutional right, whereas, both in courts of law and in the academic community the presumption must be one of innocence in the absence of evidence to the contrary.

The statement of the Association of American Universities presents the general position of some of the most important private and public universities of the country in the matter of the responsibility of the universities for the freedom of their faculty members. [8] The statement leads to the conclusion that the university presidents who stated the general view of their universities felt themselves to be on the defensive for their institutions, and that they accepted the presumption of Congress that educational policy and the limits of intellectual freedom can be set by the government and not by the citizens and their universities. In referring to a line at which freedom begins to be qualified by duty and obligation, the presidents point to the fact that the line itself is set by legislation and by the courts. "However much the location of the line may be criticized, it cannot be disregarded with impunity. Any member of a university who crosses the duly established line is not excused by the fact that he believes the line ill-drawn. When the speech, writing, or other actions of a member of a faculty exceed lawful limits, he is subject to the same penalties as other persons. In addition, he may lose his university status." [9]

[8] *The Rights and Responsibilities of Universities and their Faculties,* Statement issued March 30, 1953, by the Association of American Universities.

[9] *Ibid.,* Section III, paragraph 2.

I am not sure what would be the decision of a constitutional lawyer about this view of freedom of "speech, writing, or other actions," but by faculty members it has been interpreted to mean that the presidents are warning their faculty members to be careful not to say, think, or write anything which makes radical suggestions for changing the structure of American society or its government. If it does not mean this, then it must mean simply that the faculty member has the same rights and responsibilities as all other citizens and must take responsibility for his acts and opinions under the law, a point which is not at issue. But one responsibility which the scholar-citizen has and one which the statement does not mention is resistance to the government and non-cooperation with it when he thinks his government is mistaken. How else have changes in government policy come about? How else can we guarantee that the government will continue to be representative of the citizens and mindful of the citizens' welfare?

When placed together with another admonition later in the document, the first warning combines with a second to indicate that the presidents have, as do the Congressional committees, their own image of political orthodoxy for the proper college faculty member. Referring to the fact that universities owe their existence to legislative acts and public charters, the document states, "Legislative bodies from time to time may scrutinize these benefits and privileges. It is clearly the duty of universities and their members to cooperate in official inquiries directed to those ends. When the powers of legislative inquiry are abused, the remedy does not lie in non-cooperation or defiance; it is to be sought through the normal channels of informed public opinion." [10]

One of the Congressional committees quite rightly took this to mean the approval of its investigation by the universities and

[10] *Ibid.*, Section III, paragraph 7.

inserted the statement into its record of the hearings. Again, the presumption is made that the citizens and the universities are obliged to justify their own legitimate educational policies before their government. "Academic freedom," the statement goes on to say, "is not a shield for those who break the law. Universities must cooperate fully with law enforcement officers whose duty requires them to prosecute those charged with offenses,"[11] and "Unless a faculty member violates a law, however, his discipline or discharge is a university responsibility and should not be assumed by political authority."[12]

There is thus an additional presumption that the Congressional investigations are designed to scrutinize the benefits and privileges of the universities. Not even the committees themselves have made this claim. Although it is true that any university must co-operate fully with law enforcement officers in the event that a member of its faculty breaks the law, this is not the issue in the present instance. The issue is, what kind and degree of protection should the universities provide for a faculty member who is ordered to answer all questions about his political opinions and associations and who exercises his right not to do so? No faculty member could take much comfort from the admonition to co-operate with a committee whose stated intention is to show that he is part of a Soviet conspiracy.

What would give him more comfort would be a statement to the effect that as a respected member of a university faculty, in the exercise of his lawful right to refuse testimony against himself before a Congressional committee, he is entitled to the support and protection of his university until such time as the evidence produced in a committee of his professional peers should prove that he is no longer worthy of the respect of his institution or a post among its members. The faculty member

[11] *Ibid.*, Section IV, paragraph 4.
[12] *Ibid.*, Section IV, paragraph 4.

does not have the resources, the time, energy, money, or public relations facilities to seek remedy for the abuse of legislative powers of inquiry through the normal channels of informed public opinion. Nor does he in every instance have the kind of forthright temperament and sanguine disposition which would make him welcome an opportunity to test the powers or judicial wisdom of Congress in a court of law, or even to reveal his private opinions, personal history, and political associations to a Congressional committee, to the newspapers, and to the country.

The faculty member who looks to his colleagues among the university presidents for common cause in the matter of intellectual and political freedom has felt less secure rather than more so after the exhortation to think freely while being careful not to go too far, and after such limited support for his constitutional rights. One can only hope that a full reading of the record of the open hearings of the Congressional investigations of the colleges in order to catch the flavor, quality, intent and style of the inquiries may persuade the university presidents, who are men of probity, scholarship, and good will, to restate the issue in terms more helpful to the faculty members who are called upon to do the free thinking.

X V

There are other kinds of damage done to colleges by the current mode of political investigations. There is of course the damage done to individuals who find their careers shattered and their loyalty impugned without proof of any crime, illegal act, misdemeanor, or disloyalty to their country or to education. There is a subtle kind of damage done to the public reputation of intellectuals, educators, and the colleges themselves

by the implication that they are lacking in patriotism and are
failing in their duty to their country by having allowed the
accused teachers to remain in their faculties until "exposed"
by a Congressional committee. This can only work to the country's disadvantage in making some sections of the public lose
faith in the country's educational system, when in fact they
should be proud of it. There is damage to the fabric of education itself by the distress, anxiety and useless controversy which
the investigations have brought to the campuses. There is also
the expense involved for teachers, many of whom have not
appeared in public hearings, have engaged in no political activity, communist or otherwise, but who have had to employ
legal counsel to advise them on the procedures of Congressional
investigations.

But most of all, the damage has been done to the atmosphere
of free expression and the vitality of political thought and
action on the college campuses. On some campuses, the inhibi-
tions to free expression reached a point during the investigations of 1953 at which faculty members who had been called
as witnesses, or who believed that they might be called, or
who had political interests, refused to talk about any political
subject, whether congressional investigations or foreign policy,
to their colleagues or to their students for fear that the colleague
or the student might also be called to testify and would be asked
questions which he would then be forced to answer about the
political views he had heard expressed. Faculty members who
had lived through part of the European experience with Nazism
or who had escaped from Communist-occupied Europe refused
to discuss their own views about American policy or about the
investigations themselves, on the grounds that some difficulty
might arise about their citizenship in the United States, or that
it might become impossible to receive a passport to travel
abroad, or that someone might be forced to give testimony about

the statements they had made. They indicated to their colleagues that they had begun to have the same feelings of anxiety
in their conversations and in their teaching which they had had
in the European universities when a political authority began
to make its inroads on their freedom. It helps very little to
reassure scholars who have such feelings that there is nothing
to worry about, and that this is the United States. They simply
continue to worry and to be circumspect in their attitudes and
expression.

The effect cannot fail to be felt in the case of the students
whom we are teaching to become independent, mature and intelligent citizens, capable of open expression of their convictions and their judgments about public policy. Consider the
effect, not merely on the teachers summoned to public hearings
but on the rest of the college community which has not yet
been summoned—that body of scholars who are being exhorted
by their college presidents to be fearless, to think freely and to
speak out, and that generation of college students who are
criticized daily as the silent generation who care more for
security than for the risks of intellectual or personal adventure.
Why shouldn't they care more for silence and security? They
are being taught to be silent and cautious from day to day by
the actions and example of those responsible for their educational development. Is education in a democracy designed to
teach the young to obey authority? I think not. That is what
deprived the German youth of its independence and gave them
Nazism. American education is designed to teach the young to
be free, to teach them to accept no authority except one founded
on reason, respect for the human mind, tolerance, law, justice,
and the ideals of freedom.

The educational destiny of the student and the teacher are
in fact identical. Where teaching is cautious and inhibited,
learning is timid and ineffectual. Christopher Fry, in writing of

the effect of hostile criticism on the artist is also describing the teacher, the scholar and the student. "The artist," says Fry, "at some level of himself, will respect an adverse criticism, if he can understand it; he has no wish to get away with anything, and he is so close to his work that he is, or should be, glad of a more distant eye. . . . But creative criticism—by which I mean criticism that takes as its starting-place the individual talent it deals with, and not some ready-made rule of thumb or personal preference—creative criticism has always been rare . . . much of the rest is as boring as a small child who insists on being looked at. And everywhere today can be heard the patter of tiny criticism, the busy sound of men continually knowing what they like. How anything manages to create itself at all is a wonder. . . ."[13]

It is this atmosphere of tiny criticism, of indecision, of uncertainty, of nagging, of caution, which is created by political investigation, whether from Congress, from patriotic organizations, or from university authorities themselves. The investigations of all kinds have had an observable effect on the college campuses. They dampen the enthusiasm of faculty and students for the expression of their own views. They inhibit the natural controversies and exchange of opinions which are the nourishment of a lively college community.

XVI

We do not want a commitment to communism by American youth. We do not want teachers whose commitment to one line of thinking about communism or about anything else makes it impossible for them to remain open-minded and honest in their relations with students and other teachers.

[13] Christopher Fry, "The Artist Views the Critic," in *Atlantic Monthly,* Vol. 191, No. 3, March 1953, p. 52.

What commitment then do we want? The communists have theirs, and we are alarmed by the strength and vigor with which it carries them into action. We are also a little worried that our own commitment is too vague, ill-defined and weak to carry us through the difficulties which surround the country daily. We call upon the need for moral strength so often that we indicate the over-concern of those who are not very sure of their own ideas.

Some want a commitment to anti-communism. But does this bring to youth the positive, forceful, compassionate philosophy strong enough to sustain their belief in freedom and to keep our society open? I do not believe it can, nor that any commitment to be against something will ever serve as the basis for a satisfying life or an open society.

Others want a commitment to free enterprise, capitalism, Americanism, or the American Century. By what method is such commitment taught? By the indoctrination of students with one point of view in politics, history, and economics? The students would simply not believe it. They would become cynical of such commitment and of education itself. This begins the cycle of indoctrination by which education is not education at all but a series of messages delivered from the government or from whoever has the power to make certain that educational orders are sent, received, and executed by the citizens. The idea of free enterprise, capitalism or whatever is meant by Americanism will have to stand on its own feet and fight its own battles for acceptance by the intelligent young. So will democracy. So will communism.

We do want a commitment to democracy. But a prior commitment for which the colleges are responsible is a passionate devotion to truth and an unshakable belief in individual human rights. Without these moral values political democracy is merely an expanse of field in which nothing will grow but weeds. The commitment to truth, to freedom and to the good of individuals makes the idea of democracy a necessary outcome of personal idealism and a love of humanity. It is a form society takes to sustain the hopes and ideals of the human race. The college student learns to make such commitments to freedom, democracy and liberal ideals by living in their presence and by feeling the power and strength of the ideals themselves when they are shown in action by the writers and the teachers who hold them.

The United States can trust its colleges, its students, and its teachers as long as they trust each other. Subversive doctrine, totalitarian ideas, disloyalty to democracy cannot live in a community where people care about each other, cherish the life of the mind, say what they think without inhibition, and are unafraid of their government.

INDEX

INDEX